Practical React Native

Build Two Full Projects and One Full Game using React Native

Frank Zammetti

Apress®

Practical React Native: Build Two Full Projects and One Full Game using React Native

Frank Zammetti
Pottstown, PA, USA

ISBN-13 (pbk): 978-1-4842-3938-4   ISBN-13 (electronic): 978-1-4842-3939-1
https://doi.org/10.1007/978-1-4842-3939-1

Library of Congress Control Number: 2018963120

Managing Director, Apress Media LLC: Welmoed Spahr
Acquisitions Editor: Louise Corrigan
Development Editor: James Markham
Coordinating Editor: Nancy Chen

Cover designed by eStudioCalamar

Cover image designed by Freepik (www.freepik.com)

Distributed to the book trade worldwide by Springer Science+Business Media New York, 233 Spring Street, 6th Floor, New York, NY 10013. Phone 1-800-SPRINGER, fax (201) 348-4505, e-mail orders-ny@springer-sbm.com, or visit www.springeronline.com. Apress Media, LLC is a California LLC and the sole member (owner) is Springer Science+Business Media Finance Inc (SSBM Finance Inc). SSBM Finance Inc is a **Delaware** corporation.

For information on translations, please e-mail rights@apress.com, or visit www.apress.com/rights-permissions.

Apress titles may be purchased in bulk for academic, corporate, or promotional use. eBook versions and licenses are also available for most titles. For more information, reference our Print and eBook Bulk Sales web page at www.apress.com/bulk-sales.

Any source code or other supplementary material referenced by the author in this book is available to readers on GitHub via the book's product page, located at www.apress.com/9781484239384. For more detailed information, please visit www.apress.com/source-code.

Printed on acid-free paper

Table of Contents

About the Author

Frank Zammetti is a veteran software developer/architect with nearly 25 years of professional experience and almost 20 years of nonprofessional development work beyond that. He has written nine other technical books for Apress and has served as a technical reviewer for other publishers. Frank is also a writer of fiction, although he's still hunting for an agent to represent his work.

About the Technical Reviewer

Akshat Paul is a software architect and author of the books *React Native for iOS Development* and *RubyMotion iOS Development Essentials*. He has extensive experience in mobile and web development and has delivered many enterprise and consumer applications over the years. Akshat frequently speaks on various technologies at conferences and meetings. He has given talks at the React Native EU Conference, DevOps Showcase Amsterdam, TheDevTheory Conference, RubyConfIndia, RubyMotion #inspect, Brussels, and was the keynote speaker at technology leadership events in Bangkok and Kuala Lumpur. In addition to writing code, Akshat enjoys spending time with his family, is an avid reader, and is obsessive about healthful eating.

Acknowledgments

I would like to acknowledge everyone at Apress who helped make this book a reality, including Nancy Chen, Louise Corrigan, James Markham, and Dhaneesh Kumar (there are likely others, so if I neglected to list you, know that you have my thanks and appreciation, regardless). I'd also like to acknowledge my technical reviewer, Akshat Paul, who challenged me to make things better and kept me honest throughout the writing of this book. Thank you all; it's always a team effort, and I always have the best team when I write for Apress!

Introduction

Creating mobile apps that look, feel, and function like native apps and are also cross-platform is a difficult proposition, even after all these years of developers working to achieve this. You can write native code for each platform and do your best to make them as similar as possible, and that's certainly a good way to get native performance and capabilities into your app, but essentially, that means writing your app multiple times.

Instead, you can take the HTML route and have a single code base that works everywhere, but you will often be left out in the cold, in terms of native device capabilities, not to mention performance frequently being subpar.

Thanks to the talented engineers at Facebook, we now have another option: React Native. This platform builds on the powerful and popular React library, also courtesy of Facebook, and provides a means for you to write a single code base (more or less) that works on Android and iOS equally well, while providing native performance and native capabilities.

In this book, you'll learn React Native, by building real apps, not just simple, contrived examples (although there are a few of those early on, as concepts are introduced). As you go through the projects, you'll see how to use various capabilities of React Native, including the user interface and application programming interfaces (APIs) it provides. By the end, you'll have a good handle on what React Native offers, and you'll be in a good position to go off and create the Next Big Thing app.

I highly recommend grabbing the source code download bundle from the Apress web site for this book (or on GitHub—Apress maintains a repo there as well) and digging into it, building it, and playing with it, as you read through the book. This isn't the olden days of computers (like when I was growing up!), when you had to type in all the code from a magazine (yes, I really did that!). Now, it's all there, ready to be compiled and run, so you can spend your time learning, rather than typing.

I hope you enjoy this book and learn a great deal from it. That's definitely my intention! So, grab a snack, pull up a comfy chair, have your laptop at the ready, and get on in. Adventure awaits! (And, yes, I realize full well how corny that sounds.)

CHAPTER 1

React Native: A Gentle Introduction

Building a mobile app is no easy task! The wide variety of devices in the world makes it difficult to target them all effectively. The situation has stabilized a lot from the "olden" days (you know, like five whole years ago or so), when you had to consider iOS, Android, Windows Mobile, Blackberry OS, webOS, Tizen, and probably some others now consigned to the dustbin of history. Today, it's a two-horse race between Apple's iOS and Google's Android.

But, that doesn't automatically mean it's much easier now. After all, these two platforms are still radically different in their development methodology and supported technologies. For iOS, you're writing Objective-C or Swift, for the most part, and on Android, it's largely Java. Languages aside, the tool chains are entirely different too (and for iOS, a Mac desktop is required).

Many people have decided to go the way of using the same technologies you build web sites with: HTML5, JavaScript, and CSS, but even if you choose that route, there's still a bewildering number of options. Do you use PhoneGap (Cordova) to wrap up your app? Maybe you go with the Progressive Web App (PWA) approach that Google is pushing. Maybe you use something like Corona SDK instead. All of these have pros and cons to consider, of course, and it's hard to find a one-size-fits-all answer. Performance is frequently an issue with the web technology–oriented approach, for example (although—spoiler alert—it doesn't have to be).

You know, it didn't occur to me until recently that I have, in fact, been doing mobile development, in one form or another, for about 15 years now. I got in early on the mobile trend. Even with all that experience, I must admit that these various decision points still can be overwhelming. They should be easy, and maybe they will be some day, but this is not the case today.

1

© Frank Zammetti 2018
F. Zammetti, *Practical React Native*, https://doi.org/10.1007/978-1-4842-3939-1_1

Until the day comes, there is a (relatively) newly emerged option that's darned good right now and is becoming more popular by the day. That option is, of course, React Native. Developed by the folks at Facebook, it builds directly on another very popular framework from those same folks, called React. Many web sites are built with React these days, and Facebook's engineers decided that creating a mobile-focused version of it might be just the ticket that allows high-performance, cross-platform applications to be built, without all the typical difficulties and complexities that mobile development so often entails.

In case you hadn't guessed, that's precisely what this book is all about. Before we get too far, though, I think it's good to know a little history. So, let's see where React Native came from, to kick things off.

So, Uh, What Is React Native, Exactly?

In a nutshell, React Native is an application development framework in which you use standard web technologies (or, in some cases, something *similar to* standard web technologies) to build your application. That means HTML (sort of, as you'll see in a bit), JavaScript, and CSS (again, sort of). React Native is based on Facebook's React framework, a popular web development framework. The critical difference between the two is that plain old React targets web browsers, whereas React Native (typically, although it technically can target web browsers as well) does not (despite the aforementioned use of web technologies). How it does this is quite interesting, and you'll see that a little later in this chapter.

Note   It should be pointed out that Facebook doesn't refer to React Native, or even React, for that matter, as a "framework." Instead, it refers to it as "a library for building UIs." However, the dividing line between a library, framework, and even a toolkit can sometimes be blurry. I'm using the term *framework* here, because I think it's a little more accurate. But, in the end, the nomenclature doesn't make much difference; it's still a thing that helps you build native applications, and that's what matters most at the end of the day.

React Native allows you to create mobile applications that look, feel, and perform much more like native apps than typical web apps, because the core technology behind it actually *is* native. It allows developers to do this while continuing to use most of the same web development skills they've built up over the years and does so while allowing that development to be cross-platform. No more writing iOS apps in Objective-C or Swift and then writing that same app again in Java for Android. No, you can now write your app once, using React Native, and have it work on both platforms with minimal effort.

React Native began its life at Facebook as a side project (an internal hackathon project, in fact) to another project that was itself at one time a side project: React. That project, created by Facebook engineer Jordan Walke, was first used in 2011 for Facebook's newsfeed. Instagram began using React in 2012, and it was open-sourced at JSConf US in May 2013.

At that point, the popularity of React took off, and Facebook took notice. It didn't take long for it to realize that the core technology beyond React could solve the difficulties of mobile development as well, and with a growing developer community backing React, React Native was a natural evolution. In fact, in 2012, Mark Zuckerberg commented, "The biggest mistake we made as a company was betting too much on HTML5 as opposed to native." He promised that Facebook would soon deliver a better mobile experience, and React Native was going to be the key to that goal.

So, in January 2015, the first public preview of React Native was offered at the React. js convention. Just a month later in March 2015, at Facebook's F8 conference, it was announced that React Native was open and available on the ever-popular GitHub. At that point, React Native took off.

The developer community outside Facebook got involved, and React Native development skyrocketed (although, naturally, the Facebook engineers who birthed it are still key players). A big boost came in 2016 when both Microsoft and Samsung committed to bringing React Native support to Windows and Tizen.

React Native powers a lot of popular mobile apps nowadays, including Facebook, Airbnb, Discord, Instagram, Walmart, Bloomberg, Gyroscope, Wix, and Skype. I'd be willing to bet you use at least one of these every day and never realized it was built with React Native! That's a testament to how close to a native look, feel, and performance React Native can provide.

So, that's what React Native is and how it came to be, in a nutshell. It hasn't been around long, to be sure, but in a short time, it has gained quite the following and is frequently at or near the top of many mobile developer searches, even eclipsing searches for things such as Android and iOS.

What Does React Native Bring to the Table?

Knowing its history and such is all well and good, but why would someone want to use React Native in the first place? And, as a corollary, why might one *not* want to use it? After all, while React Native may have a lot going for it, there's almost never a perfect answer.

Pros

Some of the benefits of React Native include the following:

- The look and feel of React Native apps are typically closer to those of pure native apps than web apps. (React Native does not use WebViews like competitors, such as PhoneGap/Cordova and Ionic do. More on this later.)

- Based on React, most of its concepts transfer to React Native, so there's a lot of developer knowledge floating around to help you.

- Simultaneous development for multiple platforms with most of the code being 100% shared means faster and cheaper development (and fewer developers going bald from pulling their hair out).

- An excellent set of development tools makes working with React Native smoother and faster than many other options (hot reloading of applications is an especially nice feature, as you'll discover later).

- This one is going to blow your mind if you've ever done any native mobile development: both Apple and Google allow apps to load JavaScript-only changes in applications *without going through the app approval process*. Yes, this means that you can make changes to a React Native app (with some caveats, naturally) without having to wait for Google or, especially, Apple (given their sometimes lengthy and onerous approval process) to grant you permission. This point alone makes React Native seriously worth consideration for any project.

- All this being said, using React Native doesn't mean that you forgo *true* native code. No! In fact, React Native, optionally, allows you to write native code and then call it from the main JavaScript code. This means that if React Native doesn't support some native device capability out of the box, you have the ability to write some native code that uses it and to use that native code from your non-native code app. This is a more advanced topic that won't be covered in this book, but it's probably useful to know about it and consider it a pro in React Native's favor.

Cons

Of course, nothing is perfect, and React Native isn't without its drawbacks, although they may not be as significant as those of many other options. Here's a list of a few things you may want to consider when looking at React Native for a project:

- Because React Native isn't just rendering into a WebView and is, in a sense, absorbed more closely into the underlying operating system's APIs, there can be some length of time during which React Native doesn't support a new version of Android, iOS, or any other platform it supports. However, to temper this a bit, it's unlikely that your app will be broken outright. It's just that you might have to wait to take advantage of new platform APIs.

- Debugging can sometimes be difficult. This is because React Native introduces an extra layer (or three!) of abstraction to deal with. Fortunately, the error messages that you get from React Native are almost always very descriptive and helpful, but I'd be lying if I said things couldn't get dicey from time to time.

- Another new thing to learn: JSX (JavaScript XML). If that seems a little scary to you, don't worry. It's nothing to be frightened of, as you'll learn. However, that said, it certainly is one other thing you'll have to pick up, because while React Native apps *can* be built without it, they virtually never are (and in this book, I'll only be dealing with JSX).

- Depending on your needs, you may still have to do some native coding anyway. If React Native doesn't offer something you need, you can create some native code and then make it available inside React Native. (Fair warning: that's something that will *not* be covered in this book.) With luck, you won't have to do this, but if you do, the promise of entirely avoiding native code with React Native is broken, so I think it's fair to call a con, even if only a potential one.

If it feels like this section and the last have flown by, that's by design. I want to get you to the fun stuff as soon as possible. And besides, a lot of the core concepts of working with React Native will be exposed naturally as you go forth, so any questions you may have now will be answered along the way, I suspect (and, indeed, hope). You'll gain a deeper understanding of many of the things I've discussed here as you do, to the extent you require, in order to develop with React Native anyway.

Getting Started with React Native

Generally, it is easy to get started with React Native, which has very few prerequisites. It doesn't assume any particular integrated development environment (IDE) and, in fact, throughout this book, I'll be dealing with a command-line interface only. Note that I am primarily a Windows user, so the screenshots will be from Windows. That said, there should not be much difference if you're a Mac or *nix user, at least nothing substantive that you won't be able to figure out on your own, such as using / instead of \, and those sorts of typical platform differences (and if there are exceptions, I'll be sure to point them out).

Prerequisites

As with so very many things these days, React Native requires you to have Node.js (or just plain Node, from here on out) and Node Package Manager (NPM) installed. If you are already familiar with this, and you already have them set up, skip to the next section; otherwise, read on for a crash course in Node and NPM and getting them set up.

Node

Ryan Dahl. That cat has some talent, I tell ya!

Ryan is the creator of a fantastic piece of software called Node. Ryan first presented Node at the European JSConf in 2009, and it was quickly recognized as a potential game-changer, as evidenced by the standing ovation his presentation received.

Node is a platform for running primarily server-side code that is high-performance and capable of handling tons of request load with ease. It is based on the most widely used language on the planet today: JavaScript. It's straightforward to get started with and understand, yet it puts tremendous power in the hands of developers, in large part thanks to its asynchronous and event-driven model of programming. In Node, almost everything you do is non-blocking, meaning code won't hold up processing of other request threads. This, plus the fact that to execute code Node uses Google's popular and highly tuned V8 JavaScript engine, the same engine that powers its Chrome browser, makes it very high-performance and able to handle a large request load.

It's no wonder that so many significant players and sites have adopted Node to one degree or another. Moreover, these aren't minor outfits either. We're talking about names you doubtless know, including DuckDuckGo, eBay, LinkedIn, Microsoft, Walmart, and Yahoo, to name just a few examples.

Node is a first-class runtime environment, meaning that you can do such things as interact with the local file system, access relational databases, call remote systems, and much more. In the past, you'd have to use a "proper" runtime, such as Java or .Net to do all this; JavaScript wasn't a player in that space. With Node, this is no longer true.

To be clear, Node isn't in and of itself a server, although it is most frequently used to create servers. But as a generic JavaScript runtime, it's the runtime that a great many non-server tools run in, and if you're now guessing that the React Native tool chain does precisely that, then pat yourself on the back.

That's Node in a nutshell. Please be aware that this section isn't meant to be an exhaustive look at Node. There's so much more to Node than this, and if you're new to it, I encourage you to peruse the Node site (`nodejs.org`). For the purposes of this book, however, this basic level of understanding will suffice.

Getting, installing, and running Node are trivial exercises, regardless of your operating system preference. There are no complicated installs with all sorts of dependencies, nor is there a vast set of configuration files to mess with before you can run a Node app. It's a five-minute exercise, depending on the speed of your Internet connection and how fast you can type. There's only one address to remember: `http://nodejs.org`. That's your one-stop shop for all things Node, beginning, right from the front page, with downloading it, as you can see in Figure 1-1.

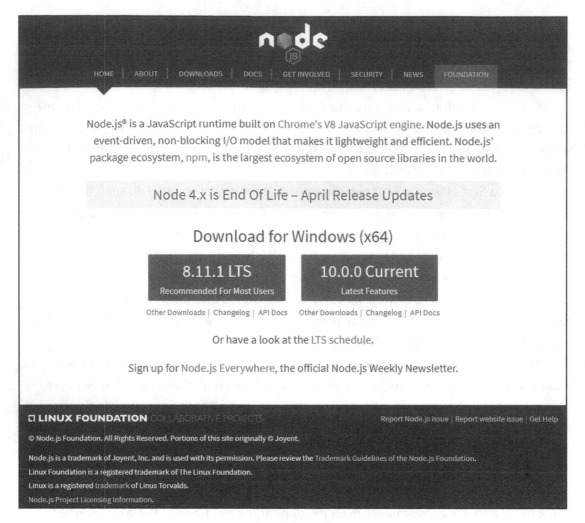

Figure 1-1. *Node has a simple web site, but it gets the job done*

Usually, I would tell you to install the latest version available, but in this case, it might be better to choose a long-term support (LTS) version, because they tend to be more stable. However, it *shouldn't* (he said, with fingers crossed) matter which you choose, for the purposes of this book. For the record, however, I developed all the code using version 8.11.1, so if you encounter any problems, I would suggest choosing that version. You can get it from the Other Downloads link and then the Previous Releases link, from which you'll be able to download any past version you like.

The download will install in whatever fashion is appropriate for your system, and I leave this as an exercise for the reader. For example, on Windows, Node provides a perfectly ordinary and straightforward installer that will walk you through the necessary (and extremely simple) steps. On Mac OS X, a typical install wizard will do the same.

Once the install completes, you will be ready to play with Node. The installer should have added the Node directory to your path. So, as a first simple test, go to a command prompt, type "node," and press Enter. You should be greeted with a > prompt. Node is now listening for your commands in CLI mode. To test this, type the following: "console.log("test");".

Press Enter, and you should be greeted with something like what you see in Figure 1-2 (platform differences excepted).

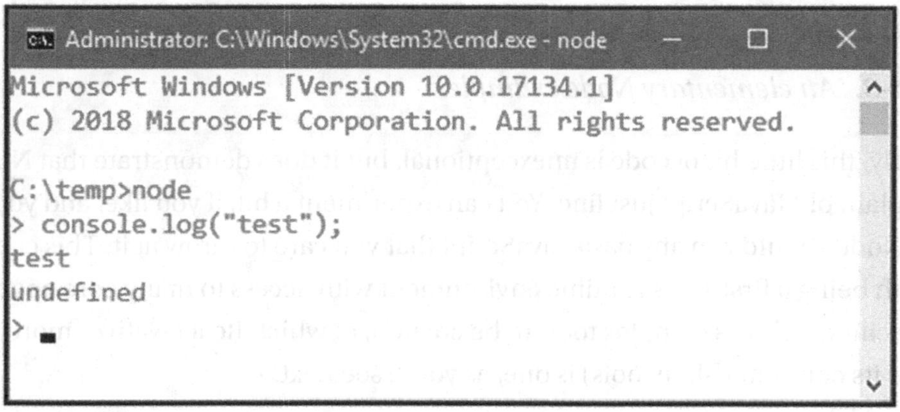

Figure 1-2. *Say hello to my little friend, Node*

Interacting with Node in CLI mode is fine but limited. What you really want to do is execute a saved JavaScript file using Node. As it happens, that's easy to do. Simply create a text file named listing_1-1.js, for example, type the code in Listing 1-1 into it, and save it.

Listing 1-1. A Quick Node Test

```
var a = 5;
var b = 3;
var c = a * b;
console.log(a + " * " + b + " = " + c);
```

To execute this file, assuming you are in the directory in which the file is located, you simply have to type this: "node listing_1-1.js".

Press Enter after that, and you should be greeted with an execution, such as the one you see in Figure 1-3.

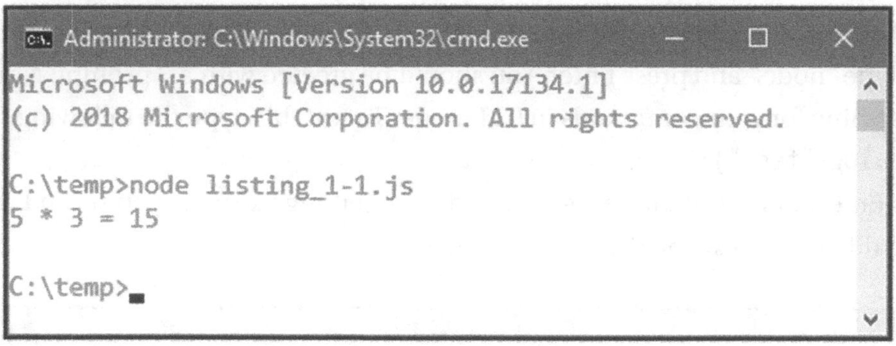

```
Administrator: C:\Windows\System32\cmd.exe                    —    □    ×
Microsoft Windows [Version 10.0.17134.1]
(c) 2018 Microsoft Corporation. All rights reserved.

C:\temp>node listing_1-1.js
5 * 3 = 15

C:\temp>_
```

Figure 1-3. *An elementary Node example*

Clearly, this little bit of code is unexceptional, but it does demonstrate that Node can execute plain old JavaScript just fine. You can experiment a bit, if you like, and you will see that Node should run any basic JavaScript that you care to throw at it. This capability, along with being a first-class runtime environment with access to many core operating system facilities, allows complex tools to be created, of which React Native (more precisely, its command-line tools) is one, as you'll see next.

How to Get React Native

Once you have Node installed, you also, in fact, have NPM installed, because NPM is packaged with Node. Now, what good does NPM do us? Well, for one thing, it makes getting started with React Native a piece of cake. To do so, at the command prompt, execute this command:

npm install -g create-react-native-app

If you're new to NPM, what that does is connect to a central repository of online packages, of which there are thousands, and finds the one named create-react-native-app (I'll explain what that is next). This command tells NPM to install this package globally (-g), which means it will be available from anywhere on your system. This is opposed to dropping the -g, which would install it in the current directory.

That is, in fact, how you'll want to install packages more times than not, as part of your project, which lives in a specific directory. In this case, however, we do want it globally, so that it isn't tied to any specific project.

That's because the `create-react-native-app` package is a tool (remember when I said that Node is also useful for building tools?) that is used to—wait for it—create React Native apps! (I know, totally unexpected, right?) The thing that makes this tool so useful is that it will allow you to do React Native development on this newly created project without having any sort of development tools installed. That means no Xcode for iOS development and no Android Studio for Android development. What this tool creates will be self-contained and, in a sense, include its own tools, as you'll see.

With that done, you're ready to create a React Native app, and, in keeping with the best traditions of computer science, we'll make that first app Hello World!

Baby Steps: A First App

So now, at a command prompt again, choose a directory in which you want your app to live. Then, execute this command:

```
create-react-native-app HelloWorld
```

It may take a few minutes to finish, because a whole bunch of packages will be installed courtesy of NPM, but before long, you'll find that a directory named HelloWorld has been created. Inside it, you'll find several files and a subdirectory, such as what is shown in Figure 1-4.

Name ▲	Size	Type	Modified	Attr
node_modules		File Folder	Today 12:22:48.6...	-------
.babelrc	130 bytes	File	Today 12:22:07.7...	-a-----
.gitignore	248 bytes	File	Today 12:22:07.7...	-a-----
.watchmanconfig	3 bytes	File	Today 12:22:07.7...	-a-----
App.js	580 bytes	JavaScript File	Today 12:22:07.7...	-a-----
app.json	47 bytes	JSON File	Today 12:22:07.7...	-a-----
App.test.js	228 bytes	JavaScript File	Today 12:22:07.7...	-a-----
package.json	625 bytes	JSON File	Today 12:22:07.6...	-a-----
README.md	12 KB	MD File	Today 12:22:07.7...	-a-----
yarn.lock	258 KB	LOCK File	Today 12:22:48.7...	-a-----

Figure 1-4. *Our first React Native app in the flesh, so to speak*

The node_modules directory is where all the packages required by this project and that NPM downloaded for us live. As mentioned, this is what happens without the -g option to NPM, and, by and large, you don't have to think about what's in there; you just let Node and NPM deal with it.

Most of the files here, such as .babelrc, .gitignore, .watchmanconfig, and yarn.lock are configuration and/or state files for various tools that you can safely ignore (and, generally, you'll always be able to, except in specific situations that won't be covered in this book). The README.md file is also not terribly important for our purposes, so you can ignore that too. The App.test.js file is a file that configures tests for the app that are run with a tool called jest. Testing can be an expansive topic and, as such, won't be covered here. As a result, you can move this file into the "safe to ignore" category as well, although, in general, you may indeed want to have tests for the apps you create, so it may be something you want to consider after you finish this book.

The other files—App.js, app.json, and package.json—however, matter to us. The package.json file is a configuration file for NPM's use. It defines the name of your project, its version and source code repository location, what JavaScript file represents as its main entry point, the dependencies it has, and more (most of which are optional, by the way). Basically, it contains all the relevant metadata about your project. A lot of this is boilerplate and not particularly relevant to this book, but given that it's not React Native-specific, that's okay. The only thing worth mentioning, I think, is the dependencies section you'll find if you open the file and read it. If your project winds up requiring an additional library, you'll frequently add it here, then execute npm install from a command prompt. NPM will read the package.json file and install any dependencies that aren't already present. You'll also frequently see people execute a command-line npm install -save XXX, in which XXX is the name of a package. That will install the package and automatically add it to the package.json file.

Note   The reason the package.json file is so important is because it allows other developers to quickly and easily get the same development environment as you. If you hand this directory off to someone, minus the node_modules directory (because that's not part of your source code, it makes sense not to include it), he or she only has to run npm install in the project directory, and NPM will dutifully download all the packages. The user then will be all set up to work, matching what you have.

The `dependencies` section also lists the version(s) of each dependency, using a technique called semantic versioning (often called SemVer). SemVer versions are in the form major.minor.patch. To give you a very brief overview, here are some of the most common dependency versions you might see (where XXX is the name of a dependency):

- `"XXX"` : `"1.2.3"`: NPM will grab this specific version only.

- `"XXX"` : `"~1.2.3"`: NPM will grab the most recent patch version. (So, `~1.2.3` will find the latest 1.2.x version but not 1.3.x or anything below 1.2.x.)

- `"XXX"` : `"^1.2.3"`: NPM will grab the most recent minor version. (So, `^1.2.3` will find the latest 1.x.x version but not 1.3.x or anything below 1.x.x.)

- `"XXX"` : `"*"`: NPM will grab the latest version available. (There is also an explicit latest value that does the same thing.)

There's quite a lot more to SemVer than this (and there's also no shortage of criticism and folks who aren't exactly fans of it), but this should cover the most common features you're likely to encounter. Indeed, this should be all you will need for this book (primarily because, for the most part, we won't have to deal with many dependencies).

The `app.json` file provides configuration information about your app specifically for React Native and something else involved here: Expo. What's that, you ask? Expo is a free and open source tool chain built around React Native that helps you create iOS and Android apps without the native tools for those being installed. Expo also provides some additional APIs that you can make use of optionally. Expo is not a product of Facebook, as React Native is. It's a separate company that has grown up around React Native. However, the React Native documentation that Facebook provides directs people by default to use Expo (as a consequence of using `create-react-native-app`), as the best and preferred way to create a React Native app. You aren't *required* to use Expo, because you aren't *required* to use `create-react-native-app`, but it is considerably better to do so—certainly, it's much easier and faster (as executing a single command, as you've seen demonstrated).

I suppose the docs don't tell you about Expo because, by and large, it won't matter to most people, but there are some consequences to be aware of. Perhaps most important is that your project isn't 100% React Native when you use `create-react-native-app`. It will have a dependency on Expo, its software development kit (or SDK, which gets installed automatically as part of `create-react-native-app`), and the company that maintains it. That said, there is a capability called *ejecting* that removes Expo from your project and leaves you with a pure React Native app, so it's not the end of the world. Ejecting is a topic beyond the scope of this book, but I think it's something you should be aware of and can look it up, if and when you need it.

Another consequence is that you can't use native modules from an app using Expo. This means that your app must be 100% JavaScript-based and additional modules written in native code won't be available to you. Depending on the type of app you're writing, this may or may not be a deal breaker.

All of this, I think, is acceptable generally and definitely, for the purposes of this book, because using `create-react-native-app` and Expo really does make everything far simpler. However, I do want to point all this out, so your eyes are open, because as you go further with React Native, I think it's important to realize that what you're going to learn here will make you dependent on Expo. While in many cases that won't actually matter and may be exactly what you want, when it does matter, you'll want to know, and that's a bit of a gap in what you'll find online, because it's not often stated, in my experience.

But, okay, all of that aside, how *does* Expo make things easier? Well, for one thing, it gives us the ability to do this (from the `HelloWorld` directory that was created for your project):

```
npm start
```

The result of that should be like what you see in Figure 1-5. In short, Expo has spun up a small server from which your app can be served. More than that, however, it has started up some debugging services, so that your app remains connected, in a sense, to that server. That means that any log messages and errors and such will show up there, in the console.

```
cmd npm

C:\temp\HelloWorld>npm start

> HelloWorld@0.1.0 start C:\temp\HelloWorld
> react-native-scripts start

13:10:31: Starting packager...
Packager started!
```

```
Your app is now running at URL: exp://10.0.75.1:19000

View your app with live reloading:

Android device:
  -> Point the Expo app to the QR code above.
     (You'll find the QR scanner on the Projects tab of the app.)
iOS device:
  -> Press s to email/text the app URL to your phone.
Emulator:
  -> Press a to start an Android emulator.

Your phone will need to be on the same local network as this computer.
For links to install the Expo app, please visit https://expo.io.

Logs from serving your app will appear here. Press Ctrl+C at any time to stop.

> Press a to open Android device or emulator.
> Press s to send the app URL to your phone number or email address
> Press q to display QR code.
> Press r to restart packager, or R to restart packager and clear cache.
> Press d to toggle development mode. (current mode: development)
```

Figure 1-5. *The Hello World app, ready to run*

Now, at this point, you'll, of course, want to run the app, probably on a real device, and because of what Expo has done for us, you can do exactly that. First, head to the app store appropriate for your platform on the mobile device of your choosing, search for the Expo app, and install it. Once that's done, and assuming you're on the same local network as the machine the Expo server is running on, you can scan the QR code shown here from the Expo app, or you can enter the URL shown directly. Either way, the app will be downloaded and launched, and, as a result, you should see something similar to what is shown in Figure 1-6.

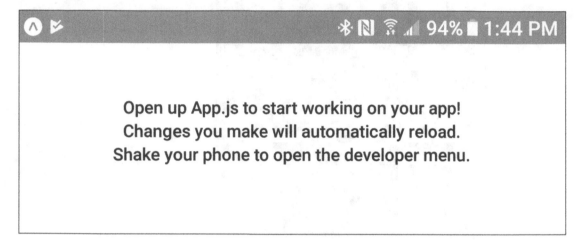

Figure 1-6. *It's not much to look at, but big things sometimes have small beginnings*

Note   At the time of writing, the latest Expo client app for iOS was forced by Apple to remove the QR scanning capability. That's unfortunate, but the Expo team added a feature to the server that provides the ability to send the URL to your device. You have only to hit the S key (one of the items listed in the menu that you should see when the app starts up) and provide either a phone number or e-mail address. The URL will then be sent via either SMS or e-mail, and you'll be able to tap the received link to open the app. It's a little less convenient, although not hugely so, but that's why you won't see a QR code scan option in the iOS Expo app, as you do in the Android app.

Now, it doesn't literally say "Hello, World!" right now, but we can fix that. Helpfully, what it *does* say gives us a clue for how to do that, by telling us about that last file I haven't mentioned yet: App.js. That's where the code of the app lives. Right now, it should look something like this:

```
import React from 'react';
import { StyleSheet, Text, View } from 'react-native';

export default class App extends React.Component {
  render() {
    return (
      <View style={styles.container}>
        <Text>Open up App.js to start working on your app!</Text>
        <Text>Changes you make will automatically reload.</Text>
        <Text>Shake your phone to open the developer menu.</Text>
      </View>
    );
  }
}

const styles = StyleSheet.create({
  container: {
    flex: 1,
    backgroundColor: '#fff',
    alignItems: 'center',
    justifyContent: 'center',
  },
});
```

I'm going to begin to dissect that in the next section, but for now, to make this a true, "standard" example, do you see the three lines with <Text> tags? Go ahead and delete any two, then change the text between <Text> and </Text> on the one remaining line to the more standard "Hello, World!" Next, assuming that you still have the app open on your mobile device, you should see it automatically update with the next text. Neat, right? If it doesn't update automatically, there will be an option to reload the app somewhere. On Android, try pulling down on the notification shade and look for the reload icon on the Expo notification that you should see. On iOS, long-press with two fingers to reveal a menu that includes a refresh option. That's another benefit of using Expo like this: fast and "hot" updating of code. No compiling, no redeploying; it's all transparent and fast.

Okay, so, we've got a real Hello World example working. Now, let's look at the code and get into some of the core concepts that make React Native work.

Tip   There are some issues you might encounter while getting this first example to work. First, if you have a firewall on your system, ensure that it is either temporarily disabled; otherwise, you'll have to open the port shown when you execute npm start. Second, if you have multiple network adapters in your system, you might find that the IP address shown isn't actually valid for your local network, and you won't be able to reach the Expo development server from your mobile device as a result. In this case, you can create an environment variable named REACT_NATIVE_PACKAGER_HOSTNAME and set its value to the IP address of the host machine. Third, ensure that the Expo app on your mobile device is up to date. Finally, if you just can't seem to get anything to work with errors, try executing npm --force cache clean, followed by npm install, from inside the project directory, to clear our NPM's cobwebs and make sure all the proper dependencies are installed.

The Core Concepts You Need to Know

Let's now have a look at the code that create-react-native-app generated for us and see what's going on. To be able to do that, though, you must understand some concepts on which that code is based, starting with the key to what React Native does: Virtual DOM.

Virtual DOM

If you've ever done any web development (and I assume you have, for the purposes of this book), you are familiar with the Document Object Model, or DOM. This is an inverted tree structure that represents all the elements on the page. It consists of a document object at the top that has children, like a head and body, which correspond to the familiar <head> and <body> HTML tags. Then there are a multitude of children under those, perhaps a `<div>` element under `<body>`, an `<h1>` under that, and so on. Anytime you use JavaScript to alter something on the page, or anytime the user does something that results in a change, the DOM is updated, and the browser uses the DOM to render the changes. Depending on the nature of the change that triggered it, the DOM might change *a lot*, forcing the browser to re-render a big chunk of the page, which can be quite slow, despite the best efforts of the browser vendors.

It's the nature of DOM in the browser that causes problems, because any changes make it complicated and expensive to update on the screen. The browser parses the HTML document and creates a DOM tree, a tree in which every tag on the page corresponds to a node in the tree. A second tree, the render tree, is created alongside it. This includes all the style information related to the tags. Every time the style information is processed, a process, called an attachment, occurs, using the appropriately named `attach()` method, and that's where problems come in, because every call to the `attach()` method is synchronous. Every time a new node is inserted, `attach()` is called. Every time one is deleted, `attach()` is called. Every time the state of an element is changed, `attach()` is called. All that might be bad enough, except for one additional fact: changes in one element can lead to changes in others, perhaps many others, because the layout has to be recalculated and re-rendered. And again, each of these operations, which could be in the hundreds or thousands, depending on what was done, will incur a synchronous call that also happens to be potentially expensive to execute. Houston, we have a problem!

Fortunately, we have a solution too: virtual DOM.

In the case of a virtual DOM, the browser doesn't use it to render anything directly or to calculate anything. It's a layer of abstraction on top of the browser's own DOM, yet it's still a DOM such as you're familiar with conceptually, in terms of it being a tree, but it's made up of simple, lightweight POJOs (plain old JavaScript objects, to use the Java term). But, the critical difference is that anytime you make a change to the virtual DOM, some code is executed before the browser deals with it. That code uses various diffing algorithms, to try and batch the necessary changes, so that all those changes can be done in the actual browser DOM in one pass. It also works to ensure that as little of the real DOM as possible is updated, which makes it much more efficient. This means that the code, React itself, in this case, can calculate the differences between the existing virtual DOM and whatever changes your code made intelligently. That way, it can make the minimal number of changes to the actual DOM and do them all at once, making the performance much better than changing the browser's DOM directly. It's a much more efficient approach, especially when page complexity increases. (It may not matter so much for small pages, but the benefit can come into play pretty quickly as a page gets more complex.)

With React Native, something interesting happens beyond this: when it comes time for changes in the virtual DOM to be displayed on the screen, instead of writing to a browser's DOM and having the browser render the screen based on that, React Native instead creates platform-native components and draws them on the screen, using platform-native methods. So, with plain React on the Web, where a <div> tag will result in a <div> element in the browser DOM being rendered to the screen, a <View> element in a React Native app (which you'll learn about later) gets rendered as a UIView component on iOS and a View component on Android. Those are native components now, not elements in a browser. That's a big difference! Despite such a big difference, you still write what looks a whole lot like writing plain old web apps, despite the syntax being a little odd, as you'll see soon.

Note   It doesn't affect learning React Native, but for the more curious among you, it's interesting to realize that virtual DOM is nothing new. You could always do what it does essentially, by creating a DOM fragment using DOM JavaScript methods, then inserting the fragment as a single unit into the DOM. That's been done for a long time and is undoubtedly more efficient than adding each node that the fragment contains into the DOM individually, because while layout and re-rendering might be more significant, they'll only have to be done once per update. And, if your code is efficient, it already considers modifying things as little as necessary up front, so the browser must make fewer of those synchronous calls, even in the context of a single update. Also, if you've ever done any game programming, you might recognize that virtual DOM is essentially a form of double buffering. The changes destined for the screen are rendered into a buffer first, then the buffer is moved en masse to the screen, leading to better performance and smoother animation. It's the same concept. So, why use virtual DOM, if you could do it directly with DOM methods? You do it to centralize the code that manages DOM fragments, and that deals with diffing the current DOM from the updated DOM (which is how the number of changes is minimized—only those things that really are changed by the update are actually updated). The virtual DOM approach also means that many parts of your app can update the DOM at once and that centralized code will manage that and, assuming it's implemented well, make it as efficient as possible (and avoid potential conflicts, of course). Writing robust virtual DOM code isn't necessarily easy, but, of course, you do not have to do it when you use React Native, so this is all just presented as an interesting technical aside, not something you will have to be directly conscious of as we move forward.

Bridges to Everywhere

The way React Native, and, indeed, React generally, works is that underneath the Virtual DOM is a render bridge. This is some code that knows how to render what the virtual DOM represents onto the screen. Think of it this way: the virtual DOM tells React Native what the screen is *supposed* to look like, but what it *actually* looks like is determined by the render bridge, and what it talks to. In the case of React for the Web, the virtual DOM "talks," so to speak, to the browser DOM. But, with React Native, the render bridge talks to the platform's native APIs, using them to create native components and rendering them onscreen.

This opens some great possibilities, because it means that if a render bridge exists, the app can be rendered to any platform it supports. If someone writes a render bridge for an old Commodore 64, you could conceivably have a modern React Native app running on a 36-year-old computer!

React Native ships with render bridges for Android and iOS, and other platforms can be supplied by the React Native developer community or companies that want apps written for their platform. It's the virtual DOM and the usage of render bridges underneath it that makes this flexibility possible.

To give a little more detail on this, the bridge sits between two main components: native modules (written in Java for Android and Objective-C or Swift for iOS, and perhaps something else for another platform) and the JavaScript virtual machine. The virtual machine is where all the JavaScript that makes up your application runs and is provided by the powerful and highly performant JavaScript Core engine, which is the same JavaScript engine that powers Safari on iOS as part of that platform. For Android, the engine is bundled with your app, which is why you'll often find that the app size of a React Native app on Android is quite a bit larger than on IOS, by three or four megabytes even. The native modules and the JavaScript VM are run on separate threads (the native queue thread and the JS queue thread, respectively), and they communicate with one another via the bridge, using a custom protocol. When the app starts up on a device, it's a bit of native code that kicks off first. It then spawns the JavaScript VM, which then loads the code for your application (which will have been bundled into a single file by the React Native tools under the covers). As the app runs, the code running in the JavaScript VM thread issues instructions to the native modules, via the bridge, to do such things as create components, show views, etc. The native modules do their thing and send a response back through the bridge to the JavaScript VM, to indicate the operation has completed.

JSX

Now, as we begin to look at the actual code, let's address the elephant in the room: that code looks *weird*! It's not everyday JavaScript, although we see elements of JavaScript, obviously. It's also not HTML, though there are elements of that too. There's also some elements of CSS in there. It kind of looks like a jumbled mess!

Well, welcome to the wonderful world of JSX!

JSX stands for JavaScript XML and is a combination of all three of the things I mentioned: JavaScript, HTML (XML, to be more specific), and CSS. More precisely, JSX is a way to embed XML inside JavaScript, without being bashed upside the head by all sorts of syntax errors.

This JSX code gets processed by React Native and transformed into plain old JavaScript, to be executed at runtime. In fact, you *can* skip JSX entirely and write a React Native app in pure JavaScript, if you wish, but that's not typically the way React Native apps are written and not an approach I'll be covering in this book. JSX, as it happens, makes things quite a bit easier and more straightforward, and positively less verbose, compared to writing it in pure JavaScript.

To put this in more concrete terms, you *could* write all your React Native code in this form:

```
React.createElement(
  "div", null,
  React.createElement("img", { src : url, className : "contactPhoto" }),
  React.createElement("span", { className : "contactName" }, firstName +
  lastName)
);
```

At this point, it's not important that you understand that code, although I'm sure that if you look at it enough, you can make some perfectly reasonable guesses about what's going on and come to a rough understanding of it. However, compare that code to the following, which is the same but in JSX form:

```
<div>
  <img src={url} className="contactPhoto" />
  <span className="contactName">{firstName + lastName}</span>
</div>
```

Now, again, you don't yet understand React Native, but that probably makes this a good test: is this code a bit more obvious? Does it seem a bit more clear and pure to your eyes? Most people, once they get past the initial revulsion most feel about JSX because it seems to mix HTML and JavaScript in weird ways, tend to feel that this is a cleaner way to write code. That's the promise of JSX: it tends to be less verbose and clearer to read, which is why it has become the de facto standard way to write React Native apps.

JSX code, as in the first app, is contained in a `.js` file, and that code starts off, naturally enough, with a typical JavaScript `import` statement that brings in the core React classes that React Native is built on top of. Another `import` statement is then used to bring in specific React Native components, which is a separate concept all its own that I'll be discussing next. In this case, this simple app requires three components: `StyleSheet`, `Text`, and `View`. These, too, are things I'll be addressing soon.

The line beginning with `export default class` is where things start to look really weird, because if you're thinking of plain JavaScript, you'll immediately think "that won't work; it's syntactically invalid!" And you would be correct. In the world of JSX, however, it's perfectly valid, odd though it may seem. I'll discuss exactly what's going on there in the next section.

As in HTML or XML, tags in JSX can contain content (`<Text>Hello</Text>`) and, therefore, have an opening and closing tag, or they can be self-closing (`<View />`). Tags in JSX can have attributes such as HTML or XML tags, but I am going to be talking about that in more detail later, so let's not go any further for now. Finally, tags in JSX can have children, and those children can be text, JavaScript expressions, or other JSX tags.

Many other frameworks provide a templating language of some sort that allows you to embed code within the templates. That's what HTML is when you think about it. It's a markup format, but you can embed JavaScript snippets into it. React Native turns that on its head, though. Now, you're writing code that has markup embedded within it.

Besides that flipping of forms, so to speak, it may take some getting used to if you've done a lot of web development. We're so used to separating things into `.js` files, `.css` files, and .html files, but JSX forces us to combine those (or, at least, *strongly suggests* we do). JSX doesn't care about separating technologies, which is really what the typical web development approach is, and, instead, favors separating concern, where the word *concern* really means a component, which just so happens is what I'm discussing next.

Components

Ah, components. You've seen that word a few times already, but what does it really mean? Everything you do in the world of React Native will be within the context of components.

In short, React components (because components aren't specific to React Native) are self-contained chunks of code that encapsulate the visual description of a visual element—its current state, its attributes, and the operations it can perform. Because React Native components map to native platform components, when you write something such as a `<View>` tag in JSX, you're, in essence, describing for React Native what you want the underlying native component to look like and how you want it to work.

All components in React Native extend from the base `React.Component` class (though not necessarily directly; this is object-orientation, after all!), and they'll always, at minimum, provide a `render()` method, both of which you can see in the generated code. The `render()` method returns some XML that describes the component and itself can include other components, which is exactly what you see here: we have a `<View>` component that then has three (at least, initially) `<Text>` components as children. In fact, the `render()` method must always return a single component, whether it be something that React Native provides, something you created, or something a third-party library offers (something you'll see later in this book). If this were plain React, you could, in fact, return HTML directly, because what React is working with is ultimately plain old HTML, but in React Native, because we're dealing with native components, it needs to be a component. When what you want to display is an amalgamation of components, which it frequently will be, they all still must be wrapped up in some single component, which is precisely what you see in this sample code. A `<View>` element is very similar conceptually to a `<div>` tag in HTML, as it acts as a container for other components, here `<Text>` components, which work like `<div>` tags, with some text between the opening and closing tag.

Components have attributes that describe them, called props, which is something we'll get into in more detail shortly. They also have behaviors, in the form of event handlers (which are still considered props). Some components also have methods that you can call to perform various functions.

What's interesting to think about is that with React Native, by extension, all you'll ever do is build components. That such a simple statement can lead to complex apps is kind of amazing, no?

Render Life Cycle

Components in React, and, hence, React Native, have a well-defined life cycle of events that fire at specific times. Figure 1-7 shows this life cycle.

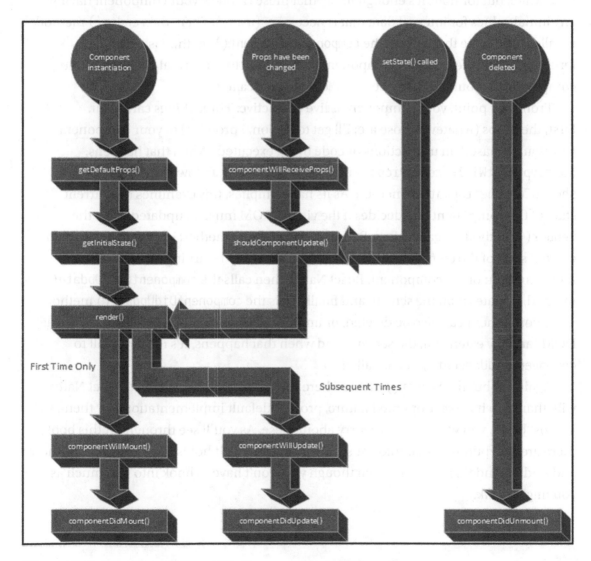

Figure 1-7. *The React/React Native component life cycle*

Along with those events are methods that you can (optionally) include in your components. As previously mentioned, render() is the only one that's required, and that makes sense, if you think about it: a component that doesn't render anything probably isn't much use. All the others, however, may or may not matter to what your component has to do.

When your component is first instantiated (as results from the code generated, based on your JSX executing), the getDefaultProps() method is called, followed by getInitialState(). Props and state are related concepts that I'll be discussing in a little while, but for now, it's enough to say that these result in your component having any initial values for internal data that is necessary (if any). Then, the render() method is called, and once that's done, the componentWillMount() method is called. The term *mounting* refers to your component being added to the virtual DOM. After the component is mounted, componentDidMount() gets called.

From that point, your component is live and active. Three things can occur. First, the props (whatever those are; I'll get to it soon, I promise) of your component can change, based on user actions or code being executed. When that happens, the componentWillReceiveProps() method is first called, followed by the shouldComponentUpdate() method. As its name implies, this examines the current state of the component and decides if the virtual DOM must be updated. If so, the render() method is again called. Because the render() method is designed to take the current state of the component into account, it winds up returning an updated visual representation of the component. React Native then calls the componentWillUpdate() method, updates it on the screen, and finally calls the componentDidUpdate() method.

A component can also be deleted, or unmounted, which removes it from the virtual DOM (and, by extension, the screen), and when that happens, it's merely a call to componentDidUnmount() that is called.

Again, all but the render() method here can be skipped, and, in fact, React Native will, thanks to its object-oriented nature, provide default implementations for them, so, in most cases, you won't have to worry about these. As you'll see throughout this book, there are exceptions to that rule, for sure, but, in general, it holds true. It's useful to know and understand this life cycle, even though you won't have to hook into it as much as you might think.

Props and State

In the previous section, two things, props and state, were mentioned, but I haven't talked about what those are yet. Fortunately, this could hardly be simpler.

Props and state are related, in that they represent data contained within a component, but they differ, in that props are generally regarded as being static, whereas a state is expected to change. Generally, props define an attribute of a component, and a state more directly represents data inside a component.

For example, think of a plain old HTML input field—let's say, one of type text. It has some attributes available, such as maxlength and readonly. It also has a value associated with it, of course. In the case of a React Native, there is a TextInput component that serves much the same purpose. For that component, there are props instead of attributes. Here, maxLength and editable are similar to the maxlength and readonly attribute of the HTML input element, and just like that element, the TextInput has a value associated with it called its state.

Just as you set attributes on an HTML input element

```
<input type="text" maxlength="10" readonly>
```

you likewise set props on a React Native component

```
<TextInput maxLength={10} editable={false}>
```

Oh, hold up now, what's this braces stuff? In JSX, anything between braces is considered a JavaScript expression and will be interpreted, and the outcome inserted, as the value. You don't have to use braces for many props; you can put static values surrounded by quotes as well. However, using expressions such as this is extremely common and extremely powerful, because it allows you to use variables and therefore modify the appearance and functionality of the component on the fly. It's often suggested always to use the expression form like this, advice I generally agree with.

Remember, though, that because these are JavaScript expressions, you can do pretty much anything within them that you can typically do in JavaScript. That includes accessing the props of the component, which is available through this.props. Let's say, for example, that we create a component name Person:

```
export default class Person extends React.Component {
  render() {
    return (
```

```
    <Text>My name is {this.props.name}</Text>
  );
 }
}
```

Then, we can do this as another component.

```
export default class MyComponent extends React.Component {
  render() {
    return (
        <Person name="Delenn" />
    );
  }
}
```

Now, when MyComponent is rendered, a Person component will be created as well, because it's used within the rendered output of MyComponent. The prop value name will be passed into Person, and it can then be accessed using this.props.name, as you see. We'll wind up with "My name is Delenn" on the screen, as a result of all of this. Perhaps not that impressive (unless you happen to be named Delenn), but it demonstrates props in their simplest terms.

It is generally expected that props do not change over time, but what if you need there to be some data within the component that does change over time? What if, for example, you want to be able to change the name of your Person component? In that case, state is what you're looking for. Take a look at this bit of code.

```
class Person extends React.Component{
  constructor (props) {
    super(props);
    this.state = { name : "" };
  }
  render () {
    return (
        <Text onPress={() => setState({ name : "Delenn"})}>My name is
        {this.state.name}</Text>
    );
  }
}
```

There are a few things to talk about here. First is the fact that a component can have a constructor function. It's optional, but for dealing with state, it's typically required. The constructor is passed an object containing all the props written on the component's JSX tag, and because React Native is built on an object hierarchy, we have to give the parent of the component a chance to handle the props too, hence the `super(props);` call first. After that, an object is created and appended as an attribute of the component itself and named `state`. Here, I can set any default state values I want.

Now, the `<Text>` component that my `render()` method returns uses the `this.state. name` value rather than the prop value you saw earlier. This is important, because it allows me to do what you see in the `onPress` prop.

That, by the way, is something else that's new: props aren't necessarily just simple static values or even values that are the output of some JavaScript expression. Sometimes, they are event handler functions, as `onPress` is. Obviously, this code will be executed when the user clicks the `<Text>` element, and when that happens, the `setState()` method is called, passing in an object with whatever changes to the component's state make sense. Note that for any attribute of the state object that you don't pass in on, the object passed to `setState()` will remain unchanged. The objects are intelligently merged by `setState()`.

The call to `setState()` triggers a call to the `render()` method, as per the life cycle previously discussed, which then reflects the new name on the screen (which, initially, would have just said "My name is," with no name, because the name attribute in the state object starts out as an empty string, as per the constructor).

It's important to note that you should never try to change the value in your state object directly, even though there's nothing to stop you from doing so. The `setState()` method has a lot of "plumbing" that takes care of ensuring that your state is consistent and always current. If you try to go around it, you'll cause your components not to work as expected, or at least you run the risk of having that happen.

So, just remember that famous historical quote (that I may or may not be remembering precisely): "Give me `setState()` or give me death" (in the form of potentially corrupt data).

That, in a nutshell, is props and state, which along with components form the core of what you'll be doing most of the time with React Native.

Styling

Up to now, you should have realized that in React Native, when using JSX, at least, your markup and code are intertwined. It's all in the same source file. When you understand that you're building components, and components are meant to be self-contained, this should start to feel less weird, but as experienced web developers, it indeed does seem odd at the start, because we're used to breaking things up. Along with the markup and the code, your CSS in React Native also gets mixed in, and to make matters odder, your styles are going to become code.

When you write CSS in React Native, it's a subset of CSS that you're already familiar with. Lots of things are cut out, as it's unnecessary in the world of React Native, and layout is based primarily on flexbox. One upside to this, aside from simpler CSS, is that there are no cross-browser issues in React Native land. Because it's a simplified subset, and because of the structure of React Native itself, CSS works the same, regardless of where it's run. That's nice!

However, where it gets weird is that all styles in React Native are always inline. One could make a good argument that the *C* in CSS means nothing in React Native. There really isn't much in the way of cascading happening, if everything is inline, after all. But, be that as it may, you've already seen what such inlined styling looks like in the generated Hello World code.

```
<View style={styles.container}>
```

Here, the `<View>` component has a `style` prop, and the value of that prop is the expression `styles.container`. What is that? Well, if you look down a little further in the code, you'll have your answer.

```
const styles = StyleSheet.create({
  container: {
    flex: 1,
    backgroundColor: '#fff',
    alignItems: 'center',
    justifyContent: 'center',
  },
});
```

Yep, it's just a JavaScript object. The StyleSheet object is one supplied by React Native that acts as an abstraction, like the stylesheet object in plain HTML. The create() method of it accepts a JavaScript object and then returns a new instance of StyleSheet, containing the styles you define within the object passed to it. In this case, the object contains an attribute named container, which then has several CSS properties defined as attributes of that object. Unlike regular web style definitions, we're using commas here, because, remember: we're defining a JavaScript object, not a stylesheet, per se. We must also quote values, in some cases, as a result, unlike regular stylesheets, to make it valid JavaScript.

Once we have a StyleSheet object, it can be referenced in the component tags, as is done with the View component. Alternatively, you can *really* go wild with the inlining and put the styles *directly* in the component definition, like so:

```
<View style={{ flex: 1, backgroundColor: '#fff', alignItems: 'center',
justifyContent: 'center' }}>
```

The reason you may prefer the first approach is that in addition to the create() method, the StyleSheet object may provide other methods that aid in making your stylesheets more like what you're used to in the pure web world, in terms of extensibility and such. For example, there is a flatten() method that takes an array of objects containing style definitions and returns a single combined StyleSheet object. Also, because you're talking about JavaScript objects here, you can use any sort of subclassing and such that you can with any other object. The choice, however, is up to you and the specific needs you have at the time.

One thing to note is that most examples you find online will show the StyleSheet creations at the *end* of the code for a component. In fact, the generated code does exactly that: the StyleSheet is created *after* the component that uses it. This, of course, works fine, but, at least to my eyes, it looks a little weird. I prefer putting the StyleSheet definitions at the top of my source code, as I would typically put them in the <head> of an HTML document, and that's how I'll be writing it throughout the book. But, it's purely a stylistic choice. There's no real technical reason to do it either way, that I can discern. In web development, you may be able to make an argument one way or the other, based on the blocking nature of stylesheet resource retrieval requests, but no such concerns are present here, so whatever looks good to you is fine with me.

Also, note that you can achieve something approaching the sort of separation you're likely more accustomed to by merely creating a single JavaScript module that contains all your styles and then importing that, where necessary, into your component source files (which, typically, are each in their own source file). This, too, may be something you prefer to do, but it's worth noting that this in a sense breaks the core concept of React Native, that of components. Remember that components are meant to be completely self-contained entities, right down to the code level. So, if a component you create has its source in `MyComponent.js`, and you then have a global `MyStyles.js` file that `MyComponent.js` imports, you've kind of broken that self-contained approach. Still, I wanted to at least point this out, because it is, again, a bit of a stylistic choice, because there's no real technical reason you can't write your code this way. I would tend to counsel against it, but I wouldn't lose a ton of sleep if I saw your code written that way on the job, either.

I will, naturally, go into more detail about the actual styling you can and can't do in React Native, as you explore the code throughout the rest of the book. Plus, you'll get a healthy dose of flexbox layout, so if that's a new concept to you, don't worry. I got ya covered! For now, though, you know the basics of styling that you'll need to march ahead.

Summary

In this chapter, you learned quite a bit. You learned what React Native is, what it has to offer, its pluses and minuses, and how to get started with it. You learned how to use Node and NPM to set up a React Native project, and you ran your first Hello World app build with it. You then learned the basic concepts behind React Native, a bit about how it works under the covers, and generally got a basic feel for what React Native is all about.

With those preliminaries out of the way, in the next chapter, you'll see in a bit more detail what React Native offers out of the box, some new code examples, and some new concepts, all leading up to building a real app with React Native, in the following chapters.

CHAPTER 2

Getting to Know React Native

In the last chapter, you began your exploration of React Native, looking at its core concepts, a little bit about how it works, and you got started with it in (more or less) typical Hello World fashion. Now, we'll dive in deeper and survey the components and APIs that React Native supplies for us to work with.

I want to make clear, however, that this chapter is not meant to be a deep-dive into all that is available. Each component has a few available props with which to configure it; some have quite a lot. Many also have methods that you can call on instances of to perform specific actions (or act as static helper methods). And some have associated JavaScript types that get created under the covers. I will not be going over every prop and method exhaustively nor showing all the associated types and demonstrating every possible variation of a component's use. Not even close! No, quite the contrary: after reading this chapter, you'll have a good idea of what you get "out of the box" with React Native, but the details of using most of it will not be filled in. I will only call out what I suspect you'll find to be the most interesting aspects of each, and I hope that this will be sufficient to give you at least a fundamental understanding of each component and API, enough to start looking at real code throughout the remainder of this book.

First, there's *a lot* to look at, and we'd have to clear a proverbial forest of trees to provide enough pages to cover everything, more than a single chapter's worth, that's for sure. Besides, that's what the React Native docs are for, and, especially, given the pace of change in React Native, I would be foolish to attempt to cover accurately all aspects here anyway.

Second, a lot of the details will be provided in subsequent chapters, as we begin to build some apps.

© Frank Zammetti 2018
F. Zammetti, *Practical React Native*, https://doi.org/10.1007/978-1-4842-3939-1_2

Third, if you look through the React Native official docs, you'll find that some components and APIs have little more than placeholder content, and some don't even include a one-sentence "this is what this component/API is." I dropped those from this chapter, because nobody can know every single available component and API in depth, and I'm no exception. I prefer not to provide information here that I cannot vet myself. I'd rather you find that information yourself, if/when you must.

Fourth, I feel that some components are better introduced in a real usage scenario in later chapters, so I skipped them here.

Finally, I dropped any component or API that is used when writing native code projects, because that's something entirely beyond the scope of this book, and I don't want to present information here that you later find you can't use without going down a different path. That, again, is something you can tackle, if and when the need arises. (Honestly, there's not a whole lot of those components, so you aren't missing too much, but I wanted at least to make you aware that they exist.)

So, don't treat this chapter as any sort of all-encompassing, detailed reference; treat it as a survey—a 10,000-foot view of the components and APIs at your disposal, just enough to give you the foundation necessary to start building real apps in the coming chapters.

Components

To start, I would offer that there are two broad categories of "things" this chapter is concerned with: components and APIs. Components are, of course, the visual elements that you see on the screen in a React Native app, and even before you consider any third-party component libraries (something you can totally do with React Native), there are several components available to you, enough to build real-world apps with, in fact.

These components can themselves be broken down broadly into a few groupings, based on various characteristics—six groups, to be precise.

Note   React Native always required that you import any component you're going to use, and the ones described in this chapter all come from the `react-native` module. I'll refrain from showing you those imports over and over, but understand that they are required, and you can see it at the top of the components sample app for this chapter, which is, of course, included in the downloadable source bundle for this book.

Basic Components

The first of the six groups includes "basic" components. Nearly every app uses one or more basic components, and this category is a bit of a catchall for components that underlie all the others. They underlie other components either directly, in cases where other components might subclass these, or in a more generic way, in the sense that other components become children of these (or the user interface is built from these "underneath" the other types of components). In fact, one of these components isn't even a component, in the traditional sense that you would consider a component, in that it's not visual, but we'll get to that one last. Let's start with probably the single most-used component in the React Native toolbox: `View`.

View

The `View` component is perhaps the one true workhorse component, and chances are you'll use it more than any other. As described in Chapter 1, the `View` component maps to fundamental native OS components—a `UIView` component on iOS and a `View` component on Android (and, if React Native were to render to HTML in a browser, it would map to the ubiquitous `<div>` element).

The `View` component, simply put, is a container element that supports layout with flexbox, styling via CSS, some general touch handling, and accessibility controls. As such, `View` components come in many forms, but a basic usage might be as follows:

```
<View style={{ width : 200, height : 100, backgroundColor : "#ff0000" }} >
```

This creates on the screen a red box 200 pixels wide and 100 pixels high. Note that styles are shown inline here, but it's more typical to externalize them in a `StyleSheet` object, something you saw in Chapter 1 and which we'll look at a little more, later in this chapter.

A `View` can have zero or more children, and these children can create as deeply nested a hierarchy as is required to achieve the layout you want. For example, if you want to have two colored boxes in a row, you might do the following:

```
<View style={{ flexDirection : "row", height : 100, padding: 20 }}>
  <View style={{ backgroundColor : "#ff0000", flex : 0.5}} />
  <View style={{ backgroundColor : "#00ff00", flex : 0.5}} />
</View>
```

I'll be covering more about layout in the next chapter, but this starts to give you a taste.

Text

The Text component is in many ways just like the View component, except that it's specifically geared to displaying text, but like the View component, it supports styling, nesting, and some touch handling.

A Text component might be as simple as this:

```
<Text>Hello, I am a Text component</Text>
```

Or, it might have some styling:

```
<Text style={{ color : "red" }}>Hello, I am a Text component</Text>
```

By default, Text components inherit the style information from their parent Text components, but that can be overridden.

```
<Text style={{ color : "red" }}>
  <Text>I am red</Text>
  <Text style={{ color : "green" }}> I am green</Text>
</Text>
```

As you can see, a Text component doesn't necessarily have to contain text. And, as you can see, Text components can be nested within one another.

One peculiarity with the Text components is that when layout comes into play, any content inside of a Text component does not use a flexbox layout, as is the case of View and any other React Native component that supports layout. Instead, inside a Text component, text layout is used. This means that any element nested within a Text component is no longer rectangular. Instead, it will wrap when an end of line is encountered. What this means in practice is that all Text components act as if they are one big, long string of text under a common parent. For example:

```
<Text>
  <Text>I am the very model </Text>
  <Text>of the modern major general</Text>
</Text>
```

When this is displayed, if the container is wide enough to accommodate the parent Text component, the two child Text components will render as "I am the very model of the modern major general," as if it were one Text component, one string.

Text components support some touch events via the onPress and onLongPress props. Just give them a value that is a function, and you can essentially create your own buttons with a combination of text and styling (and this sort of "create your own touchable thing" is quite common in React Native development).

Text components can also be nested in typical web form, which allows for easy formatting of the text. For example:

```
<Text style={{ fontWeight : "bold" }}>I am bold
  <Text style={{ color : "#ff0000" }}>and red</Text>
</Text>
```

This will render a bold string, "I am boldand red," where the words *and red* are—wait for it—IN RED! Note that there is no space between them, as any whitespace at the end of the content of the first Text component and before the nested Text component is ignored, for the purposes of displaying them onscreen.

Image

The Image component is exactly what its name implies: it allows you to display images. This component supports images retrieved from the network, such as an HTML < img> tag, static resources read from the file system—or encoded as data URLs—or from specific locations, such as the device's camera roll. Its simplest usage might be

```
<Image source={ require("./image.png") } />
```

Assuming you have a file named image.png in the root of your application code, it will be read and displayed. Or, you might get it from the network.

```
<Image source={ uri : "https://www.etherient.com/logo.png" } />
```

You can apply styling to an Image component, using the style prop you've seen several times now.

Some event-related props are present. These include onLoad, which is a function you provide that will be executed when the image is loaded successfully (primarily useful when fetching from the network, since that could take some time, and you might want to do something when it's loaded); onLoadStart, which fires when loading begins; and onLoadEnd, which executes whether the load failed or not (and if it fails, there's onError available for you to hook into).

The Image component is the first component you've encountered that also provides some methods that can be called. All these methods are static methods on the Image object itself. So, for example, if you want to get the width and height of an image on the network, you can do like so:

```
Image.getSize("https://www.etherient.com/logo.png,
  (width, height) => { console.log(width, height); }
);
```

The Image component also offers a method prefetch(), which loads an image into memory without displaying it, and queryCache(), which allows you to determine if an image has already been loaded and cached in memory, among other methods.

One thing to notice here is my use of the console.log() function. You've almost certainly seen this in your web development work, and as such, you're used to those messages showing up in some developer tools, like Chrome dev tools, for example. By virtue of using Expo, we also have a console object with methods that you'll likely be familiar with, like log(). Where do these messages go, though? Well, it turns out they are output to the console that you started the app from with npm start. Yes, the app running on a real device can output log messages to the PC with which you're doing development. That's cool, no? It's nice, because it means most of the CLI-oriented tricks you might be used to employing can be applied here, if you pipe the output somewhere to be processed. But that aside, just being able to quickly see log messages without having to try and view them on the device itself is excellent.

ScrollView

In simplest terms, the ScrollView component is essentially just a View component that allows for scrolling. In other words, it is a container component, like View, but it allows for more content to be rendered than can be displayed onscreen at once and then allows the user to scroll through that content.

You use ScrollView precisely like View.

```
<ScrollView>
  ... some number of components, more than will fit on the screen ...
</ScrollView>
```

A ScrollView must have a bounded height, which means you must either set its height directly, which is discouraged, or its parent container (all of them, in fact) will have bounded heights. The easiest way to do this is to ensure that flex:1 is set on all parent views of the ScrollView (although it appears that if a ScrollView is the first container view, then this is automatically true).

Note that ScrollView renders all its children at once, even those not yet visible. As you can guess, this can be a performance hit, depending on the complexity of the component hierarchy. You'll meet the FlatList component later, which, for most intents and purposes, can be thought of as a ScrollView that renders its children lazily, i.e., only when scrolling makes them visible.

The ScrollView component has a wide variety of props, including:

- alwaysBounceVertical: When true, the ScrollView bounces in the vertical direction when it reaches the end of its content, even if the content is smaller than the ScrollView itself.

- showsHorizontalScrollIndicator: When true, an indicator showing horizontal scroll position is shown (there is also a corresponding showsVerticalScrollIndicator prop).

- centerContent: When true, the ScrollView automatically centers its children, as long as the content of those children is smaller than the ScrollView bounds.

- zoomScale: The current scale of the ScrollView's content (this is an iOS-only prop)

ScrollView also supports some life cycle hooks, including:

- onScroll: Fires at most once per frame whenever scrolling occurs

- onScrollEndDrag: Fires when the user stops dragging the ScrollView, and it either ends or begins to glide

Finally, ScrollView also supports a couple of methods.

- scrollTo: Scrolls to a given x/y offset location (can be done immediately with or without animation)

- scrollToEnd: Scrolls either to the bottom of a vertical ScrollView or the far right of a horizontal one

There are quite a few more props available, but this sampling should provide a general picture of what this component is about.

TouchableHighlight

The TouchableHighlight component is another workhorse that, with its related siblings TouchableNativeFeedback, TouchableOpacity, and TouchableWithoutFeedback, provides a way to make virtually any view or component respond correctly to touch events. When a TouchableHighlight component is pressed, the opacity of the wrapped view is decreased, allowing the color underlying it to show through, which darkens or tints the view.

This component must always have one and only one child component (although, if you want more than one component to be wrapped by a TouchableHighlight component, that child can be a View component, which itself can contain multiple components). Here's a simple example:

```
<TouchableHighlight onPress={() => { console.log("Pressed!"); }} >
  <Text>Tap me to hide modal</Text>
</TouchableHighlight>
```

The onPress prop is the main one you'll use, and it's the function that fires when the component is pressed.

The other components work the same but with some differences. The TouchableNativeFeedback component is an Android-only component that uses native state drawable components to display touch feedback. This gives the proper Android look and feel to touchables (the material ripple effect usually). The TouchableOpacity component uses the Animated API that you'll see later and one of the components it exports, Animated.View, which it wraps around the child component, to manipulate opacity when pressed. TouchableWithoutFeedback, as I'm sure you can guess, creates a touchable element that gives no visual feedback. The React Native docs admonish you not to use this without good reason, and I agree. Touching something should provide some visual feedback, so you should avoid using this, unless you have some specific use case that can only be solved with this component.

Data Input, Form, and Control Components

If you look in the React Native docs, you'll see what they refer to as "user interface" components. I find this a little odd, because aren't *all* components user interface components? As I looked at what's contained in this second group, it seemed to me that what we have here are components for data input, for controlling things, and which are often used in forms. So, instead of a user interface components group, I decided to go with data input, form, and control components. I suppose Facebook can send me a nastygram, if it disagrees too strongly.

TextInput

I'm sure it won't surprise you to learn that the TextInput (Figure 2-1) component allows the user to input information via keyboard. This component has several useful configuration options for things such as auto-correction, auto-capitalization, and placeholder text. Its usage is very simple.

```
<TextInput value={ this.state.textInputValue }
  style={{ width : "50%", height : 40, borderColor : "green", borderWidth : 2 }}
  onChangeText={ (inText) => this.setState({inText}) }
/>
```

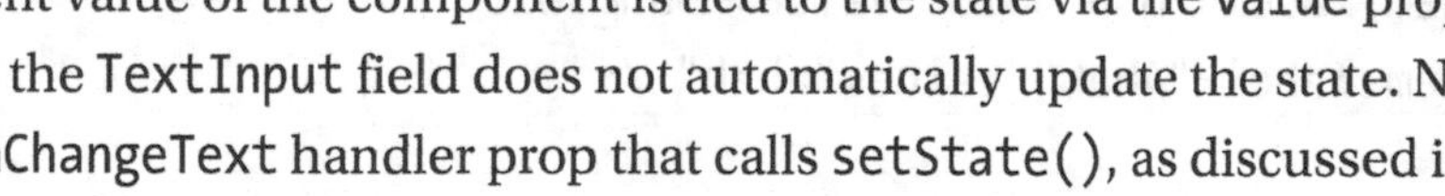

Figure 2-1. *The* TextInput *component (iOS version on the left, Android version on the right)*

The current value of the component is tied to the state via the value prop, but note that typing in the TextInput field does not automatically update the state. No, you must provide an onChangeText handler prop that calls setState(), as discussed in Chapter 1.

The TextInput component has a long list of supported props—far too many to detail here—but following is a sampling of some of the more interesting ones (in my opinion):

- autoCapitalize: Can be set to characters, to capitalize everything entered; words, to capitalize the first letter of each word; sentences, to capitalize only the first word of a sentence; and none, not to auto-capitalize anything.

41

- autoCorrect: Set to true, to enable auto-correct; set to false to disable it.

- maxLength: This sets a limit to the number of characters that can be entered.

- multiline: Set to true, to allow multiple lines of text to be entered; otherwise, set to false (which is the default).

- onFocus: A function to execute when the component gains focus

- onBlur: A function to execute when the component loses focus

- selectTextOnFocus: Set to true, to make the TextInput highlight any existing text when the field gains focus; set to false to not do this.

Picker

In the world of React Native, Picker refers to a component that allows the user to choose from a set of options. The form of this component varies between platforms, but it serves the same basic function on any platform that supports it. However, the Picker component (Figure 2-2) doesn't work without another component, Picker.Item, as you can see following:

```
<Picker selectedValue={ this.state.bestCaptain } style={{ height : 200,
width: 100 }}
  onValueChange={ (inValue, inIndex) => this.setState({ bestCaptain:
  inValue }) }
>
  <Picker.Item label="James Kirk" value="james_kirk" />
  <Picker.Item label="John Sheridan" value="john_sheridan" />
  <Picker.Item label="Han Solo" value="han_solo" />
  <Picker.Item label="Ahab" value="ahab" />
</Picker>
```

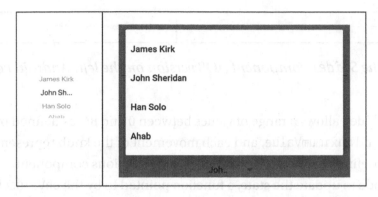

Figure 2-2. *The* Picker *component (iOS version on the left, Android version on the right)*

In this code, you create a Picker component and then nest one or more Picker. Item components under it. Each of these contains two props: label and value. The label prop is what is displayed on the screen, and value is the underlying value for a given option. As with the TextInput before it, the Picker component won't mutate state, unless you provide a handler function to do so, through the onValueChange prop, in this case. You'll see this pattern, the need to provide code to mutate state, repeated throughout React Native components, so you might as well get used to this now.

The list of props for Picker isn't very extensive. In addition to selectedValue, which gives the Picker its initial value, onValueChange, which I just discussed, and the ever-present style prop, there is also enabled, to enable (true) or disable (false) the component, mode (Android only), which determines whether the Picker is shown as a modal dialog (the default) or a drop-down anchored to the Picker's View, and itemStyle, which allows you to provide styling for the Picker.Item components in a common way.

Slider

The Slider component (Figure 2-3) allows the user to choose a value from a predefined range of values, by dragging a knob along a slider line. It has several props for defining the range and other associated attributes, as you can see following:

```
<Slider style={{ width : "75%" }} step={ 1 } minimumValue={ 0 }
  maximumValue={ 84 } value={ this.state.meaningOfLife }
  onValueChange={ inValue => this.setState({ meaningOfLife : inValue })}
/>
```

Figure 2-3. *The* Slider *component (iOS version on the left, Android version on the right)*

Here, the Slider allows a range of values between 0 and 84, as defined by minimumValue and maximumValue, and each movement of the knob represents a value change of 1, as defined by the step prop. As with the previous component, you'll have to supply some code to update the state, a function pointed to by the onValueChange prop.

In addition to these basic props, some of the others available include the following:

- disabled: One you've seen a few times and should by now realize is available on most components. It defines if the Slider is disabled (when set to true) or not (false).

- minimumTrackTintColor/maximumTrackTintColor: This allows you to specify the color to make the slider line below the knob and above the knob, respectively.

- thumbImage: This allows you to provide a custom image for the Slider's knob.

- onSlidingComplete: This is a callback function you can specify to be called when the user releases the Slider knob, regardless of whether the value has changed or not.

Switch

The Switch component (Figure 2-4) is very much like an HTML check box, in that it represents a binary choice: yes or no, on or off, 0 or 1, etc. As you might imagine, using it is quite easy.

```
<Switch value={ this.state.loveRN }
  onValueChange={ (inValue) => this.setState({ loveRN : inValue }) }
/>
```

Figure 2-4. *The* Switch *component (iOS version on the left, Android version on the right)*

There aren't too many props available for a Switch, which kind of makes sense, given what it is. Aside from value and onValueChange, which you should be pretty familiar with by now, you also have disabled and style, as do most components. There is also onTintColor, which is the color of the Switch's background when it's on. Also, you have tintColor, which is the same as onTintColor, except for the off state. Finally, there is thumbTintColor, which is the color of the foreground Switch grip (the meaning of these can vary from platform to platform, because the Switch's presentation can itself vary).

Button

A UI without buttons is one that wouldn't generally do very much. Buttons are one of the most common interface elements that provide the user a means to execute some action, and React Native offers a Button component (Figure 2-5) for precisely that purpose. Button components, of course, render in a platform-specific way, and because buttons are so common and platform-specific, React Native offers only a small number of customization opportunities. If you want or need a custom button that looks totally different from the platform default, you'll typically use the previously discussed TouchableHighlight, or it's brethren, to create a button from scratch. Here is a basic Button example:

```
<Button title="Go ahead, press me, I dare ya!"
  onPress={ () => console.log("You pressed me!"); }
/>
```

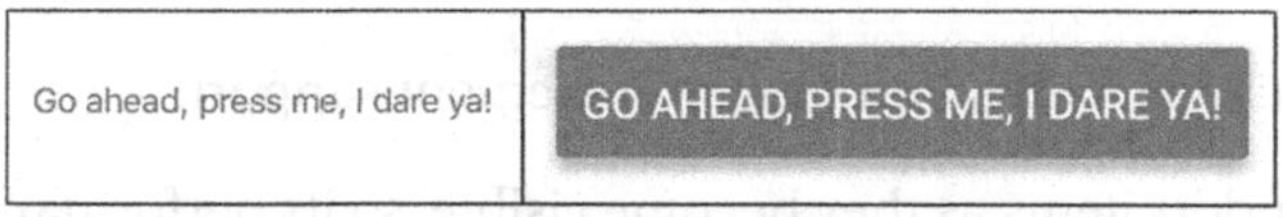

Go ahead, press me, I dare ya!   GO AHEAD, PRESS ME, I DARE YA!

Figure 2-5. *The* Button *component (iOS version on the left, Android version on the right)*

Yep, it's that simple. A `Button` without an `onPress` prop wouldn't have much purpose, and that's the one prop you'll always supply. Along with it is `title`, which is also required, and is the text to show on the button. The other props available are:

- `accessibilityLabel`: Text to display for blindness accessibility features (think screen readers, the text that they will read aloud will be defined by this prop)

- `color`: The color of the text for IOS, the background color of the button for Android

- `disabled`: Of course, you can disable a button.

List Components

Thankfully, the third group of components, the list components, is much more straightforward than the previous group. As the name implies, these are components used to show lists of items that, typically, a user can scroll through. To that end, they only render elements that are currently visible on the screen, as opposed to the previously described `ScrollView` component, which makes these much more efficient and a good choice when you have a long list of items to present.

FlatList

The `FlatList` component (Figure 2-6) is another workhorse that you'll see a lot of. It's meant for rendering simple flat lists (*flat* meaning a single dimension of data) and supports a host of features.

- `FlatList` is fully cross-platform.

- It has an optional horizontal scrolling mode, in addition to its default vertical mode.

- It has a header, footer, and separator element support.

- It only renders items as they become visible, so its performance is excellent.

- It supports the common pull-to-refresh interaction.

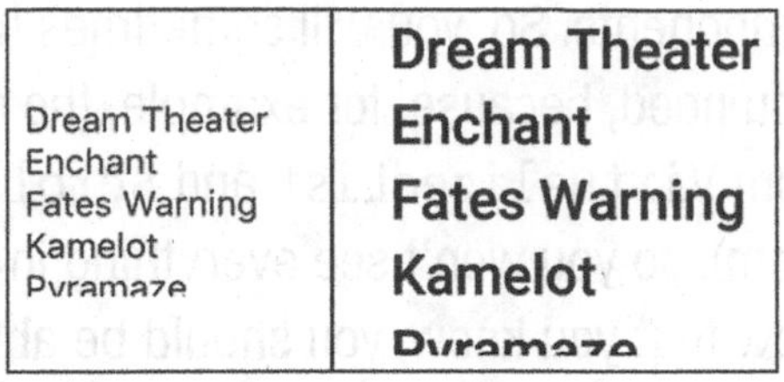

Figure 2-6. *The* FlatList *component (iOS version on the left, Android version on the right)*

In simplest terms, a FlatList can be just this:

```
<FlatList style={{ height : 80 }}
  data={[
    { key : "1", text : "Dream Theater" },{ key : "2", text : "Enchant" },
    { key : "3", text : "Fates Warning" },{ key : "4", text : "Kamelot" },
    { key : "5", text : "Pyramaze" },{ key : "6", text : "Rush" },
    { key : "7", text : "Serenity" },{ key : "8", text : "Shadow Gallery" },
    { key : "9", text : "Pink Floyd" },{ key : "10", text : "Queensryche" }
  ]}
  renderItem={ ({item}) => <Text>{ item.text }</Text> }
/>
```

You can provide data for the FlatList inline, as shown here, or you can, of course, reference an existing data structure. You provide a renderItem prop that renders each item in whatever fashion is appropriate for your app. Here, it's just a plain old Text component, but it could be any React Native component or hierarchy of components.

FlatList has a relatively long list of available props, and that list is made longer, because it is a descendant of the VirtualizedList component. VirtualizedList is a component you rarely use directly (and, hence, why I haven't listed it separately), which is itself a descendant of the ScrollView component you saw earlier. All of this means that all the props available for these two components are also available for FlatList.

Tip   It is true of all React Native components that they inherit the props of the component they extend from. Many will extend from the base component directly, which is why all components have props, such as disabled and style available to them. But the total list of props available on any component is the sum of the props of all its parent components. So, you will sometimes have to dig through the docs a bit to find what you need, because, for example, the docs for `FlatList` don't list all the props from `VirtualizedList` and `ScrollView` (or `View`, which `ScrollView` extends from), so you won't see everything in one place. That's a little inconvenient, but now that you know, you should be able to cope just fine.

By default, the `FlatList` must find a key attribute on each of the data items. This key can be any unique value you like that makes sense for your data. Sometimes, however, you may want the key to be made up by concatenating pieces of your data, or maybe you want to generate the key dynamically, based on some algorithm. Alternatively, for those cases, you can supply a function, by way of the `keyExtractor` function. This function will be called for each data item, and the return value from the function will become the key for that data item. This is a typical pattern you'll see in lots of React Native code, especially when there is no explicit key on your data items, because `FlatList` still must find a key, so you may just extract some element(s) from your data and make that the key to keeping `FlatList` happy. As a concrete example, imagine you have a set of data like this:

```
[ { firstName : "Steve", lastName : "Rogers", { firstName : "Tony",
lastName : "Stark" } ]
```

To use that with `FlatList`, each of those two objects in the array must have a key attribute. But, they don't right now, so you could either add them explicitly, or you could supply a function via `keyExtractor`. Maybe that function is

```
(item, index) => `avenger_${item.firstName}_${lastName}`
```

or, maybe it's just

```
(item, index) => recordNumber++
```

Assuming `recordNumber` was a variable accessible to that function that begins with a value of 0, each item in the array that becomes an item in the `FlatList` would have a number as its key, with each item's key being one greater than the previous item.

If you set the `horizontal` prop to `true`, the items are rendered next to each other across the screen, instead of the default vertical stacking. You can also invert the direction of scrolling by setting the `inverted` prop to `true`. You can hook some events via such props as `onEndReached` (for when the user scrolls to the end of the list) or `onRefresh` (for when a call to retrieve more data completes).

FlatList is the list component you'll likely use most, but it's not the only one. There is also the SectionList component, if you require—wait for it—*sections*!

SectionList

SectionList (Figure 2-7) is almost identical to FlatList, except that you can have a more interesting data structure in play. Here's the code for a SectionList:

```
<SectionList style={{ height : 100, borderWidth : 1, padding: 20 }}
  renderItem={ ({item, index, section}) => <Text key={index}>{item}</Text>
}
  renderSectionHeader={ ({ section : { title}  }) => (
    <Text style={{backgroundColor:"#e0e0e0",fontWeight : "bold"
    }}>{title}</Text>
  )}
  sections={ sciFiCharacters} keyExtractor={ (inItem, inIndex) => inItem +
  inIndex }
/>
```

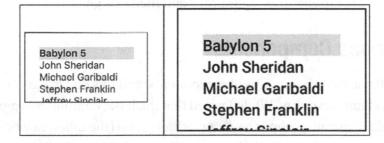

Figure 2-7. *The SectionList component (iOS version on the left, Android version on the right)*

And then there's the data that can feed it. (Here, you can see an example of *not* inlining the data. The data is just a JavaScript variable defined anywhere the component can reach it. In the sample project, it's just a module-scoped variable.)

```
const sciFiCharacters = [
  { title : "Babylon 5",
    data : [ "John Sheridan", "Michael Garibaldi", "Stephen Franklin",
    "Jeffrey Sinclair" ]
  },
```

```
{ title : "Star Trek",
  data : [ "James Kirk", "Leonard McCoy", "Hikaru Sulu", "Pavel Chekov" ]
},
{ title : "Star Wars", data : [ "Han Solo", "Luke Skywalker", "Leia
Organa" ] },
{ title : "Battlestar Galactica",
  data : [ "Kara Thrace", "Gaius Baltar", "William Adama", "Laura Roslin"
]
  }
];
```

As you can see, the top-level elements in the data are TV shows, which become sections in the SectionList, and then the data below each are characters from the shows, which become regular items in the SectionList. Note now that in addition to the renderItem prop, as you saw on FlatList, we now have a renderSectionHeader prop too, which is how those top-level data items get rendered. Here, I'm just giving them a gray background color, so that they stand out nicely from the regular data items. And, really, aside from that additional renderSectionHeader prop, there's little else different from the FlatList component, as far as props and methods go.

Miscellaneous Components

We're halfway through the six groups of components, and this one is a good old-fashioned miscellaneous group. While I noted that the basic components group is a bit of a catchall, this disparate group is *really* a catchall group (the difference being that the basic components are more foundational, whereas the miscellaneous components are somewhat higher level, conceptually). The React Native documentation itself refers to these components as "Other," but that seems even more generic than *miscellaneous* does, but if you're looking for them in the docs, that's where they'll be.

ActivityIndicator

When your app has long-running activities, such as fetching data from the network, for example, it's typical and considerate of your users to give some indication that activity is in progress. That's precisely what the ActivityIndicator component (Figure 2-8) is for. Using it couldn't be simpler.

```
<ActivityIndicator size="large" color="#ff0000" />
```

Figure 2-8. *The* ActivityIndicator *component (iOS version on the left, Android version on the right)*

This results in a circular animated "loading" indicator. None of the props this component supports is required, but you'll usually supply a value for size, which will be one of the supported values "small" or "large", with "large" being the default. Often, you'll also want to specify color. If not, the default color is gray. In addition, the animating prop, which you can change at any time, determines if the ActivityIndicator is showing (true) or not (false). Also, all the props supported by View are available here, owing to the object-oriented nature or React Native components.

Modal

Sometimes, when your user is looking at a particular screen in your app, you'll have to present some information to them "above" the current content. The perfect component for doing this is Modal (Figure 2-9), which is sometimes called a window, in other libraries. Its usage is fairly simple but quite flexible.

```
<Modal animationType="slide" transparent={ false }
  visible={this.state.modalVisible} presentationStyle="formSheet"
  onRequestClose={ () => { console.log("onRequestClose"); } }
>
  <View style={{ marginTop : 100, flex : 1, alignItems : "center" }}>
    <View style={{ flex : 1, alignItems : "center" }}>
      <Text>I am a modal. Ain't I cool??</Text>
      <TouchableHighlight style={{ marginTop : 100 }}
        onPress={() => { this.setState({ modalVisible : false }); }}
      >
```

```
        <Text>Tap me to hide modal</Text>
      </TouchableHighlight>
    </View>
  </View>
</Modal>
```

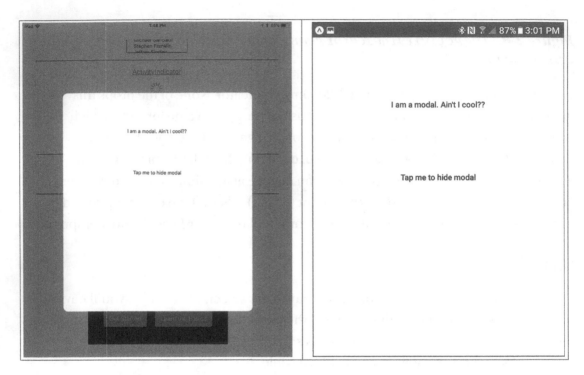

Figure 2-9. *The Modal component (iOS version on the left, Android version on the right)*

Here, you have a Modal component, which you can animate into and out of view, by setting a value for the animationType prop (support values are slide, fade, and none, where none is the default). The transparent prop, when true, makes the background transparent. You must be a bit careful with this prop, because when set to true, if your Modal content isn't designed right, you'll find that it just kind of blends in with the content behind it and will be useless. Try it in the sample app for this chapter, and you'll quickly see what I mean.

The visible prop, of course, determines whether the Modal is visible. Here, it's tied to the modalVisible attribute of the state object, which means that you can do a setState() call to hide and show the Modal. You can see that being done in the custom button, using the TouchableHighlight component. (Remember when I said you could do that? See, I was telling the truth.) The sample app has a similar TouchableHighlight to show the Modal too.

The onRequestClose prop seems to be required on Android but not on iOS, so to avoid a warning banner on the bottom, I've supplied a version here, to log a message to the console.

Finally, the presentationStyle determines how the Modal will look. Here, the formSheet value tells React Native to display it, covering a narrow-width view and centered. That means that on a larger screen device, it won't obscure the whole screen, which is the default (either fullScreen or overFullScreen, to be precise, depending on the setting of transparent, because only overFullScreen allows for transparency). Note that presentationStyle is an iOS-only property and is ignored on Android.

Inside the Modal, you can have any valid content you wish, as simple or as complex a UI as you require. Here, that's just a Text component and the aforementioned TouchableHighlight component (and another Text component nested inside that), all wrapped inside two View components, used to provide a basic layout and ensure there's some space on the top of the content inside the Modal.

In addition to the props seen here, there are a few callback handlers that you can use. The onRequestClose prop will be called when the user taps the hardware back button on Android devices or the menu button on Apple TV devices. The onDismiss prop will be called whenever the user dismisses the Modal. Correspondingly, onShow is called right after the Modal is shown.

WebView

The WebView component renders HTML content in a native web View component. Note that this includes CSS, JavaScript, and anything else you can typically display in a web browser (subject to whatever limitations might exist on a given platform). Interestingly, there are no required props for this component, because it's possible to create an empty WebView and then write dynamic content into it, which would not require you to supply props initially. However, a typical usage does require at least the source prop, like so:

```
<WebView source={{ uri : "https://facebook.github.io/react-native" }} />
```

The source doesn't have to be a network address, however. It can also be a static file included in your app. In addition, the source prop can be an object instead of a string, in which case, you can supply not only a uri but also headers for the request, as well as the

HTTP method to use and the content for the body of the request. So, if you want to make a REST call and have the response displayed in a WebView, you can do exactly that! Or, you can supply HTML content directly in the object, via an html attribute on the object, and it will be rendered into the WebView.

The list of props for this component is fairly long, but there are a few you might find most interesting. First up is injectJavaScript, which is a string that will be passed into the WebView and executed immediately as JavaScript. Next is mediaPlaybackRequiresUserAction, which determines whether HTML5 audio and video content requires the user to tap the rendered player controls in the WebView to start them playing. The onLoadStart/onLoad/onLoadEnd/onError props allow you to hook into the life cycle of the WebView (when the WebView starts loading; when it finishes loading, if successful; when it finishes loading, whether successful or not; and if an error occurs, respectively). Finally, initialScale, for Android only, tells the WebView the initial percentage to scale the content to.

iOS-Specific Components

The previous four groups had at least one thing in common: all the components in them are cross-platform. That, of course, is one of the big attractions of React Native: what you write will work across multiple mobile platforms. However, there are situations in which what you are trying to accomplish actually does require something platform-specific, and that's what the fifth group (as well as the final sixth group) is all about. React Native offers some components that are specific to iOS and wrap around UIKit classes. As I'm sure you can guess, there are also components specific to Android, but that's stealing my own thunder. Let's look at the iOS-specific components now, and we'll get to the Android-specific ones in the next section.

ActionSheetIOS

The ActionSheetIOS (Figure 2-10) component is the first component you've seen that only supplies methods. In React Native parlance, it only has an imperative UI. That means that there is no <ActionSheetIOS> tag at any time. Instead, you have to request this component in response to some action, like so:

```
<Button title="Open ActionSheetIOS"
  onPress={ () => {
    ActionSheetIOS.showActionSheetWithOptions(
      { title : "My Favorite Muppet", message : "Pick one, human!",
        options: [ "Fozzy", "Gonzo", "Kermit", "Piggie" ]
      },
      (buttonIndex) => { console.log(buttonIndex); }
    );
  }}
/>
```

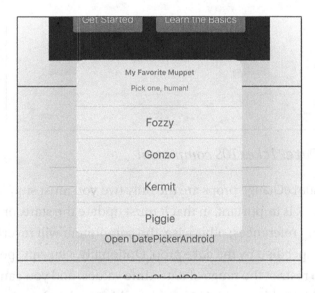

Figure 2-10. *The* `ActionSheetIOS` *component*

From the `onPress` handler of a `Button` component, the
`showActionSheetWithOptions()` method of the `ActionSheetIOS` component is called,
passing it two things: a configuration object and a callback function. The configuration
object can contain several options. In this case, it's a `title` to show above the choices
and a smaller `message` text to show below the title text. Then, an array of `options` to
display is provided.

The callback function can do whatever you like, of course; in this case, I'm just
outputting the index of the selected option to the console.

DatePickerIOS

The DatePickerIOS (Figure 2-11) component renders a date/time selector on iOS devices. Here's a basic usage:

```
<DatePickerIOS
  style={{ width : 400, height : 200 }} date={ this.state.chosenDate }
  onDateChange={ (inDate) => this.setState({ chosenDate : inDate }) }
/>
```

Sat May 26	10	26	
Sun May 27	11	27	
Mon May 28	12	28	AM
Today	**1**	**29**	**PM**
Wed May 30	2	30	
Thu May 31	3	31	
Fri Jun 1	4	32	

Figure 2-11. *The* DatePickerIOS *component*

The date and onDateChange props are the only two you must supply. The onDateChange callback is important, in that it must update the state, or whatever variable the date prop references; otherwise, the component will revert to whatever value was originally specified by the date prop. Optionally, you can specify minimumDate and maximumDate, to restrict the range of date/time values, and you can specify a mode prop with a value of date, time, or datetime (defaulting to date), to determine what information the user will select.

SegmentedControlIOS

A SegmentedControlIOS component (Figure 2-12) is another way to present the user with a selection of mutually exclusive options to choose from. You can think of it as a variation on the radio buttons common in HTML. To show this component, you do something like this:

```
<SegmentedControlIOS style={{ width : 400 }}
  values={ [ "Venus", "Earth", "Mars" ] }
  selectedIndex={ this.state.segmentedIndex }
```

```
  onChange={ (inEvent) => {
    this.setState({
      segmentedIndex : inEvent.nativeEvent.selectedSegmentIndex
    });
  }}
/>
```

Venus	Earth	Mars

Figure 2-12. *The SegmentedControlIOS component*

Only the `options` prop is required, although this component won't be of much use without an `onChange` prop as well, so you'll likely always supply that. You can have a default selection to begin with, by specifying the `selectedIndex` prop. By default, the selected item remains visibly selected, but if you just want a momentary visual change, so that the segments act more like buttons, you can specify the `momentary` prop set to `true`. The `tintColor` prop allows you to specify the color of the selected item and the text and borders. Finally, if you have to change the `selectedIndex` programmatically, you can do that just by updating the `state` variable tied to this component. React Native will see the change and take care of updating the component for you (this, by the way, is how you programmatically change most components' props, where applicable).

Android-Specific Components

The final group of components is a collection that is specific to the Android platform. These components wrap several commonly used native Android classes, things that are typically seen only on Android.

DatePickerAndroid

In a previous section, you saw the `DatePickerIOS` component that allows the user to enter a date/time on iOS. It turns out that Android has its own version of this, and it is, not surprisingly, named `DatePickerAndroid` (Figure 2-13). Unlike the iOS version, this component on Android is only activated by its imperative UI, meaning that like `ActionSheetIOS` before it, something must trigger its creation. For example, you may have a button to do so.

```
<Button title="Open DatePickerAndroid"
  onPress={ async () => {
    const { action, year, month, day } = await DatePickerAndroid.open({
      date : new Date()
    });
  }}
/>
```

Figure 2-13. *The DatePickerAndroid component*

Because getting a date is an asynchronous operation, a promise is returned by the open() call, so perhaps the best way to write the code to use it is with the async/await keywords. That way, execution halts in the anonymous function the onPress prop points until a date is selected (until the promise resolves, in other words).

This component has very little in the way of props, only two subtypes on top of the open() method. The first subtype is dateSetAction, which is used to determine when a user has selected a date. The other type is dismissedAction, which occurs when the dialog has been dismissed (canceled, without a date being selected). The way you use these is with the action value returned by the open() call. All you do is add some code immediately after the line with the open() call, like so:

```
if (action === DatePickerAndroid.dateSetAction) {
  console.log(year + " " + month + " " + day);
}
```

Thanks to the async/await usage, this if statement will only execute once a date has been selected and will, of course, log the selected date. Similarly, if you want to know when the user did not select a date, you can use dismissedAction in the same way.

```
if (action === DatePickerAndroid.dismissedAction) {
  console.log("Dismissed");
}
```

And that's all there is to this component. Note that unlike DatePickerIOS, DatePickerAndroid only lets you select a date, not a time. But, hey, time matters to us all, doesn't it? Because it does, that's what the next component is for.

TimePickerAndroid

Selecting a time on Android requires the use of TimePickerAndroid (Figure 2-14), for which there's no direct analogy on the iOS side, because there, the DatePickerIOS allows entry of both date and time. But that's okay. Right now, I'm only talking about entering a time, and it works the same as using DatePickerAndroid.

```
<Button title="Open TimePickerAndroid"
  onPress={ async () => {
    const { action, hour, minute } = await TimePickerAndroid.open({
      hour : 16, minute : 30, is24Hour : false
    });
    if (action === TimePickerAndroid.timeSetAction) {
      console.log(hour + ":" + minute);
    }
```

```
    if (action === TimePickerAndroid.dismissedAction) {
      console.log("Dismissed");
    }
  }}
/>
```

Figure 2-14. *The* `TimePickerAndroid` *component*

Here, instead of passing a date to the open() method, we give it an hour and minute as the initial time to select (or don't pass those in, if you prefer, in which case, you'll get the current time). We can also tell the picker whether we want to use an AM/PM chooser, which we get by setting is24Hour to false, or a 24-hour picker, when set to true (the default). Specifying is24Hour is optional and will use the default for the current locale, if not specified. We can also pass a mode attribute. The default value is clock, which shows an analog clock face to select the time. The other choice is spinner, which shows the time picker in spinner mode.

Regardless of those settings, the values in hour and minute are returned as 24-hour values, so 4:30 p.m. would be returned as 16 for hour and 30 for minute.

ViewPagerAndroid

The final component we'll be looking at in this chapter is the ViewPagerAndroid component. It's a simple component that allows the user to swipe between multiple pieces of content. Using it looks like this:

```
<ViewPagerAndroid initialPage={ 0 }
  style={{ flex : 1, width : "100%", height : 100 }}
>
  <View style={{ alignItems : "center", padding : 10 }}>
    <Text style={{ fontSize : 24 }}>Page{"\n"}Number{"\n"}1</Text>
  </View>
  <View style={{ alignItems : 'center', padding : 10 }}>
    <Text style={{ fontSize : 24 }}>Page{"\n"}Number{"\n"}2</Text>
  </View>
</ViewPagerAndroid>
```

The component wraps some number of View components, which can contain any content you wish. One of these Views, whichever one the initialPage prop specifies (or the first in the array of children, if you don't include this prop), is displayed. The user can then swipe left and right, to access the others.

In addition to initialPage, this component also has the following props:

- keyboardDismissMode: Determines whether the keyboard gets dismissed in response to a drag (defaults to none, and you can also specify on-drag, to dismiss the keyboard when dragging begins)

- pageMargin: This is the amount of space, if any, to show between pages when they are scrolling (the pages are still edge-to-edge when not scrolling).

- peekEnabled: When true (defaults to false), a portion of the next and last pages are shown when dragging.

- scrollEnabled: When true (the default), content does not scroll.

- onPageScroll: A callback executed when transitioning between pages

- onPageScrollStateChanged: A callback executed when the page scrolling state has changed. (The state is either idle, meaning no interaction is currently occurring; dragging, meaning there is currently a drag interaction occurring; or settling, meaning there was a drag interaction and the page opening and closing animation is completing.)

- onPageSelected: A callback executed once the component finishes navigating to a selected page

APIs

Now that I've surveyed all the components, let's look at the next topic of this chapter: APIs. APIs are, of course, collections of functions that you can call on in your application code to perform various functions. These APIs provide you access to many native device capabilities, as well as common pieces of functionality that many apps require. Each API serves a specific purpose, as you'll see.

Like components, some APIs are cross-platform, and some are specific to either iOS or Android. The names of the APIs, just as with the components, tell you which is the case: if it says IOS at the end of the name, it's iOS-specific; if it says Android, it's Android-specific. If it says neither, it is cross-platform. Also, like components, you import APIs the same way you do components, because, after all, they're just JavaScript modules.

AccessibilityInfo

The AccessibilityInfo API offers functions related to accessibility concerns, such as determining whether the device currently has an active screen reader attached. You can use it to query for the current state of the screen reader, by calling the fetch() method. Or, you can request that some code you provide be executed when the status changes, by calling the addEventListener() method and specifying a supported event (change, which fires when the state of the screen reader changes, or announcementfinished, which for iOS-only devices fires when the screen reader has finished making an announcement).

There is also a removeEventListener() method, which is typically used in conjunction with a corresponding addEventListener() call. A typical usage might be to register some code with addEventListener() in a component's componentDidMount() method, and then call removeEventListener() in componentWillUnmount(). This ensures that no memory leaks occur, something that is rather easy to do with event listeners in general.

By way of example, here's how you might use this API:

```
class ScreenReaderStatusExample extends React.Component {

  state = { isEnabled : false, };

  componentDidMount() {
    AccessibilityInfo.addEventListener("change", this.toggleState);
    AccessibilityInfo.fetch().done((isEnabled) => {
      this.setState({ isEnabled : isEnabled, });
    });
  }

  componentWillUnmount() {
    AccessibilityInfo.removeEventListener("change", this.toggleState);
  }

  toggleState = (isEnabled) => {
    this.setState({ isEnabled : isEnabled });
  };

  render() {
    return (
      <View>
        <Text>
          The screen reader is{" "}
          { this.state.isEnabled ? "enabled" : "disabled" }.
        </Text>
      </View>
    );
  }
}
```

Tip   This is also a good example of something that comes up often, which is how whitespace is ignored within Text components. See that { " " } expression after the first line? It's necessary because, without it, the words *is* and *enabled* or *disabled* wouldn't have any space between them, as whitespace at the end and beginning of content inside a Text component is ignored. This is a handy trick to keep in mind.

Alert and AlertIOS

The Alert API has a single alert() method that launches an alert dialog appropriate for the platform with a title and message displayed. A dialog can have one or more buttons, which you can specify yourself or allow the default OK button to be displayed.

A simple example could be this bit of code:

```
Alert.alert("Greetings, human!",
  "You know just how to push my buttons!",
  [ { text : "OK" } ], { cancelable : false }
)
```

Here, the title of the alert is the first argument and an optional message is second. Although it's the default, I've specified an OK button explicitly, as the third argument, which is completely okay to do, though superfluous.

Although this API is cross-platform, there are some platform-specific details to be aware of. First, on iOS, you can specify any number of buttons, and each button can define a style, which must be either default, cancel, or destructive. The destructive button is red, and the cancel button is bolded. On Android, however, there can be at most three buttons specified, and Android has the concept of a neutral button, a negative button, and a positive button. If only one button is specified, it's automatically considered positive. If two are provided, such as Cancel and OK, one is negative, and one is positive. For three buttons, each type will be represented by one button.

Also for Android, by default, an alert can be dismissed by tapping outside the alert itself. You can provide a callback handler, by supplying a fourth argument to alert(), the value of which is an object that contains options. If you provide an onDismiss attribute on that object that is the function, it will be executed when the alert is dismissed in this way.

Alternatively, you can disable the dismiss behavior completely, as shown in the sample, by providing a `cancelable` attribute set to `false`.

While showing static information in an alert is a common use case, there is also a use case in which user input is required. This, however, isn't something supported on both platforms. Only iOS has this capability, so there is, in addition to the `Alert` API, an `AlertIOS` API. This API, in addition to having an `alert()` method like the `Alert` API for displaying static information, also provides a `prompt()` method.

The `prompt()` method is passed a title and text as the first two arguments, just as with the `alert()` method, but now the third argument can be a callback function that will be passed what the user enters the alert. You can still provide custom buttons, if you wish, and there are some configuration options available, if the prompt is for sensitive information, such as passwords, so that it will be hidden when entered, for security purposes.

As an example, here's an alert prompt for entering a password:

```
AlertIOS.prompt(
  "Password", "Please enter your password",
  (inPassword) => console.log("Your password is " + inPassword),
  "login-password", "???"
);
```

Animated

The `Animated` API is a rather extensive API, designed to make animations fluid, powerful, and easy to build and maintain. It's one that could have an entire chapter dedicated to it. Many components in React Native use this API behind the scenes, although you absolutely can use it directly yourself. The basic idea behind this API is to define starting and ending points for an animation, with some number of configurable transformations between them, which run over a given period of time. In other words, you define the starting state of something, such as the color of some text, say, and the ending state, such as if you want to fade the text gradually from red to green. You tell this API those things and to transform between red text and green text over a specified period of time, and it happily does it for you, without you having to figure out the details.

Because this API is so extensive, and I know I can't do it justice in a short section such as this, I'm going to leave it as something for you to explore further on your own. That said, I'll offer you a quick example, so that you have a basic idea of what the code looks like.

```
Animated.timing(this.state.fadeAnim, {
  toValue : 1, duration : 1000, easing : Easing.inOut(Easing.ease), delay :
  1000
}).start();
```

Yep, that's it! The `timing()` method is one of the most commonly used Animated API methods, because it allows you to change the value of some variable over a given period of time, optionally using a defined `easing` curve, indicating how the value changes over time, whether via a simple linear progression or by starting slow, getting faster, then slowing down at the end. The first argument is the value to change over time, and the second argument is a configuration object. Most of the attributes in this object are optional, but here I've defined the final value that represents the end of this animation as `toValue` (this attribute is, in fact, required). I've also specified the `duration` of the animation (one second here, or 1000 milliseconds), what `easing` curve to use from one of the predefined curves in the `Easing` API (which contains just a collection of static members that are various easing functions you might use). Note that the easing function shown here is, in fact, the default anyway, so specifying it isn't necessary. There is also `delay`, which optionally tells the `Animated` API how long to wait before kicking off the animation.

Caution   As wonderful as the `Animated` API is, it's important to know that it can only be used on components that allow for animation, namely, `View`, `Text`, `Image`, and `ScrollView`, at the time of writing. You can also create your own using the `Animated.createAnimatedComponent()` method. You'll definitely want to consult the docs of this API for more information, especially given that there's every chance that what can be animated will expand as time goes on.

AppState

The `AppState` API can be used to determine if your app is in the foreground or background and can optionally notify your code when that state changes. This information is most commonly used to determine how your app should react to push notifications.

An app can be in one of the following three states:

- *Active*: The app is running in the foreground.

- *Background*: The app is running in the background (which means that the user is either in another app, is on the home screen, or, for Android, is in another activity, even if launched from the same app).

- *Inactive*: The app is either transitioning between the two previous states or there has been a long period of inactivity (as you might imagine, this and, really, the other two are somewhat platform-dependent, but React Native seeks to normalize them, so you can treat them the same across platforms, for most intents and purposes).

To use this API, you can either read the `AppState.currentState` attribute or you can use the same sort of `addEventListener()` and `removeEventListener()` logic you saw when we looked at `AccessibilityInfo`, to have some code you specify executed anytime the app's state changes.

BackHandler

The `BackHandler` API is for Android only and is exceedingly simple. It only offers `addEventListener()` and `removeEventListener()` methods (there is also an `exitApp()` method, and it's a good guess that it forces an exit from the app, but it's just that, a guess, because there's no documentation for it that I could find). You call `addEventListener()`, requesting a callback for the `hardwareBackPress` event, and implement whatever logic is appropriate when the back button is pressed, if any.

It should be noted that you can have multiple subscriptions for a given event, and the handlers are called in reverse order, that is, the last one registered is called first. They will continue to be called in reverse order, unless and until one returns `true`, in which case, the sequence ends.

Clipboard

The `Clipboard` API is a straightforward API that gives you access to the device's clipboard, using the `getString()` and `setString()` methods. So, to save a string to the clipboard you do the following:

```
Clipboard.setString("My string");
```

To retrieve a string from the clipboard, use

```
let s = await Clipboard.getString();
```

Because getString() returns a promise, using await is a good way to deal with it. Remember that for await to work, whatever function this code is within must be prefixed with async (or you can handle the promise another way, if you prefer; it's your choice).

Note that you can't store anything but a string to the clipboard with this API alone, at least not without introducing some additional native code to your project. However, if you can serialize an object to a string, you can store it on the clipboard, so Base64-encoding an image, for example, and saving it to the clipboard is a possibility.

Dimensions

The Dimensions API is a simple one that provides a means to get the dimensions of the device's screen. A call to its get() method, passing it what you want dimensions for (window being the only documented value at present), returns an object with various attributes, as you can see here:

```
{ "fontScale": 0.8999999761581421, "scale": 3.5,
  "width": 411.42857142857144, "height": 731.4285714285714 }
```

The width and height attributes are probably the ones you'll be most interested in, but who am I to judge?

Additionally, this API provides an addEventListener() and removeEventListener() pair and an event type change that fires anytime anything in the dimensions change. It may seem odd that the dimensions of a screen can vary, but there's one key instance in which they can: when the screen rotates. The width and height will, of course, swap, and you very well may want to have code that changes your layout when switching from landscape to portrait and vice versa, and this API provides a way to do that.

Geolocation

The Geolocation API is a bit of an oddball, in that it's the first component or API you've seen that you *do not* have to import explicitly. That's because this API is a browser polyfill that extends the Geolocation web spec, and, as such, it's automatically available on the navigator.geolocation global object. I haven't mentioned global scope before, and that's because, by and large, you won't use it directly in your code, but there are situations in which you will, and this API is one of them. There is quite a lot of stuff in global scope, which you can see for yourself by putting a `console.log(global);` line in some code and looking at what gets dumped to the console. The `global` variable is a special one that represents global scope, which means you could do `global.navigator.geolocation`, and it would work. But React Native works some behind-the-scenes magic to make it, so you don't have to reference attributes of global like that. You can access things like `navigator` directly.

Global scope aside, this API is straightforward. There's an optional `setRNConfiguration()` method that allows you to set configurations for location requests (currently there is only a single iOS-only option, `skipPermissionRequests`, which, when `true`, forces the user to okay the position requests). Then there's the method you'll probably be most interested in: `getCurrentPosition()`. This accepts a function to call on successful location determination, one to call if an error occurs, and options. The options include `timeout`, to set a limit on how long to wait for a location, `maximumAge`, which determines how long a cached location is good for, and `enableHighAccuracy`, which on Android only enables getting a location with higher accuracy than usual.

Alternatively, you can use the `watchLocation()` method, to call a function you supply anytime the location changes. This has the same success handler, error handler, and options parameter list as `getCurrentPosition()`, but it has a few extra options available. These are `distanceFilter` and `useSignificantChanges`, both of which, frankly, aren't documented anywhere I could find, so I can't say with certainty what they're for. But, I think their names allow for a reasonable guess, which I'll leave to you. There's a corresponding `clearWatch()` method, to stop watching location changes, and a `stopObserving()` method, which seems to do much the same thing as `clearWatch()`, except that it automatically removes any added listeners and stops the API itself from watching for location changes, whether your code is watching for them (as a power-saving measure).

By way of example, the Geolocation API can be used as follows:

```
navigator.geolocation.getCurrentPosition(
  (position) => { console.log("getCurrentPosition()", position); },
  (error) => { console.log("getCurrentPosition() error", error); },
  { enableHighAccuracy : true, timeout : 20000, maximumAge : 1000 }
);
```

And the output of this would be

```
getCurrentPosition() Object {
  "coords": Object {
    "accuracy": 65,
    "altitude": 41.38749748738746,
    "altitudeAccuracy": 10,
    "heading": -1,
    "latitude": 32.38729736476293,
    "longitude": -22.192837464023,
    "speed": -1,
  },
  "timestamp": 1527607301269.7148,
}
```

InteractionManager

The InteractionManager API is an API that allows long-running tasks to be scheduled, so that they execute only after any user touch interactions and/or animations have completed to keep everything running smoothly. It contains only a small handful of methods.

- runAfterInteractions: Schedules a given function to execute after all interactions have completed

- createInteractionHandle: Notifies the manager that an interaction has started

- clearInteractionHandle: Notifies the manager that that an interaction has finished

- setDeadline: Specifies a time-out value to schedule any tasks for after the eventLoopRunningTime hits the deadline value; otherwise, all tasks will be executed in one setImmediate batch (which is the default)

If that seems a little complicated, maybe an example will help clear it up.

```
InteractionManager.runAfterInteractions(() => {
  // Implement some long-running task here
});
const handle = InteractionManager.createInteractionHandle();
// Now run any animations you need to
InteractionManager.clearInteractionHandle(handle);
// All tasks queued up via runAfterInteractions() are now executed
```

Keyboard

The Keyboard API allows your code to listen for native keyboard events of interest and react to them in some application-specific way and also provides some control over the keyboard, such as dismissing it.

First, there is an addListener() method, which that allows you to listen for any of the following events, the names of which I think do quite a good job of telling you what they are all about:

Note   I was not able to determine what the keyboardWillChangeFrame and keyboardDidChangeFrame are really all about, but they seem to be iOS-specific. Hey, the React Native docs are pretty good, but this chapter proves there definitely are some gaps, and this is one.

- keyboardWillShow

- keyboardDidShow

- keyboardWillHide

- keyboardDidHide

- keyboardWillChangeFrame

- keyboardDidChangeFrame

There is, of course, a corresponding removeListener(), in keeping with the pattern you've seen a number of times before. This time, however, there is also a removeAllListeners() method, if brevity is your thing. Finally, the dismiss() method does exactly that: dismisses the keyboard.

It's a simple API, but then, we're talking about a keyboard, not exactly the pinnacle of human ingenuity, so it doesn't need to be super deep, I suppose.

LayoutAnimation

The LayoutAnimation API allows you to tell React Native to automatically animate views to their new positions when they move when the next layout occurs. A common use case is to call this API before a call to setState(), so that if that state change results in any views moving, they can be animated in doing so.

While there are three methods in this API, two of them, create() and checkConfig(), are optional helper methods (which happen not to be well-documented). The one essential method is configureNext(). This accepts two arguments: a config object (which can be created with that create() method, but doesn't have to be) and, optionally, a function to call when the animation ends (which is only supported on iOS). The config object contains three attributes. The first is duration, which is how long the animation will take in milliseconds. Second is create, which is an Anim type that defines the animation to use for views that are coming into view. Finally, there is update, which is similarly an Anim type but describes the animation to use for views that were already visible but have been updated.

NetInfo

The NetInfo API provides some methods and a property that allows you to determine the connectivity state of a device. The first way to use this API is via its getConnectionInfo() method.

```
NetInfo.getConnectionInfo().then((inConnectionInfo) => {
  console.log("getConnectionInfo()", inConnectionInfo);
});
```

This returns a promise that resolves to an object with two attributes, type and effectiveType. The type attribute is of type NetInfo.ConnectionType, which is an enum with values none, wifi, cellular, and unknown and three Android-only types: bluetooth, ethernet, or wimax. The effectiveType is of type NetInfo.EffectiveConnectionType and is an enum that further defines the connection type, when the type is cellular, with the values 2g, 3g, 4g, and unknown.

You can also monitor network status by using the addEventListener() method (and the corresponding removeEventListener() method, of course), to listen for the connectionChange event, which fires when the network status changes.

There is also an isConnected property that can asynchronously fetch a Boolean to determine if Internet connectivity is currently available. To use it, you write

```
NetInfo.isConnected.fetch().then(isConnected => {
  console.log(`We are currently ${isConnected ? "Online" : "Offline"}`);
});
```

Finally, this method, for Android only, provides an isConnectionExpensive() method that tells you whether the connection is metered. An sample usage looks similar to using isConnected().

```
NetInfo.isConnectionExpensive()
.then(isConnectionExpensive => {
  console.log(`Connection is ${(isConnectionExpensive ? "Metered" : "Not Metered")}`);
})
.catch(error => { console.log("isConnectionExpensive() not supported on iOS"); });
```

Of course, to keep your code cross-platform, an error handler should be used here, to avoid problems on iOS devices, hence the reason this code is slightly different from that for isConnected().

Note   In addition to isConnectionExpensive(), Android provides more information about network connectivity than does iOS, including whether the device is connected to Bluetooth, whether it's connected via Ethernet, or whether it's connected via WiMAX. You'll definitely want to check the docs for this API, to ensure that the code you write is either cross-platform or will work in iOS vs. Android.

PixelRatio

The PixelRatio API gives you access to information about the device's pixel density. This is useful, because modern apps are expected to use higher resolution images, if the device has a high-density display, so being able to determine that in your code is critical.

The methods provided by this API are

- get(): Returns the device pixel density, limited examples of which include 1 (mdpi Android devices @ 160 dpi), 1.5 (hdpi Android devices @ 240 dpi), 2 (iPhone 4/4S/5/5c/5s/6), 3 (iPhone 6 plus), and so on

- getFontScale(): Returns the scaling factor for font sizes, that is, the ratio used to calculate absolute font size (or the device pixel ratio, if a font scale is not explicitly set) for Android only. (It reflects the user preference Settings ➤ Display ➤ Font size, and on iOS, it will always return the default pixel ratio.)

- getPixelSizeForLayoutSize(): Converts a layout size (dp) to pixel size (px) (guaranteed to return an integer number)

- roundToNearestPixel(): Rounds a layout size (dp) to the nearest layout size that corresponds to an integer number of pixels

As you can probably guess from the types of values shown here, you absolutely must refer to the documentation to determine what values you really can get on a given device and how to deal with them. In fact, this is one time I'm going to quote directly from the React Native docs, because I don't think I could explain it any better.

Fetching a correctly sized image

You should get a higher resolution image if you are on a high pixel density device. A good rule of thumb is to multiply the size of the image you display by the pixel ratio.

var image = getImage({

width: PixelRatio.getPixelSizeForLayoutSize(200),

height: PixelRatio.getPixelSizeForLayoutSize(100),

});

<Image source={image} style={{width: 200, height: 100}} />

Pixel grid snapping

In iOS, you can specify positions and dimensions for elements with arbitrary precision, for example, 29.674825. But, ultimately, the physical display only has a fixed number of pixels, for example, 640×960 for iPhone 4 or 750×1334 for iPhone 6. iOS tries to be as faithful as possible to the user value, by spreading one original pixel into multiple ones to trick the eye. The downside of this technique is that it makes the resulting element look blurry.

In practice, we found out that developers do not want this feature, and they have to work around it by doing manual rounding, in order to avoid having blurry elements. In React Native, we are rounding all the pixels automatically.

We have to be careful when to do this rounding. You never want to work with rounded and unrounded values at the same time, as you're going to accumulate rounding errors. Having even one rounding error is deadly, because a one-pixel border may vanish or be twice as big.

In React Native, everything in JavaScript and within the layout engine works with arbitrary precision numbers. It's only when we set the position and dimensions of the native element on the main thread that we round. Also, rounding is done relative to the root, rather than the parent, again to avoid accumulating rounding errors.

Platform

The Platform API is something you'll wind up using a fair bit in those places where you must branch your code, based on what platform it's running on. The API is straightforward, providing three primary things.

First, is a static member named OS that tells you the name of the platform (a string with a value of either ios or android). There is also a Version attribute that provides information about the version of the platform (for Android, it will be the API level; for iOS, it's a string in the form major.minor, 10.3, for example). You can, of course, write any sort of branching logic with these values as you see fit. For example, you may have to adjust the height of a style, based on the platform.

```
const styles = StyleSheet.create({
  height : Platform.OS === "ios" ? 250 : 125,
});
```

Or, maybe you need to use an API that is only available on certain versions of Android:

```
if (Platform.Version === 25) {
  // Make version-dependent call here
}
```

One other thing this API provides is a select() method. This is frequently used in style definitions, such as the preceding example, but is a little different.

```
const styles = StyleSheet.create({
  container : {
    flex : 1,
    ...Platform.select({
      ios : { backgroundColor : "#ff0000" },
      android: { backgroundColor : "#00ff00" }
    })
  }
});
```

The result of this will be a StyleSheet (the next API we'll be looking at) that has a flex of 1 and a red background in iOS and a green one in Android. Which branching method you use is really a matter of preference.

One final way that this API can be used is to select a platform-dependent component.

```
const Component = Platform.select({
  ios: () => require("ComponentIOS"),
  android: () => require("ComponentAndroid"),
})();
<Component />
```

In this way, you can alter the layout and component hierarchy, based on what platform the app is running on. As I'm sure you can guess, you'll be seeing more of this API in action in later chapters, as it's key to making an app that works properly across multiple platforms.

StyleSheet

You've already seen the StyleSheet API in action by way of the StyleSheet.create() method, so you already know that it takes in a JavaScript object and returns a new StyleSheet object from it.

Why do we do this in the first place? Well, for a couple of reasons. First, as with CSS on the Web, you make your code easier to understand by not having all the styles inlined in the render() method. It also provides a more generally better accepted organization and separation of concerns. Also, by naming the styles, you help add meaning to the low-level component in the render() method. Third, when you inline styles, a new StyleSheet object is automatically created behind the scenes, which means anytime the render() method is called, which means anytime the layout changes, which means this can happen a lot! That's not good for performance. Finally, when styles are defined in this manner, they are sent through the render bridge only once and cached with subsequent usages looking them up by ID. (That said, this appears to be something that isn't quite implemented yet, according to the docs at the time of writing.)

In addition to create(), there is also a flatten() method that takes in an array of styles and returns a single object with all the styles concatenated. For example:

```
const stylesAPITest = StyleSheet.create({
  style1 : { flex : 1, fontSize : 12, color : "red" },
  style2 : { color : "blue" },
});
const stylesAPITestNew =
  StyleSheet.flatten([stylesAPITest.style1, stylesAPITest.style2]);
console.log("stylesAPITestNew", stylesAPITestNew);
```

This will display

```
stylesAPITestNew Object {
  "flex": 1,
  "fontSize": 12,
  "color": "blue"
}
```

Note how the color attribute takes on the value of the last item in the array.

ToastAndroid

As the name implies, this API is for Android only and provides access to the toast message facility that platform offers. These are short pop-up messages that typically alert the user to some action having been completed. Showing them with the following API is very easy:

```
<Button title="Show Toast Message (Android Only)"
  onPress={ async () => {
    ToastAndroid.show("I am a short message", ToastAndroid.SHORT);
    ToastAndroid.showWithGravity(
      "I am a message with gravity, centered",
      ToastAndroid.SHORT, ToastAndroid.CENTER
    );
    ToastAndroid.showWithGravityAndOffset(
      "I am a message with gravity, offset from the bottom",
      ToastAndroid.LONG, ToastAndroid.TOP,
      -75, Dimensions.get("window").height / 2
    );
  }}
/>
```

Here, three different toast messages are shown. The API automatically queues these up, so that the second doesn't show up until the first is dismissed (either automatically after some period of time or via the user clicking it), and the third likewise doesn't show up until the second is gone.

You can see that there are three different methods available. The first, and the one you'll probably use most, is show(). It just shows the message specified near the bottom of the screen, which is the most typical location for toast messages to appear, and for a specified duration in milliseconds. (You can use one of the constants defined as attributes of ToastAndroid, SHORT or LONG, or you can specify a value yourself.) There is also showWithGravity(), which allows you to determine the layout gravity, which is an overly complicated way of saying where the message will appear. (There are two constants for this, CENTER and BOTTOM, which are self-explanatory. Note that TOP also works, although it's not documented). Finally, there is showWithGravityAndOffset(), which does the same as showWithGravity() but additionally allows you to specify offset X and Y values. In this example, I have the third message appearing near the top, but then moving it left 75 pixels and down half the height of the window (which is determined using the Dimensions API discussed previously).

Vibration

The final API to consider is the Vibration API. This is a very simple API that contains a total of two methods, vibrate() and cancel(), and which is concerned with haptic feedback. For devices that don't support vibration, any calls to this API are safely ignored, so you don't have to wrap the calls in any sort of platform determination logic.

To use this API, you simply call the vibrate() method.

```
Vibration.vibrate([ 250, 2000, 250, 1500, 250, 1000, 250, 500 ]);
```

The method accepts as its first argument either a single number, which is the duration to vibrate for (which only has meaning on Android; iOS does not allow you to configure the duration, and it will vibrate for around 500ms, regardless of what you pass in here) or can be an array of values. When it's an array, as in the example, the values alternate between some number of milliseconds to wait and some number of milliseconds to vibrate for. So, on Android, this example will wait 250ms, then vibrate for 2000ms, then wait for 250ms, then vibrate for 1500ms, and so on. You can also optionally pass a Boolean as a second argument, and if it's true, the pattern will repeat until the cancel() method is called.

Summary

Whew, this chapter was a whirlwind! In it, you took a trip through React Native land, examining each of the components and APIs it offers by default (meaning without adding any extra libraries on top of it). This gives you a good foundation from which to go forward and build apps.

In the next chapter, we'll begin building one such app, and in the process, you'll learn new concepts about React Native, such as how to structure a React Native app and the navigation between parts of the app. And, of course, you'll start to gain real experience in working with the components and APIs you saw briefly in this chapter.

Hang on to your hats; it's going to be quite a ride!

CHAPTER 3

Restaurant Chooser, Part 1

Alright, now the fun begins! In the previous two chapters, you got an introduction to React Native, and I surveyed what it has to offer. You even saw a first simple Hello World–type app. Now, with those preliminaries out of the way, it's time to get to the meat of this book—writing some real apps, beginning with Restaurant Chooser.

Before I get too far, I want to note that the code in this book has been condensed for the printed page. Spacing has been altered, comments removed, and some reformatting of lines has been done, in the interest of saving space. Rest assured, however, that the actual code—the real content—appears here as it appears in the download bundle, and that's what matters.

With that said, let's get right to it, beginning with an obvious question.

What Are We Building?

The Restaurant Chooser app seeks to solve a real-world problem that I suspect many have been through: the contest that ensues when you ask a group of people the simple question, Where would you like to go for dinner?

This is a frequent problem with my family, because one kid says, "I don't like the Mexican place!" and another admits, "I don't know what I want!" and then my wife declares, "I don't care," none of which helps to reach a decision. So, I wrote this app to solve the problem.

In simplest terms, you create people and restaurants in the app, and then you let the app choose an eatery for you, with some caveats. First, you select the people who are going to eat, then the group you're trying to feed can do some pre-filtering, if it wants. So, for example, if everyone magically agrees that they want Chinese food, that's good,

© Frank Zammetti 2018
F. Zammetti, *Practical React Native*, https://doi.org/10.1007/978-1-4842-3939-1_3

because it narrows the choices (unless you've only got one favorite Chinese restaurant, in which case, there's still a decision to be made). Perhaps you only want to patronize a top restaurant, so you prefer to pre-filter by star rating. Then, once that's done, and the app makes a selection, each person in the group gets one veto. So, if a majority chooses a Greek restaurant, but Mister "I don't like Greek food" objects, he can exercise his veto, and the app will choose another restaurant. Once a restaurant is selected that no one vetoes—or when everyone has vetoed once—that restaurant is the final outcome, like it or not.

It's not a complicated app, but it legitimately can be useful, and regardless of its utility, it will serve as an excellent, not overly complicated app to learn some React Native with.

So, what does it look like? Well, it all begins with a splash screen when the app is starting up, as shown in Figure 3-1 (with the iOS version on the left and Android version on the right).

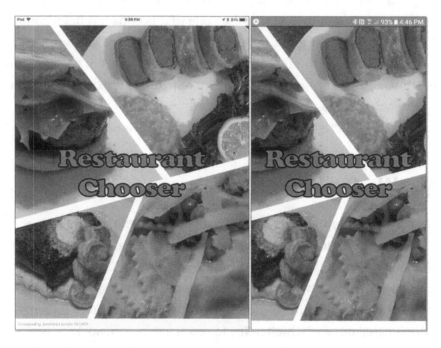

Figure 3-1. *Splash screen (cheap plug: with my wife's cooking shown)*

Once the app loads, the users initially find themselves on the It's Decision Time screen, as shown in Figure 3-2.

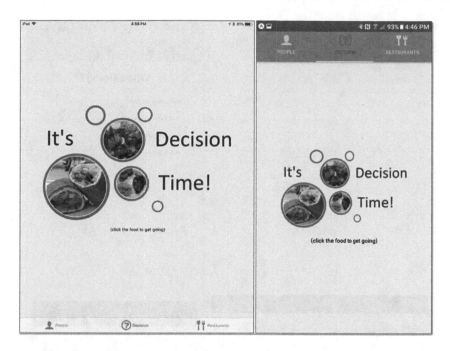

Figure 3-2. *Where it all begins*

You'll notice right away that there is a tabbed interface to do this, and that's because there are essentially three different screens at a high level: the People screen, which is where you create people who will be eligible to be involved in a decision; the Decision screen, which is actually a collection of a number of sub-screens, so to speak, as you'll see later; and the Restaurants screen, which is like the People screen but for maintaining your list of restaurants.

Assuming people and restaurants have already been created and you're ready to make a decision, you have only to tap the big graphic, and you'll wind up on the Who's Going screen, as shown in Figure 3-3.

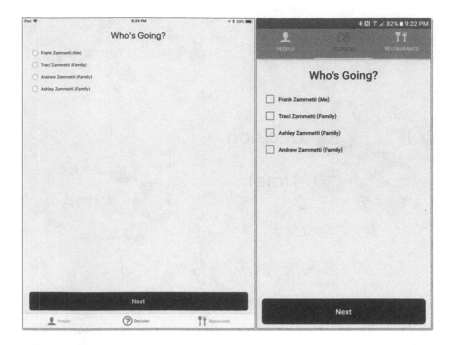

Figure 3-3. *Who's Going screen*

The Who's Going screen presents a list of people for you to choose from. Once you've selected one or more people, you hit the Next button, and you wind up on the Choice Screen, which is shown in Figure 3-4.

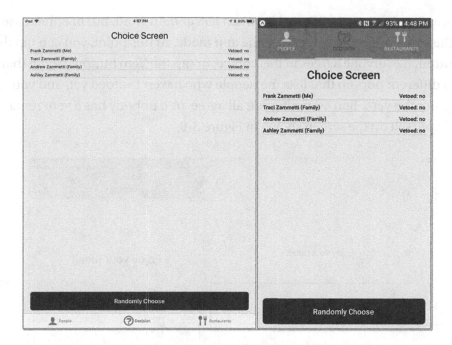

Figure 3-4. *Choice Screen*

That big Randomly Choose button at the bottom is the one you tap to make a choice, which results in the Decision screen shown in Figure 3-5.

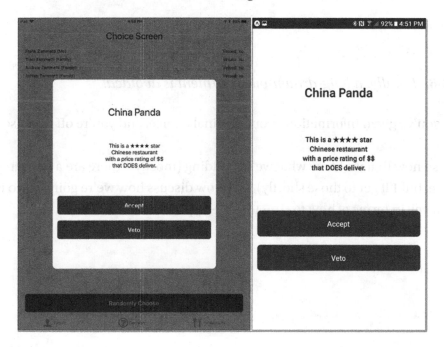

Figure 3-5. *Decision screen*

The presentation is a bit different between iOS and Android, but in either case it conveys the same thing: the choice that the app made. At this point, you can tap the Accept button, if everyone agrees to this choice, or tap the Veto button. Doing that latter presents a different pop-up that lists the people who haven't vetoed yet, and you can tap one to register the veto. But, assuming you all agree, or if nobody has a veto remaining, you'll find yourself on the screen shown in Figure 3-6.

Figure 3-6. *Finally, a long-drawn-out argument is avoided!*

Here, you've given information about the final choice, and you're off to get some grub.

Okay, so now that we know what we're building (mostly—there are a few screens not shown here, but I'll get to those shortly), let's now discuss how we're going to do it, at a very high level, in terms of how to structure the application.

Ruminations on Application Structure

Before we go too far, we must talk a bit about how to structure a React Native app. This can be a terse conversation: there are no rules.

In fact, React Native doesn't really force any particular structure on you, nor does Expo on top of React Native. Oh, to be sure, there are some things that you must do and have. For one, you're going to need an app.json file to describe your app to Expo, and you'll have an App.js file that is your main entry point into your app's code. As discussed in Chapter 1, when you run create-react-native-app, you'll get these files, plus a few others, and you'll get a node-modules directory, of course, but beyond that, you're free to structure your code however you wish.

If you want to put all your code in App.js, you absolutely can (that's how the Hello World app from Chapter 1 and the Components app from Chapter 2 were written, after all), but that's not usually a great approach, unless it's an especially trivial app. No, more often than not, you'll want to add some directories, to keep things organized, and that's precisely what I've done for Restaurant Chooser, as Figure 3-7 shows.

Name ▲	Size	Type		Modified		Attr
components		File Folder	Wednesday	3:55:57.8...	-------	
images		File Folder	Tuesday	2:26:38.7...	-------	
node_modules		File Folder	5/14/2018	4:04:43.7...	-------	
screens		File Folder	Wednesday	5:39:13.2...	-------	
.babelrc	130 bytes	File	5/1/2018	12:58:54.6...	-a-----	
.flowconfig	2.14 KB	File	5/1/2018	12:58:54.6...	-a-----	
.gitignore	248 bytes	File	Today	10:07:04.3...	-a-----	
.watchmanconfig	3 bytes	File	5/1/2018	12:58:54.6...	-a-----	
App.js	2.52 KB	JavaScript File	Wednesday	2:21:34.0...	-a-----	
app.json	464 bytes	JSON File	Wednesday	1:42:17.8...	-a-----	
appIcon.png	313 KB	PNG image	Tuesday	11:58:18.3...	-a-----	
package.json	761 bytes	JSON File	5/14/2018	4:00:07.5...	-a-----	
package-lock.json	374 KB	JSON File	5/14/2018	4:04:44.4...	-a-----	
README.md	13.1 KB	MD File	5/1/2018	12:58:54.6...	-a-----	
splash.png	9.73 MB	PNG image	Tuesday	3:06:11.5...	-a-----	

Figure 3-7. *Restaurant Chooser app's directory structure*

In addition to `app.json` and `App.js`, you'll also find `.babelrc`, `.flowconfig`, `.gitignore`, and `.watchmanconfig`, all of which you can happily ignore, as they are files associated with tools that React Native and Expo use under the covers. The `appIcon.png` file is an added one that will be discussed later, which is also true of `splash.png`. The `README.md` file is created for you but is irrelevant to this project (though you're free to replace the useful information it has by default with whatever you might find helpful). The `package.json` and `package-lock.json` files are also files you can ignore, as they're for NPM's use.

Aside from the files, there are a few directories. The `images` directory is—you guessed it—where I've put images, including the icons on the three tabs and the graphic for the It's Decision Time screen. You already know what `node_modules` is, which just leaves `components` and `screens` directories, both of which are directories I added and directly relate to application structure, as I'm discussing here.

The `components` directory is where I store two custom components that you'll see later, and this is a good practice to get into. Working with React Native is, as you now know, based entirely on the notion of components. Often, you'll be using components that React Native itself supplies, sometimes, as you'll see later, components that third-party libraries provide, and sometimes you'll create your own. The latter is the situation here, and in that directory, you'll find two files: `CustomButton.js` and `CustomTextInput.js`. As I said, I'll get to these later, but I'd bet good money you can figure out what they might be, based on the names alone.

The `screens` directory hints at how the app is fundamentally organized: by "screens." Now, what constitutes a screen isn't necessarily straightforward, and that's the case with Restaurant Chooser. There are three screens at a high level: the People screen, the Decision screen, and the Restaurants screen. However, the preceding screenshots show that there are more than three unique screens here. The Decision screen has several what you might call sub-screens. But, I still consider these to be part of the Decision screen, and so they all live in the same source file in the `screens` directory, aptly named `DecisionScreen.js`. Similarly, there is a `PeopleScreen.js` file and a `RestaurantsScreen.js` file that house the code for the People and Restaurants screens, respectively, and which later you'll find contain more than one sub-screen, in a sense. You might call the sub-screens views instead, and I considered doing that but decided not to, to avoid conflicts with the `View` component, but at the end of the day, what really matters is that the app is broken into some number of "screens," and each winds up having its own source file. The sub-screens are also contained in them, though one could make an argument that they should also each be contained in their individual source files as their own discrete components, and I wouldn't argue too strongly against that (although it would complicate a few things, which is why I didn't do it).

Critically, however, remember when I said there were no set rules for React Native app structure? This is what I meant. We can debate one structure vs. another, but you aren't *required* to choose one vs. another, beyond the few requirements I mentioned earlier. Whatever makes sense to you and whatever organizes your code in a way that is logical to you is fine. React Native doesn't care, nor does Expo. If you've got an App.js file to kick things off, the rest is up to you.

Note   As previously mentioned, in this book, I've chosen to focus on React Native development using Expo, because it makes most things easier and provides some additional capabilities (and it also happens to be the path the React Native docs themselves lead you down by default). However, in talking about application structure, it should be noted that if you don't use Expo and ask React Native to stub out an application for you, the structure you get is a bit different. If you "eject" your app from Expo, that is, remove Expo from the mix and make it a "naked" React Native app, you'll be fitted into that structure as well. I'm not going into that structure here, but I wanted to mention it, because if you go looking at React Native samples on the Web, you may well run into that structure, and now you'll have some understanding of why that's the case.

Getting Started

Getting this project off the ground is as easy as running the following:

```
create-react-native-app RestaurantChooser
```

That's all I did to start this project, and that gives us the skeleton of our app. Well, more precisely, it gives us a full working app that you could go ahead and run immediately. Of course, it's not Restaurant Chooser yet (although that would simultaneously be extremely cool and put us all out of work), so we have to start writing some code. While app.json and App.js files were generated for us, we must start our work by replacing their content with code more appropriate to our needs. So, let's start with app.json.

app.json

The `app.json` file is concerned with configuring your app and is the one-stop shopping location for telling React Native and Expo about your app. This file is just a plain old JSON file, as you can see here:

```
{
  "expo": {
    "name": "Restaurant Chooser",
    "description": "Takes the pain out of making a decision!",
    "icon": "appIcon.png",
    "splash" : { "image": "splash.png", "resizeMode": "cover" },
    "version": "1.0.0",
    "slug": "restaurantChooser",
    "sdkVersion": "23.0.0",
    "ios": { "bundleIdentifier": "com.etherient.restaurantChooser" },
    "android": { "package": "com.etherient.restaurantChooser" }
  }
}
```

This file allows for many configuration options under the top-level expo key, but only a few of them are required: `name`, `slug`, and `sdkVersion`.

The `name` attribute is simply the name of your app. The `sdkVersion` attribute is the version of Expo the project is using, and this should match the version specified in `package.json` (which `create-react-native-app` created for you). The `slug` attribute is a name for your app that will be used to publish your app via Expo. The URL that Expo will create will be in the form expo.io/@<your-username>/<slug>, so the value of the `slug` attribute must be suitable for insertion into a URL (i.e., no spaces are allowed).

All the other attributes shown here are optional. The `description` attribute is just a description of your app, which is nice, if you have multiple apps published, to tell others (and yourself) what the apps are. The `icon` attribute is the icon that will be used in app launchers on iOS and Android to represent your app. The `splash` icon is the image that will be shown while your app is loading. The value of this attribute is the name of the image file, and the `resizeMode` attribute tells Expo how to resize your image. The default value, if you don't specify this, is `contains`, which will result in the splash screen being wholly contained within the physical screen, meaning it will cover as much of the screen as it can, after being resized in a way that keeps its proportions intact, and the rest of the screen will be uncovered. A value of cover results in the splash image being resized big enough to fill the entire screen, while allowing any portions of it that don't to "overflow" off the screen.

The version attribute is for your own use and is the version of your app. The ios and android attributes specify a bundleIdentifier and a package name, respectively, which becomes important when you ask Expo to build you a real application package (which will be covered in the next chapter). The value here should be in the typical reverse-domain name form.

There are quite a few other attributes supported in app.json—and you can even create your own, if you want to include information in your app that shouldn't be embedded in code—but those here are the ones you *must* have and the ones you're *most likely* to have, and they are all we need for this app (you can see more of what's available here: https://docs.expo.io/versions/latest/workflow/configuration).

On to the Code

With the app skeleton created and the necessary configuration out of the way, it's finally time to get to some actual code. Execution begins in the App.js file, so that's going to be our first stop.

App.js

The first thing we need to do is import all the modules the code will use, both those coming from React Native itself, things that Expo provides on top of that, as well as our own application code.

```
import React from "react";
import { Constants } from "expo";
import { Image, Platform } from "react-native";
import { TabNavigator } from "react-navigation";
import { PeopleScreen } from "./screens/PeopleScreen";
import { DecisionScreen } from "./screens/DecisionScreen";
import { RestaurantsScreen } from "./screens/RestaurantsScreen";
```

You'll always import React, because React Native is, of course, built on top of it. The Constants module is something Expo provides that makes some additional information about the device available to our code, as you'll see shortly. You've seen the Image component before, as well as the Platform module, although that was only briefly touched on in Chapter 2. This module is similar to Constants but is provided by React Native itself, and it, too, gives us additional information (and some methods, as you saw in the last chapter) about the device the code is running on. The final three imports are the three main screens of the application. It wouldn't do much without those, would it?

After the imports, a little bit of opening logging is done.

```
console.log("-------------------------------------------------------------
");
console.log(`RestaurantChooser starting on ${Platform.OS}`);
```

This gives us some information about what OS we're running on in the console and indicates that the app has started up.

After that is a simple line of code.

```
const platformOS = Platform.OS.toLowerCase();
```

This is something that arguably isn't necessary but that I think makes life simpler. Later, you'll see some code that branches based on whether the app is running on iOS or Android. I didn't want to have to worry about getting the case of those strings right, so lowercasing it allows me to avoid that. (That way, if React Native or Expo ever decides to change the case, the code still works. It would be another story, if they changed the string itself, of course.)

The code that comes next requires me to talk about something that I haven't discussed before: navigation through the screens of an app. So, I'll do that now.

React Navigation

It's not all that common to find mobile apps that consist of a single screen. So, how do you as an app developer navigate between screens? Well, because a screen is, ultimately, just a component, you could write some code that hides all the screen components, except for the current one, and keep doing that as the user moves through your app. That can work, but it's a fair bit of code you must write, and especially when you start to think about animated transitions between them, getting all of that right can be tricky, especially in a cross-platform way.

In the React Native world, and in the mobile development world more generally, there is a concept of a *navigator* that handles all those details for you. In simplest terms, you tell a navigator about your screens, and then you tell it what screen you want to show, and the navigator takes care of the transitions and all the plumbing involved in hiding the current screen and displaying the new one.

It's not a complicated concept, even if the implementation details can be, but React Native suffers, in a sense, from an embarrassment of riches. If you Google "React Native navigation," you'll be confronted with such things as React Navigation, NavigatorIOS, Ex-Navigation, Navigator, Native Navigation, React Native Router Flux, ExperimentalNavigation, React Router Native, and React Native Navigation (and probably a lot more). Which do you choose? How do you even compare them to decide?

Well, the first thing to understand is that all navigators fall broadly into two categories: JavaScript navigators, which are those that are written entirely in JavaScript, and native navigators, which are, of course, written in platform-native code. JavaScript navigators can have worse performance, but if they're written well, they're virtually indistinguishable from native navigators, in terms of performance, while having the added benefit of being a lot more customizable, generally. Another consideration is how popular each option is, because it's always nice to have a lot of support when you run into issues.

For our Restaurant Chooser app, the decision is easy, because we can eliminate the native navigators right off the bat, because when you use Expo, you don't have access to many of the native code parts of the React Native ecosystem. (That's changing a bit at the time of writing, but it's still true, in a general sense.) Once you eliminate those options, the choice becomes pretty simple, because one JavaScript-based solution has, for all intents and purposes, won in the court of public developer opinion, and that's React Navigation.

React Navigation (`https://reactnavigation.org`) is a stand-alone library, separate from React Native (and Expo). To add it to this project, you either will have to execute

```
pm install --save react-navigation
```

or you'll have to add it explicitly to `package.json` and then run `npm install`, to get it installed into the project. Once that's done, your code will have access to any of the navigators that React Navigation provides. There are a number of them, many of which you'll see in this project and the next, and the `TabNavigator` you see imported here is one.

With React Navigation, the navigators are just React Native components, and among those built in, you'll find the `TabNavigator`, which provides a tabbed interface, as seen in the screenshots of Restaurant Chooser; a `StackNavigator`, which is a simple one, in which multiple screens are "stacked" with only one showing at a time; and a draw-type navigator for control drawers typically seen in Android apps.

You can also create your own navigators or use others created by the community. The benefit of all of them is that they will use a common API, a common configuration structure, which is based on intelligent but customizable defaults that should reduce the amount of code you have to write. Speaking of code you have to write, let's see how Restaurant Chooser makes use of React Navigation.

```
const tabs = TabNavigator({

  PeopleScreen : { screen : PeopleScreen,
    navigationOptions : { tabBarLabel : "People",
      tabBarIcon : ( { tintColor } ) => (
        <Image source={ require("./images/icon-people.png") }
          style={{ width : 32, height : 32, tintColor : tintColor }} />
      )
    }
  },

  DecisionScreen : { screen : DecisionScreen,
    navigationOptions : { tabBarLabel : "Decision",
      tabBarIcon : ( { tintColor } ) => (
        <Image source={ require("./images/icon-decision.png") }
          style={{ width : 32, height : 32, tintColor : tintColor }} />
      )
    }
  },

  RestaurantsScreen : { screen : RestaurantsScreen,
    navigationOptions : { tabBarLabel : "Restaurants",
      tabBarIcon : ( { tintColor } ) => (
```

```
      <Image source={ require("./images/icon-restaurants.png") }
        style={{ width : 32, height : 32, tintColor : tintColor }} />
    )
  }
}
```

We begin by creating a TabNavigator component and passing to it configuration objects that describe each of the three top-level screens of the app. Each object has a screen attribute, which is the top-level component that contains the screen (this happens to be the name that will represent this screen internally to the TabNavigator), as well as a navigationOptions attribute that tells the TabNavigator about that screen's tab, because each screen will, of course, be represented by a tab. This includes the tabBarLabel, that is, the text shown on the tab, plus tabBarIcon, which is wrapped in a function, so that we can alter the color of the icon when it's current (you'll see more about that in the next section). Each icon specified is created via an Image component, with the source specified using a require() statement referencing the appropriate image file. Note that the style attribute references the tintColor passed into the function. That becomes important when you look at the last object passed to the TabNavigator constructor.

```
{ initialRouteName : "DecisionScreen",animationEnabled : true,
swipeEnabled : true,
  backBehavior : "none", lazy : true,
  tabBarPosition : platformOS === "android" ? "top" : "bottom",
  tabBarOptions : { activeTintColor : "#ff0000",showIcon : true,
    style : { paddingTop : platformOS === "android" ? Constants.
    statusBarHeight : 0 }
  }
}
```

Rather than defining an individual screen, this is now some information that configures the TabNavigator itself. First, the initialRouteName "DecisionScreen" is the name of the screen to show first (the term *route* is synonymous with *screen* in this context, as well as other navigators you may encounter, whether React Navigation navigators or others).

The animationEnabled : true setting determines whether TabNavigator will animate the screens into and out of view, or if they will just "pop" onto the screen.

The `swipeEnabled : true` option allows or disallows users swiping left and right to navigate between screens (if not, they will have to tap the icons directly, which is still enabled, even if swipe is as well).

The `backBehavior : "none"` option determines what happens when the hardware back button on Android devices is tapped. A setting of `none` means that the back button won't do anything. This is what I want in this application; otherwise, as the user navigates between screens, a stack will be created, and as users hit the back button, they'll navigate through that stack, even if the navigation doesn't make logical sense.

The `lazy : true` attribute tells the `TabNavigator` not to build each screen until it becomes visible, which aids in performance.

The `tabBarPosition` attribute tells `TabNavigator` whether to put the tabs on the top or the bottom. Here, I use the `platformOS` variable defined earlier, to ensure the tabs are in the platform-appropriate: on top for Android, on the bottom for iOS.

Finally, the `tabBarOptions` attribute is an object that defines the look of the tabs. The `activeTintColor : "#ff0000"` within it determines the color that the icons will be tinted to when current, in this case, red (and that gets passed into that function that wraps the `Image` component you saw earlier, so now you know why that was done that way). The `showIcon : true` attribute must be set to `true` for the icons to appear. Otherwise, only text would be shown. The `style` attribute adds some padding to the top when on Android, which keeps the tabs from being superimposed over the system's status bar (no such padding is required for iOS, hence the zero in the ternary).

That configuration is all that is needed for `TabNavigator` to work, and there are a ton more options available, far too many to go into here, but this gives you a good, basic idea of what `TabNavigator` can do.

There is one last line of code in this source file, after the `TabNavigator` configuration code, that is of crucial importance:

```
export default tabs;
```

Without that, React Native won't know what component to create when the app starts, and you'll wind up with an empty screen. I hear that's not especially good for user experience, so we should probably export the `TabNavigator` we created, by way of the `tabs` variable.

It's Custom Component Time!

If you look back on the screenshots of Restaurant Chooser from earlier in this chapter, you'll notice that the buttons appear a bit different from the buttons in the components project in Chapter 2. In that project, the buttons were Button components that React Native gives us, which are platform-specific button components when rendered. It might be possible to use simple styling to make those buttons look like what you see in Restaurant Chooser, but there's an easier and, in many respects, a better way, and that's to create a custom component that can be reused anywhere you need it.

CustomButton.js

Such a custom button is housed in the CustomButton.js file in the component directory. By doing this, we will be able to use a <CustomButton> tag anytime we need one of these special buttons.

```
import React, { Component } from "react";
import PropTypes from "prop-types";
import { TouchableOpacity, Text } from "react-native";
```

First, we must import React, as always, and we also must import Component, since we'll be extending that to make a new component. The PropTypes module is something we'll require, in order to have custom properties available on our CustomButton. Finally, to build a button, we're going to use two other React Native components: TouchableOpacity and Text. You've seen Text before, it's just to be able to put some text on the screen, but TouchableOpacity is new. In short, it allows us to create an area of the screen that reacts to touch events and provides some visual feedback when it occurs via a gradual opacity change. That sounds like something a button should do, right?

```
class CustomButton extends Component {

  render() {

    const { text, onPress, buttonStyle, textStyle, width, disabled } =
    this.props;
```

This destructuring assignment is responsible for taking the values of several props that this component can have, props that aren't available as a result of extending

97

Component, and putting them into some variables that we can use in the remainder of the code.

Here's the deal: you can attach arbitrary props to a component you create without ill effect, and the code inside the component can gain access to them through this.props. However, that's error-prone, because a user of your component won't know what type a given prop expects. That's where something called propTypes comes in. Here's a chunk of code that comes after the render() method:

```
CustomButton.propTypes = {
  text : PropTypes.string.isRequired, onPress : PropTypes.func.isRequired,
  buttonStyle : PropTypes.object, textStyle : PropTypes.object,
  width : PropTypes.string, disabled : PropTypes.string
};
```

You attach this propTypes attribute to your custom component, and within it, you define each of the additional props your component supports, and for each, you specify a function that will validate the prop. Here, I'm using some existing validators that the PropTypes module provides. This module provides quite a few validators, such as string, array, bool, and number, just to name a few. Also, some variants include isRequired as well, so string.isRequired, for example as you see here, tells React Native that the text prop must be present and must be a string. We'll get a very helpful error if validation fails for any prop, making it a lot easier to spot problems. This also serves as a form of self-documentation, as the props that represent the API of the custom component don't have to be guessed; they're well-defined, thanks to propTypes.

Now, it comes time to define the component.

```
  return (
    <TouchableOpacity
      style={ [
        { padding : 10, height : 60, borderRadius : 8, margin : 10, width
        : width,
          backgroundColor :
            disabled != null && disabled === "true" ? "#e0e0e0" :
            "#303656",
        },
        buttonStyle
      ] }
```

```
        onPress={ () => { if (disabled == null || disabled === "false") {
        onPress() } } }
      >
        <Text style={ [
          { fontSize : 20, fontWeight : "bold", color : "#ffffff",
            textAlign : "center", paddingTop : 8
          },
          textStyle
        ] } >
          {text}
        </Text>
      </TouchableOpacity>
    );

  }

}
```

This is the same basic idea as when we create a component: create a class that extends from some component, here, the literal Component class, and build a render() method. Our CustomButton is just a y component wrapped around a y component. As you can see, there is some styling applied to the TouchableOpacity, to give it some padding, static height, and rounded corner. Now, a button also has a static width, at least our CustomButton instances do, but you'll notice that the width style attribute's value is taken from the variable width.

The final style attribute is backgroundColor, and here we use some logic to determine whether the button should be grayed out (disabled is true) or should be blue (active, disabled is false, or not supplied). Similar logic is used next in the onPress prop, so that only an active button responds to touch.

You should also notice that the style attribute is a little different from anything you've seen before, in that it seems to use array notation, as indicated by the use of brackets. Yes, you can apply multiple styles to a component in this way, and the point to doing it here is so that the styles of the button can be overridden or customized further by a developer using CustomButton, by supplying a buttonStyle prop.

The Text component is inside the TouchableOpacity and is little more than some basic styling, again using array notation (with which the textStyle can override or extend the base styling), so that those styles can be changed or extended, as required, and then the text itself, taken from the text prop defined earlier.

It's not really a sophisticated piece of code by any stretch, but it shows quite a bit about creating custom components. However, there's one last thing we must do, and I suspect you know what it is: export the component.

```
export default CustomButton;
```

React Native will take care of adding CustomButton to its internal registry of components when you import this module into another, which is what makes <CustomButton> work, as you'll be seeing very soon.

CustomTextInput.js

There's one other custom component used in Restaurant Chooser, and that's CustomTextInput, the code for which is found, obviously enough, in the CustomTextInput.js file. It has, by and large, the same basic aim as CustomButton, but with a little more going on, though not *much* more.

```
import React, { Component } from "react";
import PropTypes from "prop-types";
import { Platform, StyleSheet, Text, TextInput, View } from "react-native";
```

We start with the same two lines as before, importing React, Component, and PropTypes. Then, we must also import some other components that this new component will be built from. The Platform module will allow us to do some branching, based on what OS the app is running on. StyleSheet is, of course, how we'll define a stylesheet the component will use. The Text component will be necessary, so that we can have a label attached to the TextInput, so that is also imported. We're also going to require a container for everything, and that's where the View component comes in.

The first thing to do is to define a stylesheet.

```
const styles = StyleSheet.create({

  fieldLabel : { marginLeft : 10 },

  textInput : {
    height : 40, marginLeft : 10, width : "96%", marginBottom : 20,
    ...Platform.select({
```

```
    ios : { marginTop : 4, paddingLeft : 10, borderRadius : 8,
      borderColor : "#c0c0c0", borderWidth : 2
    },
    android : { }
  })
}

});
```

The fieldLabel style is going to apply to the Text component that will serve as a label for the field. Indeed, the label is the raison d'être for this custom component in the first place. I, of course, could have just put a Text component, followed by a TextInput component, on any screen where I wanted to have a label and a text entry field, but the problem is that the components would wind up lining up differently between iOS and Android. In fact, that's the reason for the branching logic in the textInput style: the styles necessary for iOS in order for the fields to line up with the labels (as well as some that are nonessential but nice to have to add visual flair, such as rounded corners and coloring) aren't required on Android. I could have replicated this styling on every individual TextInput and avoided creating a custom component, but then I wouldn't have had a chance to show you custom components. Besides, I do generally try and follow the DRY (Don't Repeat Yourself) principle, when possible, and this was an excellent place to do so. I thought.

With the styles defined, we can get on to building the component.

```
class CustomTextInput extends Component {

  render() {

    const {
      label, labelStyle, maxLength, textInputStyle, stateHolder,
      stateFieldName
    } = this.props;

    return (
      <View>
        <Text style={ [ styles.fieldLabel, labelStyle ] }>{label}</Text>
```

```
    <TextInput maxLength={ maxLength }
      onChangeText={ (inText) => stateHolder.setState(
        () => {
          const obj = { };
          obj[stateFieldName] = inText;
          return obj;
        }
      ) }
      style={ [ styles.textInput, textInputStyle ] }
    />
  </View>
);


}


}
```

Once again, we have some custom props available: label is the label text; labelStyle is any additional style we want to apply to the label; maxLength allows us to have a maximum length of text the user can enter; textInputStyle lets a developer override or extend the base styling of the TextInput.

The stateHolder and stateFieldName props are references to the object that is storing the state for the TextInput component, and stateFieldName is the name of the field on that object, respectively. This is necessary for the code in the onChangeText prop function to work right in all cases, because the object might not necessarily be what the this keyword references (if we didn't use fat arrow notation) or even what the function is bound to if we tried to do it with a classic-style function. Providing these props, and making them required, ensures that this component will be usable in any situation, regardless of how state data is being stored in any component that uses it.

The content that's rendered is a View component at the top level, a Text component for the label, and the TextInput component itself within the View. You can see how stateHolder and stateFieldName are used within onChangeText to update the value when the value within the TextInput component changes.

Of course, this component, like CustomButton, has a propTypes defined after the render() method.

```
CustomTextInput.propTypes = {
  label : PropTypes.string.isRequired, labelStyle : PropTypes.object,
  maxLength : PropTypes.number, textInputStyle : PropTypes.object,
  stateHolder : PropTypes.object.isRequired, stateFieldName : PropTypes.
  string.isRequired
};
```

This time, we require `label` text, as well as `stateHolder` and `stateFieldName`. After that, we just have to export

```
export default CustomTextInput;
```

and that's another custom component, ready to go!

Now, let's look at the code for the Restaurants screen, which will include the use of both of these custom components.

Our First Screen: RestaurantsScreen.js

The Restaurants screen is where the user enters the names of restaurants from which selections will be made later. It consists of two sub-screens, so to speak: the list screen and the add screen. The list screen is shown in Figure 3-8.

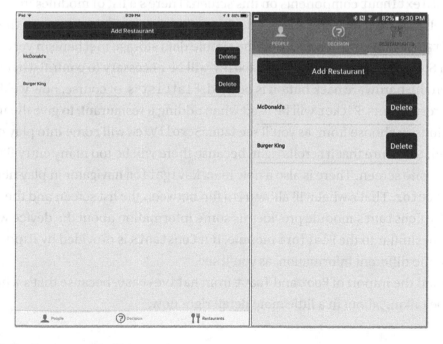

Figure 3-8. *Restaurants list screen*

It's a simple enough screen, consisting of a button at the top that leads the user to the add screen, to add a new restaurant, and the list of existing restaurants, with the ability to delete one. The ability to modify a restaurant isn't provided. The user would have to delete and re-add to make a change, but, hey, maybe this would make for a good task for you to do on your own, to gain some experience, hint, hint.

The code is likewise reasonably simple, beginning with some imports.

```
import React from "react";
import CustomButton from "../components/CustomButton";
import CustomTextInput from "../components/CustomTextInput";
import { Alert, AsyncStorage, BackHandler, FlatList, Picker, Platform,
ScrollView,
  StyleSheet, Text, View
} from "react-native";
import { StackNavigator } from "react-navigation";
import { Root, Toast } from "native-base";
import { Constants } from "expo";
```

React, StyleSheet, and Platform you're already pretty familiar with, ditto Text and View. As mentioned in the previous section, we'll be making use of the CustomButton and CustomTextInput components on this screen. There's a list of modules from React Native itself that we'll be using. Alert will allow us to show some messages to the user. AsyncStorage will provide us access to the simple data storage mechanism very much like Local Storage in the browser. BackHandler will be necessary to control what Android does when the hardware back button is pushed. FlatList is, of course, how we'll display the list of restaurants. Picker will be used when adding a restaurant, to give the user a list of options to choose from, as you'll see later. ScrollView will come into play on the add screen, to ensure that it scrolls right, because there will be too many entry fields to show on one screen. There is also a new react Navigation navigator in play here: StackNavigator. That's what will allow us to flip between the list screen and the add screen. The Constants module provides us some information about the device we're running on, similar to the Platform module, but Constants is provided by Expo and gives us some different information, as you'll see.

I skipped the import of Root and Toast from native-base, because that's what I'm going to be talking about in a little more detail right now.

Third-Party Components: NativeBase

While React Native offers an excellent collection of components to build your app from (and though you haven't seen any, Expo provides a few more), and while you can create your own custom components, as you saw in the previous section, sometimes it's best to look to third-party libraries for components. If you choose a good library, you can gain access to a lot of outstanding, solid components that will significantly expand the pallet from which you build apps.

One of the most popular third-party libraries available is NativeBase (`https://docs.nativebase.io`). This is a free and open source library that not only provides some new and handy widgets but, at its core, is built with the intent of making the components styleable, without modifying the code behind them.

As with most libraries, to use NativeBase requires that you install it with NPM, either with

```
npm install --save native-base
```

or by adding it to `package.json` and then doing an NPM install to download it. Either way, once done, you'll find a whole host of new components available to you, including (but not limited to)

- `Accordion`: Multiple sections of content in which the visibility of sections can be toggled by clicking a header above them

- `Badge`: Shows notification icons, such as number of e-mails, on icons (or other elements)

- `Card`: A content container typically seen on Android devices

- `FABs`: Floating action buttons, usually a circular button floating above the UI that gives the user access to various functions

- `Layout`: I discuss layout in React Native in Chapter 4 (and I'll touch on it a bit here), but this component provides an arguably easier and more flexible way to do layout than with what you get in React Native by default (and, as a preview, that's flexbox).

- `SearchBar`: A specialized entry field with applicable iconography for performing searches

- **Segment:** An alternate to tabs, segments look like two (or more) buttons munged together, which, when tapped ,become highlighted (while the others are un-highlighted, if they previously were).

- **SwipableList:** A list of components that allows the user to swipe left and/or right on items, to reveal action buttons or other content

- **Typography:** Not a specific component, but a group of components that allows you to do HTML-like headings, using H1, H2, and H3 tags

This is just a sampling of the components Native Base provides, and, in fact, you're about to see two others—the ones imported in the Restaurants screen code, Root, and Toast. But, let's not get too far ahead of ourselves; there's a bunch more code to see.

The List Screen

As I mentioned, the Restaurants screen (as well as the People and It's Decision Time screens) are really made up of a number of what I would call sub-screens, and the first of these for Restaurants is the list screen. So, to build this screen, we begin, as we always do, by creating a component.

```
class ListScreen extends React.Component {

  constructor(inProps) {
    super(inProps);
    this.state = { listData : [ ] };
  }
}
```

Anytime you build a component and must do something at construction time (which isn't required but probably is necessary more often than not), you'll begin by passing the object referenced by the inProps argument, which contains all the props specified on the tag for the component and is passed into the constructor by React Native, to the superclass's constructor. In fact, if you *don't* do this, you're likely to run into problems with things simply not working, so as a general rule, you'll always have to do this. (There may be some cases in which you don't have to or want to, but they're likely to be so few and far between that it's better to not even consider the possibility, unless you *really* must.)

The constructor is typically where you define a state attribute on the component, too, if you need one at all (not all components require state, remember). Here, the state object will contain an array of objects that will be the data the list renders.

Speaking of the list and rendering, after the constructor comes our friendly neighborhood render() method. Take a look at the whole thing, and then we'll break it down together.

```
render() { return (

  <Root>

    <View style={styles.listScreenContainer}>

      <CustomButton text="Add Restaurant" width="94%"
        onPress={ () => { this.props.navigation.navigate("AddScreen"); } } />

      <FlatList style={styles.restaurantList} data={this.state.listData}
        renderItem={ ({item}) =>
          <View style={styles.restaurantContainer}>
            <Text style={styles.restaurantName}>{item.name}</Text>
            <CustomButton text="Delete"
              onPress={ () => {
                Alert.alert("Please confirm",
                  "Are you sure you want to delete this restaurant?",
                  [
                    { text : "Yes", onPress: () => {
                      AsyncStorage.getItem("restaurants",
                        function(inError, inRestaurants) {
                          if (inRestaurants === null) {
                            inRestaurants = [ ];
                          } else {
                            inRestaurants = JSON.parse(inRestaurants);
                          }
```

```
                            for (let i = 0; i < inRestaurants.length; i++) {
                              const restaurant = inRestaurants[i];
                              if (restaurant.key === item.key) {
                                inRestaurants.splice(i, 1);
                                break;
                              }
                            }
                            AsyncStorage.setItem("restaurants",
                              JSON.stringify(inRestaurants), function() {
                                this.setState({ listData : inRestaurants });
                                Toast.show({ text : "Restaurant deleted",
                                  position : "bottom", type : "danger",
                                  duration : 2000
                                });
                              }.bind(this)
                            );
                          }.bind(this)
                        );
                      } },
                      { text : "No" }, { text : "Cancel", style : "cancel" }
                    ],
                    { cancelable : true }
                  )
                } } />
            </View>
          }
        />
      </View>
    </Root>
  ); }
```

First, we have something you haven't seen before: a Root element. This is a NativeBase component that is necessary in order for the Toast component, which we'll use to show messages, to work. It provides a container element that NativeBase controls and augments, as required, to enable Toast to work. (It's also necessary for some other NativeBase components. You'll have to consult the docs to determine which components require it.)

Inside the Root element, we have a View that will provide a container we can style appropriately to implement the layout desired. What styling, you ask? Well, it's the listScreenContainer style here:

```
listScreenContainer : { flex : 1, alignItems : "center", justifyContent :
"center",
  ...Platform.select({
    ios : { paddingTop : Constants.statusBarHeight },
    android : { }
  })
}
```

As I mentioned earlier, layout is a topic I'm going to address in detail in Chapter 4, but for now, I'll tell you that this style configuration ensures that this View fills the entire screen (flex : 1) and that any children within it are centered both horizontally (justifyContent : "center") and vertically (alignItems : "center"). The Platform. select() method is used to set a paddingTop attribute for iOS but not Android, so that the container doesn't overlap the status bar.

Next up is the Add Restaurant CustomButton component. It's a simple bit of configuration, but the onPress handler gives you something new to see. As you'll discover near the end of this chapter, the list screen (as well as the add screen that we'll talk about next) are housed inside a React Navigation StackNavigator. This navigator provides a way to have multiple components, our list and add sub-screens, stacked on top of one another, so that only one is visible at any given time, and we can call some methods to flip between them. React Navigation will automatically add a navigation attribute to the props collection of the top-level component. That attribute is an object that contains some methods we can call, one of which is navigate(). What we provide to it is the name of the screen that the StackNavigator includes that we want to show, and the navigator takes care of flipping between them.

After that comes a `FlatList` component. We looked at this in Chapter 2, but as a refresher, it's a component that renders a simple list of items. The item that will be rendered is specified by the `data` attribute and references the `listData` array in the `state` object for this component. Don't worry about how the data gets into that array; we'll see that after we're done with the `render()` method.

The `FlatList` also has a style applied, and that style is simply this:

```
restaurantList : { width : "94%" }
```

The preceding is done to ensure that there is some space on both sides of the list, which I just felt looked more pleasing. This works because the parent `View`'s style centers its children, remember, so we'll wind up with 3% of the screen's width on either side of the `FlatList`.

The `renderItem` prop on the `FlatList` is a function you, as the developer, supply that the `FlatList` calls to render each item. As you can see, the `item` is passed into this function, and you can return virtually any structure you could from a `render()` method, because under the covers, React Native is creating a component on the fly from what you provide here. In this case, a `View` is created, to contain the item, because there will be multiple parts to it. This `View` has the following style applied:

```
restaurantContainer : { flexDirection : "row", marginTop : 4,
marginBottom : 4,
  borderColor : "#e0e0e0", borderBottomWidth : 2, alignItems : "center"
}
```

If you've never seen flexbox in action before—again, we'll be looking at this in Chapter 4—I don't want to leave you high and dry here, so I'll tell you that `flexDirection`, when set to `row`, means that the children of this `View` will be laid out in a row, side by side across the screen. The rest of the attributes are to ensure that there is some space above and below each item, that each item has a light gray border that is two pixels thick, and that the children within the `View` are centered horizontally.

Speaking of children, the first is a `Text` component that is simply the name of the restaurant, taken from the object passed into the `renderItem` prop method. This has a simple style applied too.

```
restaurantName : { flex : 1 }
```

Yes, more flexbox! This is so that the name of the restaurant will take up as much space as it can, minus the space for the Delete CustomButton, which is the second child inside the View. The button will automatically size to its text, so it effectively has a defined width, which means that the name Text component will fill whatever horizontal space remains after the button is rendered.

Now, inside that button is an onPress handler, and there's some exciting stuff happening there. First, the Alert API is used to ask the user to confirm the deletion. Three buttons are present: Yes, No, and Cancel. Pressing any of them (or tapping outside the pop-up on Android, thanks to the cancelable attribute being set to true) will dismiss the pop-up without anything happening. It's the code inside the Yes button handler that does all the work, as you'd expect.

That work is performed in two parts. First, the restaurant must be deleted. This is done by using the AsyncStorage API, to retrieve the list of restaurants. AsyncStorage is very much like Local Storage in a web browser in that it's a simple key-value data store. You can only store strings in it, so you'll have to serialize and deserialize anything to and from a string, such as a JavaScript object, as is the case here. The getItem() method is called to get the object under the key restaurants. If there is none yet, meaning the user hasn't created any restaurants, an empty array is created. Otherwise, the string retrieved is deserialized into an object using the well-known (and available in React Native code) JSON.parse() method. After that, it's a simple matter of iterating the array and finding the restaurant with the key (which all restaurants have) that matches the key of the item of the FlatList item being rendered and removing it from the array.

With it removed from the array, the next step is to write the array back into storage, using AsyncStorage.setItem(), using JSON.stringify() to serialize the restaurants array into a string for storage. Note that both getItem() and setItem() are asynchronous methods, so you'll have to provide a callback handler for each, and the deletion from the array and the call to setItem() is done in the callback for the getItem() call.

Finally, in the callback handler for the setItem() call, the NativeBase Toast API is used to show a message indicating that the deletion was successful. This takes the form of a little banner that appears on the bottom of the screen, specified for a period of two seconds, which will be read because of having set the type to danger.

The final part of the equation is something I alluded to earlier, namely, getting the data into the FlatList in the first place. That's done in the componentDidMount() method, which React Native will call once the top-level component has been created.

```
componentDidMount() {

  BackHandler.addEventListener( "hardwareBackPress", () => { return true; } );

  AsyncStorage.getItem("restaurants",
    function(inError, inRestaurants) {
      if (inRestaurants === null) {
        inRestaurants = [ ];
      } else {
        inRestaurants = JSON.parse(inRestaurants);
      }
      this.setState({ listData : inRestaurants });
    }.bind(this)
  );

};
}
```

First, we must consider what should or shouldn't happen when the user presses the hardware back button on an Android device. By default, the user will go back through every screen he or she has navigated to in reverse order (a stack is built as you transition from screen to screen, so hitting back just pops off screens that stack). This is frequently precisely what you want to happen, but in this app, it didn't strike me as working how you'd logically expect, so I wanted to disable that functionality. To do that, you attach an event listener using the BackHandler API, and the function that executes just has to return true, and the navigation that usually occurs will be stopped.

With that out of the way, it's time to get the data into the FlatList. It's sitting there in AsyncStorage, of course, so it's just a simple matter of using the same getItem() method you saw just a moment ago, doing the same check for null to avoid errors, and then calling setState() on the component and passing the list of restaurants as the listData attribute. React Native takes care of everything else.

The Add Screen

Being able to list restaurants wouldn't be very useful if we couldn't create restaurants to list. That's where the add screen, which you get to by clicking the Add Restaurant button on the list screen, of course, comes in. Figure 3-9 shows you that screen.

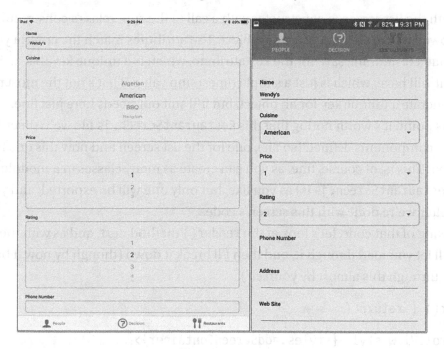

Figure 3-9. *Restaurants add screen*

Each restaurant can have several attributes, including its name, type of cuisine, star rating, price rating, and phone and address information. These are entered using various data entry fields, including the CustomTextInput component we built earlier and React Native's own Picker component.

But, before we get to those, let's see how this component begins.

```
class AddScreen extends React.Component {

  constructor(inProps) {
    super(inProps);
    this.state = { name : "", cuisine : "", price : "", rating : "",
```

```
      phone : "", address : "", webSite : "", delivery : "",
      key : `r_${new Date().getTime()}`
    };

  }
```

As with the list screen, a constructor with a call to the superclass's constructor is first, followed by the creation of a state object. The attributes match the criteria you can enter about a restaurant, save for the key attribute, which is a unique key that an added restaurant will have, which is just a simple timestamp value. That's not the most robust way to generate a unique key for an object, but it'll suit our needs here just fine.

At this point, it's worth noting that this `RestaurantScreen.js` file we've been looking at has two components defined (so far), one for the list screen and now this one for the add screen. This is, of course, fine, as you can create as many classes in a module (which is what `RestaurantScreen.js` is) as you like, but only one will be exported, and you'll see that after we're done with this screen's code.

Speaking of that code, let's look at the `render()` method next, and as with the list screen, I'll let you read through it, and then I'll break it down (though by now, I bet you can work through this almost by yourself).

```
  render() { return (

    <ScrollView style={styles.addScreenContainer}>
```

Because there are quite a few entry fields, it's almost guaranteed that the device's physical screen won't be big enough to show them all at once, so we have to allow for scrolling. That's where the `ScrollView` component that houses all the other components comes in. This is a container component that allows the user to drag it to scroll. It's like a `FlatList`, in a sense, but where `FlatList` renders specific components, and does so bit by bit as they come into view, the `ScrollView` renders all of its children at once and doesn't do so with a defined function to render each. Being so simple means the only thing we must consider is that the `ScrollView` will overlap the status bar if we don't deal with that, and that's where the style applied to it comes into play.

```
addScreenContainer : { marginTop : Constants.statusBarHeight }
```

The Expo `Constants` API is again used to get the height of that status bar, and a simple `marginTop` style gives us the necessary spacing.

```
<View style={styles.addScreenInnerContainer}>

  <View style={styles.addScreenFormContainer}>
```

Now, if you think about this screen, there are really two parts to it: the data entry components and the Cancel and Save buttons at the bottom. In order to style these as unique entities, we're going to create another `View` inside the `ScrollView` (so that we can style both sections as a whole as well) and then create two more `View`'s inside that one, one for the entry components and one for the buttons. So, the `ScrollView` has a `View` as its first child, and that one has the following style attached:

`addScreenInnerContainer : { flex : 1, alignItems : "center", paddingTop : 20, width : "100%" }`

This ensures that its children are centered and fill the screen horizontally. There is also some additional padding on the top, to ensure that when the content scrolls, it doesn't scroll over the status bar.

Then, inside of that `View` is another, the first of the two I mentioned, this one for the entry components. It has a style applied as well.

`addScreenFormContainer : { width : "96%" }`

Using a `width` of 96% places some space around the sides of the components, just as was done on the list screen.

```
          <CustomTextInput label="Name" maxLength={20}
            stateHolder={this} stateFieldName="name" />

          <Text style={styles.fieldLabel}>Cuisine</Text>
          <View style={styles.pickerContainer}>
            <Picker style={styles.picker} prompt="Cuisine"
              selectedValue={this.state.cuisine}
              onValueChange={ (inItemValue) => this.setState({ cuisine :
              inItemValue }) }
            >
              <Picker.Item label="" value="" />
              <Picker.Item label="Algerian" value="Algerian" />
```

```
        <Picker.Item label="American" value="American" />
        ...
        <Picker.Item label="Other" value="Other" />
        ...
      </Picker>
    </View>
```

Now, we're three `View` containers deep into the layout, and at this point, we can start adding entry components, the first of which is a `CustomTextInput` component. This is for the restaurant's name, so we supply the appropriate label text via the `label` prop, tell it what the maximum entry length is (20), and tell it what object stores the state of this component (`this`, which is a reference to the `AddScreen` class instance itself, and React Native knows to look for a `state` attribute on it) and the attribute on that `state` object, name.

After that comes the entry of the restaurant's cuisine type. This is done via a `Picker` component, one that React Native comes with. It's a simple spinner control on iOS, and a pop-up dialog with a scrollable list of clickable options on Android, the point of which is to force the user to select an option from a list of available options. But, just putting a `Picker` component wouldn't suffice, because the user wouldn't know what it's for necessarily, so we'll add a `Text` component before it as a label, and to that `Text` component, we'll apply this style:

```
fieldLabel : { marginLeft : 10 }
```

The goal here is to ensure that the label lines up with the left side of the `Picker`'s box, which it won't, if we don't apply this style.

The `Picker` itself is wrapped in a `View` component, so that the following style can be applied to it and for it to have the desired effect:

```
pickerContainer : {
  ...Platform.select({
    ios : { },
    android : { width : "96%", borderRadius : 8, borderColor : "#c0c0c0",
    borderWidth : 2,
      marginLeft : 10, marginBottom : 20, marginTop : 4
    }
  })
}
```

And that desired effect is primarily to give the `Picker` a border. In addition, the width is set to 96%, which the `Picker` will fill, and some padding added around it, all of which goes to making the `Picker` look nice and fit on the screen. However, note that `Platform.select()` is used here again, because, on iOS, these styles aren't necessary. As it happens, to make the `Picker` look similar on both platforms, the `View` was required around the `Picker`, but to complete the task, we must also apply some styling to the `Picker` itself.

```
picker : {
  ...Platform.select({
    ios : { width : "96%", borderRadius : 8, borderColor : "#c0c0c0",
    borderWidth : 2,
      marginLeft : 10, marginBottom : 20, marginTop : 4
    },
    android : { }
  })
}
```

In this case, it's iOS that needs the styling, where Android does not. When these styles are applied to the containing `View` and the `Picker`, and the `Platform.select()` statements considered, we wind up with the screen looking pretty much the same across both platforms, which is the goal. They can't look perfectly identical, simply because a `Picker` on iOS fundamentally looks and works differently from one on Android, but this styling gets them looking reasonably alike, which is what I wanted.

The `Picker` definition itself is, I think, pretty obvious. The `prompt` prop is for Android only, because when the `Picker` is clicked, Android opens a pop-up for the user to use to make their selection, and this prop ensures that the label on the add screen is replicated onto that pop-up. The `selectedValue` prop ties the `Picker` to the appropriate state object attribute, and `onValueChange` handles updating that value when it changes. Then the `Picker` gets some child components defined under it, `Picker.Item` components to be precise, in which each is given a label and a value, the latter being what will be set in state. In the following code, I've cut down the items in the list a bit with the ellipses, just to save a little space, but trust me, they're included in the real code.

```
<Text style={styles.fieldLabel}>Price</Text>
<View style={styles.pickerContainer}>
  <Picker style={styles.picker} selectedValue={this.state.price}
```

```
          prompt="Price"
          onValueChange={ (inItemValue) => this.setState({ price :
          inItemValue }) }
      >
          <Picker.Item label="" value="" />
          <Picker.Item label="1" value="1" />
          <Picker.Item label="2" value="2" />
          <Picker.Item label="3" value="3" />
          <Picker.Item label="4" value="4" />
          <Picker.Item label="5" value="5" />
        </Picker>
    </View>

    <Text style={styles.fieldLabel}>Rating</Text>
    <View style={styles.pickerContainer}>
      <Picker style={styles.picker} selectedValue={this.state.rating}
        prompt="Rating"
        onValueChange={ (inItemValue) => this.setState({ rating :
        inItemValue }) }
      >
          <Picker.Item label="" value="" />
          <Picker.Item label="1" value="1" />
          <Picker.Item label="2" value="2" />
          <Picker.Item label="3" value="3" />
          <Picker.Item label="4" value="4" />
          <Picker.Item label="5" value="5" />
        </Picker>
    </View>
```

After the cuisine field comes an entry field for price (which indicates how expensive the restaurant is) and one for rating—both Pickers—and both fundamentally the same pattern as you saw with cuisine, so there's no point digging through them again here.

```
<CustomTextInput label="Phone Number" maxLength={20}
stateHolder={this}
  stateFieldName="phoneNumber" />
```

```
<CustomTextInput label="Address" maxLength={20}
stateHolder={this}
  stateFieldName="address" />

<CustomTextInput label="Web Site" maxLength={20}
stateHolder={this}
  stateFieldName="webSite" />
```

After the two `Picker` components are three more `CustomTextInput` fields, one each for the restaurant's phone number, address, and web site. As with price and rating, they are not much different from the name field we looked at earlier, so I think it's safe to skip over them here now as well.

However, did you happen to notice that none of these fields is required? Well, they aren't! You can, in fact, create a restaurant with no name and no data, which makes it pretty much useless. I did this very much on purpose, though, just so that I could suggest this: why don't you take a little break here and see if you can figure out how to make the fields required? Does React Native offer any sort of "make this field required" flag? Or do you have to write some code, say, in the Save button, that we'll look at shortly, to do the validation and show a message if something is missing (that may or may not be a hint)? Are there actually multiple ways to do it that you might choose from, perhaps including some third-party libraries? I've left this as an exercise for you, dear reader.

```
<Text style={styles.fieldLabel}>Delivery?</Text>
<View style={styles.pickerContainer}>
  <Picker style={styles.picker} prompt="Delivery?"
    selectedValue={this.state.delivery}
    onValueChange={ (inItemValue) => this.setState({ delivery :
    inItemValue }) }
  >
    <Picker.Item label="" value="" />
    <Picker.Item label="Yes" value="Yes" />
    <Picker.Item label="No" value="No" />
  </Picker>
</View>

</View>
```

Rounding out the restaurant information fields, there's one other data entry field—another `Picker`—and it's for entering whether the restaurant delivers. It's another basic `Picker`, the same as the others, except for the options available, naturally, so we won't linger here, because there's one more important thing to look at, and that's the buttons.

```
<View style={styles.addScreenButtonsContainer}>

  <CustomButton text="Cancel" width="44%"
    onPress={ () => { this.props.navigation.navigate("ListScreen"); } } />

  <CustomButton text="Save" width="44%"
    onPress={ () => {
      AsyncStorage.getItem("restaurants",
        function(inError, inRestaurants) {
          if (inRestaurants === null) {
            inRestaurants = [ ];
          } else {
            inRestaurants = JSON.parse(inRestaurants);
          }
          inRestaurants.push(this.state);
          AsyncStorage.setItem("restaurants",
            JSON.stringify(inRestaurants), function() {
              this.props.navigation.navigate("ListScreen");
            }.bind(this)
          );
        }.bind(this)
      );
    } }
  />

</View>

</View>

</ScrollView>

); }

}
```

The buttons are contained in the second View that is a child of the master View we created earlier (which is itself a child of the ScrollView, remember?). This View has the following style applied:

```
addScreenButtonsContainer : { flexDirection : "row", justifyContent :
"center" }
```

Now, here, I want the buttons to be side by side, laid out in a row, hence the flexDirection value of row. I still want the buttons themselves centered, however, so justifyContent is set to center (and once more, I'll let you know that we'll get into all this flexbox and layout stuff in more detail in the next chapter, but in large part, you've already seen the most important basics throughout this chapter).

Inside this View goes two CustomButton components, for Cancel and Save, respectively. The buttons are sized to 44% the width of the screen, which leaves 12% of the width for spacing. Because the parent View is laying these out centered in a row, that means 4% of the width of the screen will be on either side of the buttons and also between them (all must total 100%, after all).

The Cancel button doesn't have much work to do: it just navigates back to the list screen, by making a navigate() call on the props.navigation attribute of the top-level component, just as you saw in the Add Restaurant button's onPress handler.

The Save button has some more work to do, though, namely, saving the restaurant the user just entered information for. To do that, we first must retrieve the list of restaurants from AsyncStorage, just as you saw on the list screen. Once that's done, all we have to do is push the state object for the top-level component onto the array of restaurants, because it contains all the data we're saving, and write it back to AsyncStorage. Finally, we navigate back to the list screen, via our StackNavigator, and React Native will take care of updating the list, by virtue of the componentDidMount() method of the list screen's component firing again.

And, As Steve Used to Say, Just One More Thing

There's one last little bit of code here that we must look at, and while it's very little code, it is absolutely key. Remember when I said that you could only export one component from the module? And remember when I said that we're using a StackNavigator to flip between the list and add screens by passing a name to the navigate() method? Well, here's where both those statements come into play:

```
const RestaurantsScreen = StackNavigator(
  { ListScreen : { screen : ListScreen }, AddScreen : { screen :
  AddScreen } },
  { headerMode : "none", initialRouteName : "ListScreen" }
);

exports.RestaurantsScreen = RestaurantsScreen;
```

This code creates a StackNavigator component and exports it, and the configuration passed to it defines two screens, ListScreen and AddScreen. For each, we point it to the component for the screen, the result of which is that the navigator now knows these screens by name, and that's how we can navigate between them. We also tell the navigator that we do not want any sort of header displayed and that the list route (screen) is the default one to display, exactly as we want in Restaurant Chooser.

And that, as they say, is a wrap! Well, until the next chapter, anyway.

Hey, What About the People Screen?

At this point, you may be looking ahead and seeing that the end of the chapter is right around a very short corner and wondering, Gee, isn't there a whole other screen to look at? And you are correct in that, yes, there is a whole *other* screen...but we're *not* going to look at it. Bad author, gipping my faithful reader out of content!

See, here's the thing: the People screen is virtually identical to the Restaurants screen, aside from the Restaurants screen having more data entry fields on the add screen. I know they're almost identical because, being a fundamentally lazy person, I wrote the Restaurants screen and then copy-and-pasted it to create the People screen. (I know, I know, copy-and-paste coding is an anti-pattern, and typically I'd agree with you, but at the time, because I wasn't sure if these two screens would diverge in any significant way initially, it made more sense to do it this way, so that possibility would be easy to deal with.) The result and only real difference is that anywhere the word *restaurants* appears, it became *people*. Otherwise, if you compare them, you'll find the same core structure, the same methods, the same variables, etc. The People screen simply has fewer fields than the Restaurants screen.

So, rather than going over what you've essentially already seen, I'll save a few pages here and use them elsewhere. I think you absolutely should have a look at the code in the download bundle, if only to convince yourself there's nothing special in this screen and also because the more you look at code such as this, the more the core concepts will embed in your brain, and especially after the explanation of the Restaurants screen, that should reinforce it all.

Summary

In this chapter, we got to work building a real app with React Native. In the process, you encountered quite a lot: navigation, custom components, third-party component libraries, usage of many components and some APIs, and one approach to structuring an application.

In the next chapter, we'll wrap up Restaurant Chooser, by exploring the largest chunk of code, that of the Decision screen. You'll learn some new things, including flexbox and layout, and I'll talk a little about testing and debugging too.

CHAPTER 4

Restaurant Chooser, Part 2

In the previous chapter, we began dissecting the Restaurant Chooser application, to see what makes it tick. You looked at the basic structure of the code at a high level, the main entry point code, and the Restaurants screens (which, by extension, effectively showed you the People screen, because the code is practically identical to that of the Restaurants screen).

That leaves a sizable chunk of the code to look at, the main code, really, in the Decision screen. This screen is, in fact, a group of screens (or sub-screens, as I've been calling them thus far): It's Decision Time, Who's Going, Pre-Filters, Choice, and Post-Choice. These are the screens, in sequence, seen as the user uses the app to decide on a restaurant. (There's also the Veto screen that may or may not come after the Choice screen.) That's what we'll be looking at in this chapter.

However, before we start tearing the code apart, I'll talk about something that I promised I'd get to in this chapter, because I don't want to make you wait any longer: layout and flexbox.

A Promise Fulfilled: Let's Talk Layout and Flexbox

In the last chapter, and in the first two chapters as well, in fact, you saw some examples of layout in React Native. You saw style attributes such as `flex`, `justifyContent`, and `alignItems`. At one point, I even said that you've already seen enough to be able to create your own layouts, and that's true. Fundamentally, React Native uses the same (mostly) Flexbox CSS that you use on the Web, and only a handful of attributes provides most of the capabilities you need to create a vast majority of layouts, both simple and complex.

© Frank Zammetti 2018
F. Zammetti, *Practical React Native*, https://doi.org/10.1007/978-1-4842-3939-1_4

But, that's not an explanation, and you deserve more. So, I'll talk about layout and flexbox in a little more detail now.

Flexbox is a layout algorithm that was introduced to CSS only a couple of years ago. It was designed with modern practices in mind, meaning such things as responsive design and layouts "flexing" (hence the name), based on the sizes of the components being laid out, even when those sizes are unknown or dynamic. When dealing with flexbox, you are concerned with some parent container element, a component in React Native, and its immediate children, and how they are arranged in one direction or another. Components that use flexbox to lay their children out can then have one or more of those children themselves use flexbox to lay *their* children out, and so on, as far as you have to go. In this way, by nesting components that use flexbox, you can achieve pretty much any layout you can envision.

All that is required to use flexbox for layout is to specify some style attributes on a component. As mentioned before, the most commonly used attributes are `flex`, `justifyContent`, `alignItems`, and `flexDirection`. There are a few others that are important, but somewhat less so, including `alignSelf`, `flexWrap`, `alignContent`, `position`, and `zIndex`.

By and large, if you find a reference about flexbox on the Web, it will apply to React Native as well, though there are a few differences you should be aware of. First, the defaults are a little different in React Native. With flexbox on the Web, the default for `flexDirection` is `row`, but in React Native, it's `column`. Second, the `flex` parameter only supports a single number.

Okay, that's all well and good, but what do these attributes do? Let's look at each now.

The first attribute is `flexDirection` (valid values: `row`, `column`, `column-reverse`, and `row-reverse`, with `column` being the default). This defines the direction of the main, or primary, layout axis. In other words, this determines whether the children of the container will be laid out horizontally across the screen (when `flexDirection` is set to `row`) or vertically (when set to `column`). The altered default (altered from flexbox on the Web) makes sense in this context, because most components on a mobile device are laid out vertically down the screen.

Next up is `flex`. This attribute tells flexbox how the available space along the primary axis will be apportioned to the children. This can get a little complicated, but let's start with the simple part: your main container will nearly always have a `flex` value of 1, which means it will take up the entire height of the screen (or the whole width, if you were laying out in `row` mode). Then, the children inside that container will divide the available space according to their `flex` values.

Let's say that you've got the following code:

```
import React from "react";
import { View } from "react-native";

export default class App extends React.Component {
  render() {
    return (
      <View style={{ flex : 1 }}>
        <View style={{ flex : 5, backgroundColor : "red" }} />
        <View style={{ flex : 2, backgroundColor : "green" }} />
        <View style={{ flex : 3, backgroundColor : "blue" }} />
      </View>
    );
  }
}
```

The first View has a flex value of 1, so it will fill the screen. It has three child Views, each with different flex values. How much space will they take up? Well, all three of them *combined* will fill the parent View, which means they will fill the screen, and that's because if you don't specify a height for the components, the View will stretch to fill space, based on its flex value, by default. But, how much of the screen's height will each View take? To know, you add up the flex values, ten here, and the flex value of each forms a fraction, using that value as the denominator. In other words, the first (red) child View takes up 5/10 of the screen, which means 1/2 (just reduce the fraction as you would mathematically). The second (green) child View takes up 2/10 of the screen, or 1/5. The third (blue) child View takes up 3/10 of the screen.

Let's say now that we change the flex values of the children to be 1, 2, and 3, respectively. Add those up, and we get 6, so now the first child takes up 1/5 of the screen, the second 2/5, and the third 3/5. If you did 4, 2, 4 instead, they now take up 2/5, 1/5, and 2/5, respectively. See how that works?

You can also mix flex values with static values. For example, replace the flex attribute of the first child View with height:100 and change the flex value of the other two children to 1, and you'll wind up with a red box 100 pixels in height, and the other two will evenly divide the remaining space between them. In this particular case, the actual flex values you use don't matter, only that they are the same matters. I hope that you can see why.

Keeping this train going, we next come to justifyContent (valid values: flex-start, flex-end, center, space-between, and space-around, with flex-start being the default). This attribute tells flexbox how the children are distributed across the primary axis. A value of flex-start means the children will "bunch up" (meaning with no space between them) at the top (or left, depending on the primary axis) of their parent. A value of flex-end means the exact opposite; they'll bunch up on the right or bottom. A value of center means they'll bunch up in the middle of the container, with any available unused space above and below (or left and right) of the children. A value of space-between ensures that any unused space is distributed evenly between the children (with no unused space before and after the first and last child, correspondingly), and space-around ensures that available space is allocated between all children, including before and after the first and last child.

They say a picture is worth a thousand words, so have a look at Figure 4-1, to see the effect of these settings in action (when the default flexDirection of column is used, that is).

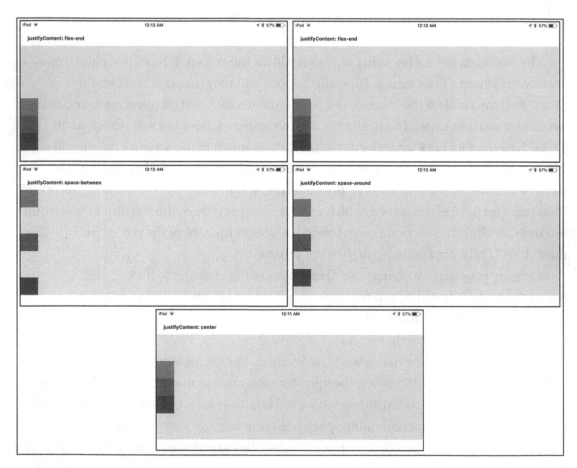

Figure 4-1. *The various settings of justifyContent*

Next up is the alignItems attribute (valid values: flex-start, flex-end, center, and stretch, with stretch being the default). This determines how the children align on the secondary, or "cross" axis. That means that, in the case of the default column layout, alignItems determines how the children align horizontally. Once again, let's go to a picture, Figure 4-2, to make these settings clear.

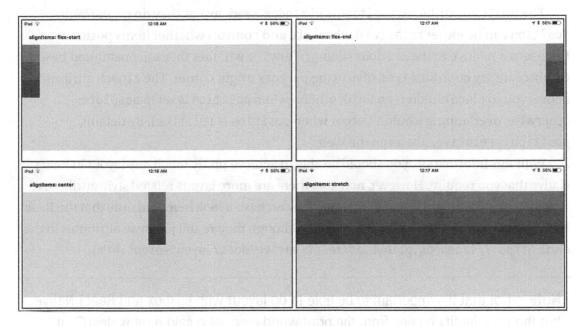

Figure 4-2. *The various settings of* alignItems

One important note is that for flex-start, center, and flex-end to work, your children must have specific widths. By contrast, they *cannot* have a fixed width, if you want to use stretch.

The alignSelf attribute (valid values: auto, flex-start, flex-end, center, stretch or baseline, with auto being the default) allows a child to define its own alignItems value for it alone, overriding the parent's alignItems value. This is a lesser used attribute, but it's there if you need it.

The flexWrap attribute (valid values: wrap or nowrap, with nowrap being the default) tells flexbox whether children are forced onto a single line, even if that means that they will flow off the screen (nowrap) or whether they can wrap onto a second line (wrap). Of course, whether your primary axis is horizontal or vertical determines whether you'll get a second row of children or a second column.

The `alignContent` attribute (valid values: `flex-start`, `center`, `flex-end`, `stretch`, `space-between`, `space-around`, with `flex-start` being the default) allows you to align the lines of children when `flexWrap` is set to `wrap` and when you wind up with multiple rows or columns. For example, if your layout flows to have two columns of children, setting `alignContent` to `center` ensures that both columns will be aligned to the center of the parent container.

The final two attributes, `position` and `zIndex`, work just as they do on the Web: `position` can be either `relative` or `absolute` and controls whether items position themselves relative to the previous sibling (if any) or whether they are positioned based on absolute x/y coordinates relative to the parent's origin corner. The `zIndex` attribute allows you to place children on top of others (when `position` is set to `absolute`; otherwise, overlapping wouldn't occur when `position` is `relative`). By default, `position` is `relative`, just as on the Web.

With this information, you should be able to achieve pretty much any layout in React Native that you require. However, note that there are more layout-related style attributes available that you might also make use of. You can have a look here (but note that the React Native docs refer to these as "Layout Props," although they're still just style attributes in the end): `https://facebook.github.io/react-native/docs/layout-props.html`.

Note   Not that it's important to be able to do layout with flexbox and React Native, but the term justify comes from the print world (see, who said print is dead?). It refers to the way in which the lines of a newspaper article fill the space available to the line evenly, something that at one point was difficult to do, before computers came along to make it a piece of cake. This results in a straight edge of content on the left and right margins, which is said to give the content a more organized layout that allows readers to move more easily between the lines of text.

To the Heart of the Matter: DecisionScreen.js

Okay, with the intro-type stuff done, it's time to get down to the code found in the `DecisionScreen.js` file, which makes up most of the code of Restaurant Chooser, where most of the action occurs. Remember here that there are effectively five screens contained in this file, or sub-screens, as I like to call them, but even before those, there's the usual boilerplate stuff you've come to know and love.

```
import React from "react";
import CustomButton from "../components/CustomButton";
import { Alert, AsyncStorage, BackHandler, Button, FlatList, Image, Modal,
Picker,
  ssPlatform, ScrollView, StyleSheet, Text, TouchableOpacity, View } from
  "react-native";
import { StackNavigator } from "react-navigation";
import { CheckBox } from "native-base";
import { Constants } from "expo";
```

We won't be using the CustomTextInput component anywhere here, but we will be using CustomButton, so that's imported. All the React Native components are ones you've already seen in one form or another, so you should recognize them at this point. The StackNavigator from React Navigation that you saw on the Restaurants screen is how we'll flip between the various sub-screens. The CheckBox component from NativeBase is imported next, and this component will be used on the Who's Going screen, to pick people who will be going out to eat. Finally, Constants from Expo will be used similarly to how it was before, that is, to get header-size information, so that some padding can be added, where appropriate, as you'll see later.

After the imports, we have three variables that will be required in this source file. They are, of course, global within this module, which means that all the sub-screen code will be able to access them, which is precisely why they're defined here. When you have to share data between data in a single module, this is an excellent way to do it.

Tip   Although true global scope, in which you can access something from any module, is generally frowned upon, it's something you can do in React Native, if you have to. There is a variable, not very creatively named global, that you can access from any module at any time, and you can attach your own data to it if you like. (It's just a JavaScript object, so attach attributes as you would any other object.) However, I would advise you to keep this as a last resort and not abuse it, if you use it. If you must, do so wisely, as in attach a single object with a name that you can be pretty sure is unique (globalData_<my app's name>, for example), to avoid any conflicts and problems.

```
let participants = null;
let filteredRestaurants = null;
let chosenRestaurant = { };
```

The participants variable will contain an array of objects, one for each person who will be participating in the decision. The filteredRestaurants variable will be an array of objects, one for each restaurant that the app might randomly choose. As the name implies, this list will consist only of restaurants that pass any pre-filter choices made by the user. Finally, chosenRestaurant is exactly that: an object with data about the restaurant that is randomly chosen.

There is one more bit of code before we get to the screens themselves, and that's a little helper function to choose a random number.

```
const getRandom = (inMin, inMax) => {
  inMin = Math.ceil(inMin);
  inMax = Math.floor(inMax);
  return Math.floor(Math.random() * (inMax - inMin + 1)) + inMin;
};
```

It's pretty boilerplate—just a typical random number generator that accepts a minimum value and maximum value and returns a random number within that range (inclusive). Because potentially it will have to be called later several times inside a loop, it makes sense to extract the code into a function such as this.

Now, on to the screens!

The DecisionTimeScreen Component

The first screen to look at is the It's DecisionTimeScreen component, which is where the user starts out when the app first launches. It's nothing but a logo and some text, all of which is tapable to initiate a decision. Have a look at the code here (and, yes, this is *all* of it).

```
class DecisionTimeScreen extends React.Component {

  render() { return (

    <View style={styles.decisionTimeScreenContainer}>
      <TouchableOpacity style={styles.decisionTimeScreenTouchable}
        onPress={ () => {
```

```
AsyncStorage.getItem("people",
  function(inError, inPeople) {
    if (inPeople === null) {
      inPeople = [ ];
    } else {
      inPeople = JSON.parse(inPeople);
    }
    if (inPeople.length === 0) {
      Alert.alert("That ain't gonna work, chief",
        "You haven't added any people. " +
        "You should probably do that first, no?",
        [ { text : "OK" } ], { cancelable : false }
      );
    } else {
      AsyncStorage.getItem("restaurants",
        function(inError, inRestaurants) {
          if (inRestaurants === null) {
            inRestaurants = [ ];
          } else {
            inRestaurants = JSON.parse(inRestaurants);
          }
          if (inRestaurants.length === 0) {
            Alert.alert("That ain't gonna work, chief",
              "You haven't added any restaurants. " +
              "You should probably do that first, no?",
              [ { text : "OK" } ], { cancelable : false }
            );
          } else {
            this.props.navigation.navigate("WhosGoingScreen");
          }
        }.bind(this)
      );
    }
  }.bind(this)
);
```

```
      } }
    >
      <Image source={ require("../images/its-decision-time.png") } />
      <Text style={{paddingTop:20}}>(click the food to get going)</Text>
    </TouchableOpacity>
  </View>

);  }
```

We start out with a container View, the typical pattern in React Native, and to that View is applied the decisionTimeScreenContainer style.

```
decisionTimeScreenContainer : { flex : 1, alignItems : "center",
justifyContent : "center" }
```

Given the discussion that began this chapter, you now know what this is all about. It's a simple flexbox layout that makes this View fill the entire screen and centers its children both vertically and horizontally on it.

Into this View goes, first, a TouchableOpacity component. You'll recall that this component is a generic container, like View, but which responds to touch events and allows us to hook code into those events. This component gets a style attached as well.

```
decisionTimeScreenTouchable : { alignItems : "center", justifyContent : "center" }
```

This configuration is necessary, because the styles on the parent View centers this TouchableOpacity component within it, but then the children within the TouchableOpacity have to be centered as well. Otherwise, the Image and Text won't be centered as we expect.

Most important, this TouchableOpacity has an onPress prop attached, but I'll come back to that in just a moment and instead move down to see the Image component that is its first child. The Image component references the its-decision-time.png image, using relative path notation, because it's in the images directory, and right now, the execution context of this file is the screens directory. In other words, if we just did

```
<Image source={ require("its-decision-time.png") } />
```

then React Native would look for that file in the screens directory and not find it, of course, and we'd have a problem. You must always consider the execution context of the source file your code is in when referencing resources that are part of your code base, as this is.

Right after that Image component is a Text component that gives the user a hint of what to do. Some padding is added as an inline style, to separate the Image from the Text. I left it as an inline style, first to remind you that you can do that, but also because you always have to decide whether it makes sense to extract your styles into a separate object. *Usually,* it does, but sometimes the styling is so minor and feels conceptually as if it should be part of the object being styled (and it's not something that you would want to change either at all or globally). This is a case in which adding a new style feels a bit superfluous to me, so I didn't do it.

Now, back to that onPress handler on the TouchableOpacity component. This, of course, is where the real work for this screen is, and that work begins by using the AsyncStorage API that by now you're quite familiar with, to retrieve a list of people who the app is aware of. If there are none, the user is told that he or she can't yet make a decision. After all, if *you alone* can't decide where to go to eat, then no app in the world is going to help you! No, this app is for helping *a group of people* make a decision, and as such, there obviously has to be people to choose from.

By the same token, if the user hasn't yet created any restaurants, there's nothing the app can do then either, so the restaurants are retrieved next from storage, and if there are none, the user is told about that too.

Finally, if there is at least one person and at least one restaurant, we call React Navigation's this.props.navigation.navigate() method, passing it the WhosGoingScreen, to navigate to the next screen, where the user can pick who's going to be involved in the decision.

Note   This screen doesn't have to do any work when it's created, which is why there's no componentDidMount() here. In fact, most of the sub-screens that are in the DecisionScreen.js file are like this. Remember that it's an optional method, after all. But it's an optional method that can be very handy for making initial remote API calls to get initial values to populate the screen or to do any sort of setup tasks that might be necessary. You'll see examples of this throughout the book, but this is one method you'll likely use a great deal in your work, so keep it in mind.

The WhosGoingScreen Component

After users click the giant graphic on the It's Decision Time screen (Figure 3-2 in Chapter 3, if you need a refresher), the next screen they find themselves at is the Who's Going screen, for which they select the people involved. This screen is contained in the WhosGoingScreen component (which is still a part of the DecisionScreen.js file), and it starts off just like any other React Native component would.

```
class WhosGoingScreen extends React.Component {

  constructor(inProps) {
    super(inProps);
    this.state = { people : [ ], selected : { } };
  }
```

The props are passed to the superclass constructor, and then a state object is attached, to hold the state for the components that will make up this one. We have two pieces of information to keep track of here: the people who the user can choose from and an array that will record which of those are selected. It would have been possible to store that selected state within the objects in the people array itself, but I felt it was cleaner to not modify those objects, because whether they are selected is a temporary state for this screen, so separating those concerns seemed appropriate. The people array will be populated in the componentDidMount() method, but I'll be getting to that after the render() method, and speaking of the render() method, here it comes now:

```
  render() { return (

    <View style={styles.listScreenContainer}>

      <Text style={styles.whosGoingHeadline}>Who's Going?</Text>

      <FlatList style={{width : "94%"}} data={this.state.people}
        renderItem={ ({item}) =>
          <TouchableOpacity
            style={styles.whosGoingItemTouchable}
            onPress={ function() {
              const selected = this.state.selected;
              selected[item.key] = !selected[item.key];
              this.setState({ selected : selected });
```

```
        }.bind(this) }
    >
        <CheckBox style={styles.whosGoingCheckbox}
            checked={this.state.selected[item.key]}
            onPress={ function() {
                const selected = this.state.selected;
                selected[item.key] = !selected[item.key];
                this.setState({ selected : selected });
            }.bind(this) } />
        <Text style={styles.whosGoingName}>
            {item.firstName} {item.lastName} ({item.relationship})
        </Text>
    </TouchableOpacity>
    }
/>
```

I'll split this discussion into two parts, the first part beginning with a View that contains the entire screen and which has this style applied:

```
listScreenContainer : { flex : 1, alignItems : "center", justifyContent :
"center",
  ...Platform.select({ ios : { paddingTop : Constants.statusBarHeight },
  android : { } })
}
```

As per the earlier discussion on flexbox, you know now that the flex, alignItems, and justifyContent attributes are responsible for ensuring that the View fills the screen and that its children are centered both vertically and horizontally. There's also a need to add some padding to the top, so the View doesn't overlap the status bar, and that's where using the Platform.select() method comes into play, because that padding is only needed on iOS, not Android. The height of the status bar is obtained with Constants.statusBarHeight, as you've seen before, and that becomes the paddingTop value.

The first child is a Text component that is a title, or headline, for the screen. This is a common pattern you'll see going forward, and for the text to look like a title, we need the following style applied:

```
whosGoingHeadline : { fontSize : 30, marginTop : 20, marginBottom : 20 }
```

A bump in font size gives us some text that looks like a heading, and some margin on the top and bottom ensures there's space around it when further components are added to the outer container View.

As it happens, there are only two other children, the first of which is the FlatList you see, and, of course, that's how the list of people is displayed. The FlatList itself is given a width of 94%, so that it doesn't bump up against the edges of the screen, and its data prop points to the people array in the state. For each item, we supply a renderItem prop that is a function to be called to render each item. What's rendered here is a TouchableOpacity component and within it is a CheckBox component from NativeBase and a Text component to show the name. They are both nested inside the TouchableOpacity, so that touching the text will allow us to check the box as well. Otherwise, the user would have to tap the CheckBox specifically, making it a little annoying to use.

Because that TouchableOpacity is the container for the CheckBox and the Text components, we need to lay them out inside of it, so this style is used:

```
whosGoingItemTouchable : { flexDirection : "row", marginTop : 10,
marginBottom : 10 }
```

The flexDirection attribute is set to row, so that the two components are placed side by side, and marginTop and marginBottom give some space between each person on the list.

Look at the onPress prop for both the TouchableOpacity and the CheckBox. Notice anything about them? Yep, they're identical. Aside from the question of whether this should or shouldn't be pulled out into a separate function (probably yes, but for something so trivial like this, I don't think it's essential), they are identical, because if they weren't, you would find that touching the CheckBox doesn't result in the CheckBox state changing.

Conceptually, you would imagine that the onPress of the TouchableOpacity is what would be triggered on a touch event. This makes sense, if you envision this in physical terms. Imagine the TouchableOpacity as a transparent plastic box, and in that box is a Checkbox (maybe you 3D-printed an actual check box). If you try to press down on the Checkbox, your finger actually makes contact with the TouchableOpacity first (and *can't* touch the check box *at all*, in fact). Therefore, you would put the onPress handler on the TouchableOpacity, and things would work as you'd expect.

But, that's not what happens.

What happens, or, at least, how it acts, is as if the TouchableOpacity somehow *knows* there's a check box underneath it and delegates to its onPress handler. In our physical version, it's as if the plastic box magically allows your finger to pass through it to touch the check box below, but only where the check box is. If you press anywhere else on the box (or on the TouchableOpacity), your finger doesn't go through, and the onPress of the TouchableOpacity fires.

To be honest, I'm not sure why it works this way. I wasn't able to determine an answer. But, in the end, the solution to the problem is simply to attach the same handler to both the TouchableOpacity and the CheckBox. That way, the user can tap anywhere on the item and get the desired effect: toggling of the check box.

The handler itself is trivial. Get a reference to the selected array in state (which you'll see initially populated very soon), toggle the item in the array associated with the item the user tapped based on its key attribute, then do a setState(), to reflect the update. Because the CheckBox's checked prop is tied to the entry in the selected array for that person, the CheckBox's visual state is updated automatically. And, speaking of that CheckBox, it has a simple style applied.

```
whosGoingCheckbox : { marginRight : 20 }
```

That's to ensure that there is some space between the CheckBox and the person's name, which is housed in a Text component after the CheckBox component and has this style applied:

```
whosGoingName : { flex : 1 }
```

That will force the Text component to fill the remaining horizontal space on that row. The Test component's value is simply a concatenation of the firstName, lastName, and relationship attributes from the object in the people array.

One thing I've glossed over is why bind() is sometimes used on event handlers and why sometimes it's not. The simple answer is that I did it both ways in various places to demonstrate to you that you can, in fact, do it either way. However, you will find some situations in which you *can't* use fat arrow notation, or else you won't have a proper reference to the component via this inside the function. In those cases, you'll have to use traditional function notation as is done for these onPress handlers and then bind() that function to the component through this.

That rounds out the FlatList code. What's next is the button below that list.

```
<CustomButton text="Next" width="94%"
  onPress={ () => {
    participants = [ ];
    for (const person of this.state.people) {
      if (this.state.selected[person.key]) {
        const participant = Object.assign({}, person);
        participant.vetoed = "no";
        participants.push(participant);
      }
    }
    if (participants.length === 0) {
      Alert.alert("Uhh, you awake?",
        "You didn't select anyone to go. Wanna give it another try?",
        [ { text : "OK" } ], { cancelable : false }
      );
    } else {
      this.props.navigation.navigate("PreFiltersScreen");
    }
  } }
/>
</View>

); }
```

It's the onPress prop that we really care about here and that's responsible for creating an array of people who will participate in this event, hence the variable name participants. It's a simple matter of iterating through the people array in state and, for each, looking up in the selected array to see if that person's entry is true. If it is, the person is copied into the participants array, and a vetoed attribute set to no is added (which will become relevant on the following screens). Now, if we do that and find that there are no entries in the participants array, then, naturally, the user hasn't selected any, so an alert is popped to tell them. Otherwise, we use the usual React Navigation method to transfer the user to the Pre-Filters screen, which is what we'll be looking at next.

Before that, though, we have one last bit of code to look at for this screen, and that's the componentDidMount() method that I promised you to see soon. Here it is.

```
componentDidMount() {
  BackHandler.addEventListener("hardwareBackPress", () => { return true; });
  AsyncStorage.getItem("people",
    function(inError, inPeople) {
      if (inPeople === null) {
        inPeople = [ ];
      } else {
        inPeople = JSON.parse(inPeople);
      }
      const selected = { };
      for (const person of inPeople) { selected[person.key] = false; }
      this.setState({ people : inPeople, selected : selected });
    }.bind(this)
  );
};
```

The task here, because this method fires when the component is created (which means when the screen is shown), is to populate the list of people in state, pulling it from AsyncStorage. You've seen this same code before in the Restaurants screen, though we were loading restaurants there, of course, so it should look familiar. Once that array is produced, the selected array is then created, with an entry for each person in the inPeople array, with a value set to false, to indicate that they aren't yet selected. Finally, both are set into state, and this screen is good to go!

The PreFiltersScreen Components

The Pre-Filters screen (which is the PreFiltersScreen component) is the screen the user sees after selecting who's going, and it allows them to filter out restaurants from consideration. I'm going to break the code down into chunks for you, to make it a little easier to digest, starting with the constructor.

```
class PreFiltersScreen extends React.Component {

  constructor(inProps) {
    super(inProps);
    this.state = { cuisine : "", price : "", rating : "", delivery : "" };
  }
```

No surprises here. Just a quick call to the superclass constructor and defining a state object. There are four criteria according to which a restaurant can be filtered: cuisine type, price (less than or equal to), rating (greater than or equal to), and whether it has delivery service. Those values are represented in the state object and will, of course, be set by the data entry fields as the user mutates them.

Next up is the render() method.

```
render() { return (

  <ScrollView style={styles.preFiltersContainer}>
    <View style={styles.preFiltersInnerContainer}>
      <View style={styles.preFiltersScreenFormContainer}>

        <View style={styles.preFiltersHeadlineContainer}>
          <Text style={styles.preFiltersHeadline}>Pre-Filters</Text>
        </View>
```

First, as usual, we have a container element, in this case, a ScrollView. This is so that we have a scrolling component, because the components rendered will wind up longer than pretty much any device's screen out there today, and without this, the user wouldn't be able to scroll down to see more of them. The style applied to this component is simple.

```
preFiltersContainer : { marginTop : Constants.statusBarHeight }
```

Just as you saw on the previous screen, a little space at the top is necessary, to avoid overlap with the status bar. A View is then nested inside of that one, with which we can introduce some layout. While it would be possible to apply the necessary styles to the ScrollView itself, doing it as a child of the ScrollView affords us the opportunity to separate the styling between the two, giving us a little more flexibility if this screen should ever be expanded upon. The style applied to this child View is also pretty basic.

```
preFiltersInnerContainer : { flex : 1, alignItems : "center", paddingTop :
20, width : "100%" }
```

With `flex:1`, it will fill its parent, and its children will be centered, thanks to the `alignItems` setting. A little more padding is added. This is necessary because, when the user does scroll, the padding on the `ScrollView` will scroll out of view, and items will overlay the status bar. Adding padding here ensures that doesn't happen. Finally, giving this `View` the entire width of the display ensures that we have the maximum space available to work with to start.

Inside this `View` is yet another `View`, a container for the data entry controls (our pre-filter "form," so to speak). This is done so that the following style can be applied to provide padding on both sides of the screen.

```
preFiltersScreenFormContainer : { width : "96%" }
```

Inside this third-level `View` is another `View`, which has a `Text` component inside of it. This gives the screen a headline heading, just as with the previous screen. The styles for this `View` and `Text` component, respectively, are

```
preFiltersHeadlineContainer : { flex : 1, alignItems : "center",
justifyContent : "center" }
preFiltersHeadline : { fontSize : 30, marginTop : 20, marginBottom : 20 }
```

The View's style is necessary because, by default, its parent container, styled with `preFiltersScreenFormContainer`, will align left (remember, `flex-start` is the default), but we want it centered, so the `Text` component is wrapped in a `View` and center alignment is added to it. The `Text` component is styled the same way as the heading on the previous screen.

So far, so good. Now, we can start putting in the data entry components for filtering, beginning with the one for cuisine type.

```
<Text style={styles.fieldLabel}>Cuisine</Text>
<View style={styles.pickerContainer}>
  <Picker style={styles.picker} selectedValue={this.state.cuisine}
    prompt="Cuisine"
    onValueChange={ (inItemValue) => this.setState({ cuisine :
    inItemValue }) } >
      <Picker.Item label="" value="" />
      <Picker.Item label="Algerian" value="Algerian" />
      <Picker.Item label="American" value="American" />
      ...
```

143

```
                <Picker.Item label="Other" value="Other" />
                ...
            </Picker>
        </View>
```

Every filter field is, in fact, a combination of a Text component, serving as a field label, and the data entry component itself, a Picker in this case. The style applied to the label (all of them, not just this one) is

```
fieldLabel : { marginLeft : 10 }
```

This serves to put a little space to the left, so that the label lines up with the edge of the Picker box, just as was seen on the Restaurants Add screen.

The Picker itself is tied to the cuisine attribute in the state object and is wrapped in a View with this style applied:

```
pickerContainer : {
  ...Platform.select({
    ios : { },
    android : { width : "96%", borderRadius : 8, borderColor : "#c0c0c0",
    borderWidth : 2,
      marginLeft : 10, marginBottom : 20, marginTop : 4 }
  })
}
```

You saw this same styling earlier on the Restaurants Add screen, so there's no need to dwell on it here. Similarly, the picker style applied to the Picker itself is the same as glimpsed on the Restaurants Add screen, but here it is again, just so you don't have to take my word for it.

```
picker : {
  ...Platform.select({
    ios : { width : "96%", borderRadius : 8, borderColor : "#c0c0c0",
    borderWidth : 2,
      marginLeft : 10, marginBottom : 20, marginTop : 4 }, android : { }
  })
}
```

Note that I've cut down the list of Picker.Item children elements, just to save a little space, but they're all there, as you'd expect. The onChange handler simply sets the new value of the Picker into the state object.

After the cuisine type Picker comes a Picker for the price, rating, and delivery. But, given that they are just straight copies of the cuisine type Picker, aside from getting and setting the price, rating, and delivery attributes of the state object, respectively, let's skip over them. (Do grab the download code bundle, however, and have a look at them, just to be sure.) That brings us to the Next button at the bottom of the screen that users tap when they've made their pre-filter selections. It's where all the real action for this screen lives.

```
<CustomButton text="Next" width="94%"
  onPress={ () => {
    AsyncStorage.getItem("restaurants",
      function(inError, inRestaurants) {
        if (inRestaurants === null) {
          inRestaurants = [ ];
        } else {
          inRestaurants = JSON.parse(inRestaurants);
        }
        filteredRestaurants = [ ];
        for (const restaurant of inRestaurants) {
          let passTests = true;
          if (this.state.cuisine !== "") {
            if (Object.keys(this.state.cuisine).length > 0) {
              if (restaurant.cuisine !== this.state.cuisine) {
                passTests = false;
              }
            }
          }
          if (this.state.price !== "") {
            if (restaurant.price > this.state.price) { passTests =
            false; }
          }
          if (this.state.rating !== "") {
```

```
                      if (restaurant.rating < this.state.rating) {
                      passTests = false; }
                    }
                    if (this.state.delivery !== "") {
                      if (restaurant.delivery !== this.state.delivery) {
                      passTests = false; }
                    }
                    if (this.state.cuisine.length === 0 && this.state.price
                    === "" &&
                      this.state.rating === "" && this.state.delivery === "") {
                      passTests = true;
                    }
                    if (passTests) { filteredRestaurants.push(restaurant); }
                  }
                  if (filteredRestaurants.length === 0) {
                    Alert.alert("Well, that's an easy choice",
                      "None of your restaurants match these criteria. Maybe " +
                      "try loosening them up a bit?",
                      [ { text : "OK" } ], { cancelable : false }
                    );
                  } else {
                    this.props.navigation.navigate("ChoiceScreen");
                  }
                }.bind(this)
              );
            } }
          />
        </View>
      </View>
    </ScrollView>

  ); }
```

The onPress handler is where it's at, of course, and the work there begins by pulling the list of restaurants from AsyncStorage, as you've seen a few times before in various places. Once we have them in the inRestaurants array, the next step is to create an empty filteredRestaurants array. Recall that this is a variable global to this module, so we're just ensuring it's an empty array at this point. (There really shouldn't be any way for it not to be, but a little defensive programming never hurt anyone.)

Next, we iterate the list of retrieved restaurants. For each, the passTests flag is set to true, so we're going to assume, to begin with, that every restaurant is included in the final array. Then the tests are performed, based on the selected filter criteria, if any. Each is checked for a blank, which indicates the user didn't set a value for a given criterion, and for any that isn't blank, the appropriate logic is executed and passTests is set to false for any that fails. In the end, if passTests is true, the restaurant is added to the filteredRestaurants array.

Finally, if after that iteration the array is empty, we tell the user that there's nothing for the app to do and admonish them to change the pre-filter criteria. If there is at least one, we navigate the user to the Choice screen, which is the next chunk of code for us to look at.

The ChoiceScreen Component

Next up on the hit parade of code is the ChoiceScreen component. It's where the app chooses a restaurant and shows it to the user. This screen uses a Modal component, a pop-up dialog window, to show the selected restaurant. It also uses a Modal when someone in the party decides to veto the choice, and both of these Modals are part of this code. Before we get to any of that, let's see how the component starts off. By now, it's nothing new.

```
class ChoiceScreen extends React.Component {

  constructor(inProps) {
    super(inProps);
    this.state = { participantsList : participants,
    participantsListRefresh : false,
      selectedVisible : false, vetoVisible : false, vetoDisabled : false,
      vetoText : "Veto"
    };
  }
```

Yep, just the usual call to the superclass constructor and a state object. The attributes of this state object are

- `participantsList`: The list of people participating in the decision. This is used to list the people on the main screen (the part that isn't in a `Modal`) and indicate whether any has exercised a veto.

- `participantsListRefresh`: A Boolean flag that is necessary for the list of people to be updated after a veto. (Don't worry, I'll explain that when I talk about the code for the list.)

- `selectedVisible`: A Boolean that tells React Native whether the `Modal` that shows the chosen restaurant is visible.

- `vetoVisible`: A Boolean that, like `selectedVisible`, tells React Native if the `Modal` in which the user selects the person who vetoed is visible or not.

- `vetoDisabled`: A Boolean that determines if the Veto button on the chosen restaurant `Modal` is disabled or not. (If there's nobody left who can veto, it should be disabled.)

- `vetoText`: This contains the text for the Veto button, which will be changed to "No Vetoes Left" when there's nobody left who can veto. (This is better than just disabling the button, because this way, the user doesn't wonder why it's disabled.)

Now, let's get on to the `render()` method. I'll break this down into bite-sized pieces for your code-consuming pleasure, beginning with this chunk:

```
render() { return (
```

```
<View style={styles.listScreenContainer}>
```

As always, we have a container element, and, as is typical, it's a `View` component. It has the same style applied as the container `View` on the Who's Going screen, so you can refer to that section, if you don't remember.

After that comes the first of the two `Modal` components. The following is used to display information about the randomly chosen restaurant:

```
<Modal presentationStyle={"formSheet"} visible={this.state.
selectedVisible}
```

```
    animationType={"slide"} onRequestClose={ () => { } } >
    <View style={styles.selectedContainer}>
      <View style={styles.selectedInnerContainer}>
        <Text style={styles.selectedName}>{chosenRestaurant.name}</Text>
        <View style={styles.selectedDetails}>
          <Text style={styles.selectedDetailsLine}>
            This is a {"\u2605".repeat(chosenRestaurant.rating)} star
          </Text>
          <Text style={styles.selectedDetailsLine}>
            {chosenRestaurant.cuisine} restaurant
          </Text>
          <Text style={styles.selectedDetailsLine}>
            with a price rating of {"$".repeat(chosenRestaurant.price)}
          </Text>
          <Text style={styles.selectedDetailsLine}>
            that {chosenRestaurant.delivery === "Yes" ? "DOES" : "DOES
            NOT"} deliver.
          </Text>
        </View>
        <CustomButton text="Accept" width="94%"
          onPress={ () => {
            this.setState({ selectedVisible : false, vetoVisible :
            false });
            this.props.navigation.navigate("PostChoiceScreen");
          } }
        />
        <CustomButton text={this.state.vetoText} width="94%"
          disabled={this.state.vetoDisabled ? "true" : "false"}
          onPress={ () => {
            this.setState({ selectedVisible : false, vetoVisible : true });
          } }
        />
      </View>
    </View>
  </Modal>
```

The `presentationStyle` prop is used to control how the `Modal` appears. For the most part, this will only have a tangible effect on larger devices, such as iPads, because, on others, it will appear full-screen, regardless of the setting (or with only a subtle visual difference). The setting of `formSheet` is one of four that shows the `Modal` as a narrow-width view centered on the screen. The other settings are

- `fullScreen`: I would hope the meaning of this setting is obvious.

- `pageSheet`: This partially covers the underlying view and is centered.

- `overFullScreen`: This is the same as `fullScreen`, but it allows for transparency.

The `visible` prop for this `Modal` is tied to the `selectedVisible` attribute in the `state` object, so the way to show the `Modal` is to change that value in `state`. This will be true of the other `Modal` as well, using the `vetoVisible` attribute.

The `animationType` attribute determines what sort of animation is used to show the `Modal`. A value of `slide` causes the `Modal` to slide in from the bottom (a value of `fade` causes it to fade into view, and a value of `none` causes it to appear without animation, and this is the default).

The `onRequestClose` prop allows you to execute some code when the `Modal` is closed. As it happens, we don't need anything to happen, in this case; however, this prop is required, and we'll get a YellowBox warning, if we don't provide one, hence the empty function. (Errors and warnings are discussed in the "Debugging and Troubleshooting" section of this chapter, so the term *YellowBox warning* will be discussed. In short, it's a warning that appears on the screen when you run the app, and, yes, it's in the form of a yellow box.)

Within the `Modal`, we begin its content with a `View`, with this style applied:

```
selectedContainer : { flex : 1, justifyContent : "center" }
```

A `Modal` is just like anything else you do in React Native, in that you'll have to provide a single component, which can, of course, have child components, so this is that top-level component. It's going to fill the `Modal` and center its children—horizontally. The primary layout axis is vertical, because the default layout is `column`, remember. Inside this top-level `View` is another `View`, and here we apply a style to center the children vertically.

```
selectedInnerContainer: { alignItems : "center" }
```

Within this View is first a y component whose value is the name attribute of the chosenRestaurant object. We want this to be in large text, so this style is used:

```
selectedName : { fontSize : 32 }
```

After that comes another View component, this one with this style applied:

```
selectedDetails : { paddingTop : 80, paddingBottom : 80, alignItems :
"center" }
```

This ensures that there is a good amount of space above and below the restaurant details, which are the centered children of this View. Each line of those details is a separate Text component, and because I wanted the text to be larger than usual, but not as large as the restaurant's name, this style is used on each:

```
selectedDetailsLine : { fontSize : 18 }
```

The four Text components now have a few interesting things going on. The first Text component has the following value:

```
This is a {"\u2605".repeat(chosenRestaurant.rating)} star
```

First, you can see that you can use Unicode character codes within strings, as I've done, to show a star character. Because strings in JavaScript have a repeat() method, I use that to show the appropriate number of star characters, based on the chosenRestaurant.rating attribute. The third Text component does a similar thing for the restaurant's price, but there's no need for Unicode values here, because a dollar sign is readily available (although, if this app were properly internationalized, we might well use Unicode to show the appropriate denomination symbol for the country the device is in). The fourth Text component includes a little bit of ternary logic, to display either DOES or DOES NOT deliver, as determined by the value of the chosenRestaurant.delivery attribute.

This Modal then contains two CustomButton components, the first used when the user accepts this restaurant, the latter when someone wants to veto the choice. For the Accept button, the onPress event handler updates the selectedVisible and vetoVisible attributes to false in the state object, which causes React Native to hide both of those Modals. (Remember that they exist, whether they are currently visible.) It then navigates the app to the Post-Choice screen, which is covered later in this chapter.

The second `CustomButton` gets its label text from the `vetoText` attribute of the `state` object and receives the value of its `disabled` prop from the `vetoDisabled` attribute in `state`. You'll see the code that sets those values later, but the point is that they must be dynamic, hence tying them to state attributes. The `onPress` handler simply hides this `Modal` and shows the next (for vetoing) by mutating state.

The second `Modal` is a bit more involved, and its code is as follows:

```
<Modal presentationStyle={"formSheet"} visible={this.state.vetoVisible}
  animationType={"slide"} onRequestClose={ () => { } } >
  <View style={styles.vetoContainer}>
    <View style={styles.vetoContainerInner}>
      <Text style={styles.vetoHeadline}>Who's vetoing?</Text>
      <ScrollView style={styles.vetoScrollViewContainer}>
        { participants.map((inValue) => {
            if (inValue.vetoed === "no") {
              return <TouchableOpacity key={inValue.key}
                style={ styles.vetoParticipantContainer }
                onPress={ () => {
                  for (const participant of participants) {
                    if (participant.key === inValue.key) {
                      participant.vetoed = "yes";
                      break;
                    }
                  }
                  let vetoStillAvailable = false;
                  let buttonLabel = "No Vetoes Left";
                  for (const participant of participants) {
                    if (participant.vetoed === "no") {
                      vetoStillAvailable = true;
                      buttonLabel = "Veto";
                      break;
                    }
                  }
                  for (let i = 0; i < filteredRestaurants.length; i++) {
                    if (filteredRestaurants[i].key ===
                    chosenRestaurant.key) {
```

```
                filteredRestaurants.splice(i, 1);
                break;
              }
            }
            this.setState({ selectedVisible : false,
            vetoVisible : false,
              vetoText : buttonLabel, vetoDisabled :
              !vetoStillAvailable,
              participantsListRefresh : !this.state.
              participantsListRefresh
            });
            if (filteredRestaurants.length === 1) {
              this.props.navigation.navigate("PostChoiceScreen");
            }
          } }
        >
          <Text style={styles.vetoParticipantName}>
            {inValue.firstName + " " + inValue.lastName}
          </Text>
        </TouchableOpacity>;
      }
    })
  }
</ScrollView>
<View style={styles.vetoButtonContainer}>
  <CustomButton text="Never Mind" width="94%"
    onPress={ () => {
      this.setState({ selectedVisible : true, vetoVisible : false });
    } }
  />
</View>
</View>
</View>
</Modal>
```

The `Modal` itself is defined as the previous one was, so there's nothing new to see there. It also starts off just like the other, in terms of its children, with a top-level `View` serving as a container, with the following style on it:

```
vetoContainer: { flex : 1, justifyContent : "center" }
```

That serves the same purpose as the previous `Modal`'s top-level child, that is, to fill the `Modal` and center its children along the primary layout axis. Also, just like the previous `Modal`, a second `View` is nested within the first, so we can apply some further layout configuration, as you can see in this styling:

```
vetoContainerInner: { justifyContent : "center", alignItems : "center",
  alignContent : "center" }
```

This time, we want the children centered on both axes, hence the flexbox settings you see. Those children begin with a heading `Text` component, using this style definition:

```
vetoHeadline : { fontSize : 32, fontWeight : "bold" }
```

Yep, just as on the first `Modal` as well. So far, there's not much different, but that changes with the next child component, which is a `ScrollView`. The goal here is to present a list of people, the same list as seen on the main screen underneath this `Modal`, which is the list of people participating, and then allow the user to tap one to indicate they are vetoing. Because this list can be arbitrarily long, we need a scrollable area, and a simple `ScrollView` does the trick. This `ScrollView` uses the following style:

```
vetoScrollViewContainer : { height : "50%" }
```

That's just an arbitrary height that I determined through trial and error that winds up mostly filling the area available in the `Modal` (once the headline and the button is considered).

Now, here's where it gets interesting: a `ScrollView` must have children, of course, but how do you take an array (`participants`, in this case) and generate that list of children dynamically? Well, one way you can do it is to use the `map()` method available on JavaScript arrays. This method allows you to take each element of the array, run it through a function, and return something. In this case, what we'll be returning is some good old React Native component configuration. By wrapping the `map()` call in braces, JSX knows this is an expression, and the output of the expression will be inserted in place of the expression. In this case, the expression is the result of executing the supplied function once for each member of the array. Therefore, we wind up with one or more child elements for the ScrollView.

What does the function map() execute for each item in the array return? As a top-level element, it returns a TouchableOpacity, which you've seen before. Here, however, you'll notice that it has a key prop, the value of which is taken from the key attribute of inValue, which is the object for the next person in the participants array. That key value is actually not necessary to do the work in this Modal, but without it, you'll get a warning that each item in an iterator must have a key. Therefore, we have a key prop, even though it's not required.

For every item in the participants array, we check its vetoed attribute. If it's no, this person still has a veto and, so, will be included in the list. Otherwise, he or she won't be. Once we determine that the person is to be included, the TouchableOpacity is defined, with the key and the following style:

```
vetoParticipantContainer : {paddingTop : 20, paddingBottom : 20 }
```

This inserts some space above and below the name of each person in the list. It also means that the touch target for the user is a comfortable 40 pixels in height, so most users will have no problem tapping the correct name and not hitting another by mistake.

The onPress of the TouchableOpacity is where the real work happens, and that begins by marking the person tapped as having vetoed. This means iterating through the participants array until we find the item with the key matching that of the tapped item and setting its vetoed attribute to yes. Note that it's set to either yes or no, not a Boolean true or false, which is what you would reasonably expect it to be set to, for a very good reason, one that will become apparent soon.

After that step, we must see if there is anyone left who can veto. This is done so that the Veto button can be disabled when no one is left to veto, as well as changing its label text to a more appropriate No Vetoes Left string.

After that, it's time to remove the vetoed restaurant from consideration. Recall that we copied the restaurant objects into a new filteredRestaurants array after the Pre-Filters screen, so we can do a straight delete from the array, using the splice() method, with no fear of munging any permanent data. This array and its data are only used during the decision-making process, so no worries.

As the penultimate step, we have to update the state object to reflect all of this work. That means setting selectedVisible to false, to make sure that Modal is hidden (it already would be, but again, a little defensive programming isn't a bad thing) and ditto the vetoVisible attribute. The label for the Veto button is set via the vetoText attribute to a value buttonLabel determined earlier. The vetoDisabled attribute is the inverse of the value of the vetoStillAvailable variable, which was also established in the previous step.

Finally, we have this participantsListRefresh attribute being toggled. What's this all about? Well, to explain it requires that we look at the list of people on the main Choice screen, which we haven't gotten to, so let's hold up on that for a moment. Bear in mind, however, that the value is being toggled, regardless of what happens. It's changing, and that's what matters most.

Before we get to that, we have to look at the Test component that is the child of the TouchableOpacity and has the following style applied:

vetoParticipantName : { fontSize : 24 }

The value shown is a concatenation of the firstName and lastName attributes of the current participant being rendered (as passed into the function provided to map(), via the inValue argument). That Text component concludes the ScrollView, and it leaves just a single CustomButton to deal with, which is the Never Mind button that allows the user to abort the veto, if the Veto button on the Selected Modal is hit by mistake. This has to set selectedVisible to true and vetoVisible to false in state to re-show the Selected Modal and hide the Veto Modal. By the way, this CustomButton should be centered and take up (nearly) the entire width of the Modal, so the containing View gets this style on it:

vetoButtonContainer : { width : "100%", alignItems : "center", paddingTop : 40 }

Now, with that second Modal out of the way, we can talk about the Choice screen, which is what you see when no Modal is showing (and you see part of it when a Modal is showing as well, although, then, only part of it if on a large-screen device).

<Text style={styles.choiceScreenHeadline}>Choice Screen</Text>

First, we have another heading, Text, as you've seen a few times before, and its styling is also the same as you've seen before, so let's get to more interesting things, namely, the FlatList component that comes next.

```
<FlatList style={styles.choiceScreenListContainer}
  data={this.state.participantsList}
  extraData={this.state.participantsListRefresh}
  renderItem={ ({item}) =>
    <View style={styles.choiceScreenListItem}>
      <Text style={styles.choiceScreenListItemName}>
        {item.firstName} {item.lastName} ({item.relationship})
      </Text>
      <Text>Vetoed: {item.vetoed}</Text>
    </View>
  }
/>
```

This, of course, is responsible for listing the participants in this decision. The data attribute is tied to the participantsList attribute of the state object, and it is given the following style:

```
choiceScreenListContainer : { width : "94%" }
```

You know the drill by now: 94% puts some space on both sides, since the children of the parent container are centered. Then the renderItem prop is a function that returns a component for each item in the data array. The top-level component that this function returns is a View, with this styling applied:

```
choiceScreenListItem : { flexDirection : "row", marginTop : 4, marginBottom : 4,
  borderColor : "#e0e0e0", borderBottomWidth : 2, alignItems : "center" }
```

Here, each row in the FlatList will consist of two Text components, so we have to use a flexDirection of row to place them side by side. There's some space on the top and bottom, so the items in the FlatList don't get too close together (an aesthetic choice), and then a light gray border is put on just the bottom of each item (again, just an aesthetic choice). The two Text components are, first, the name and relationship of the person, and the second is whether they have vetoed. The first Text component uses this styling:

```
choiceScreenListItemName : { flex : 1 }
```

That's to ensure that the name will fill whatever space is available to it (which will be most of the row, because the second Text component is always going to have a small width). Speaking of that second Text component, it answers the earlier question about why the vetoed attribute is set to yes or no and not true or false: it's displayed literally here, and yes or no is more user-friendly (and that's why it'll always be a small width).

If you've been paying attention, you'll no doubt be asking, Hey, wait a minute, what about that extraData prop there? Well, that's where that participantsListRefresh state attribute that I skipped earlier comes into play. So, here's the deal: when React Native sees the value of this prop change, it re-renders the list, regardless of whether the data changed. That's important, because when someone vetoes a restaurant choice, we update the vetoed attribute of the object in the participantsList array in the state object, but sometimes React Native can't notice changes to data in state when changes are made to its attributes. If you go back and look at the code in the Veto button, you'll notice that the call to setState() doesn't include setting participantsList. Doing so wouldn't cause React Native to see the change to the vetoed attribute either. Think of it this way: React Native is fantastic at noticing changes to state attributes that are *directly* an attribute of state, but it's not always so great at noticing changes to attributes of objects that are part of a collection that is itself directly an attribute of state. Point state.participantsList to an entirely new array in the Veto button's onPress handler code? React Native will notice that and re-render the list. Change an attribute of an object inside the array that state.participantsList already points to? React Native won't notice. So, you have to give it a little nudge, so to speak, with the extraData prop. It doesn't matter what you store in the prop, as long as it changes. That's enough to force React Native to re-render the list, and that's what we need here.

Finally, after the FlatList, we have a simple CustomButton that triggers the app to select a restaurant randomly.

```
<CustomButton text="Randomly Choose" width="94%"
  onPress={ () => {
    const selectedNumber = getRandom(0, filteredRestaurants.length - 1);
    chosenRestaurant = filteredRestaurants[selectedNumber];
    this.setState({ selectedVisible : true });
  } }
/>

</View>

); }
```

At last, we can see where that getRandom() function from the very beginning of Chapter 3 comes into play. A random number is chosen, then the object associated with that index in the filteredRestaurants array is stored into chosenRestaurant (one of the module-global variables from earlier, remember), and then a setState() call is done, setting selectedVisible to true, to show that Modal.

And that's all there is to the Choice screen and its associated Modals! We have only one more screen to look at, and, of course, it's what the user sees after accepting this restaurant.

The PostChoiceScreen Component

The final screen is the Post-Choice screen, the one the user sees after having accepted a choice. This screen, aside from the initial It's Decision Time screen, is straightforward and doesn't contain anything you haven't encountered multiple times previously. Here's the code for this screen:

```
class PostChoiceScreen extends React.Component {

  constructor(inProps) { super(inProps); }
```

The constructor simply calls the superclass constructor, passing in the props that were passed to it. If you go back and look at the It's Decision Time screen, you'll notice that there is no constructor. I did this on purpose, to demonstrate that, strictly speaking, you don't *have* to have a constructor, and you don't *have* to pass the props up to the superclass constructor. To be clear, however, you almost always *should*. It's only because the It's Decision Time screen's code doesn't deal with props that it works (and that it is a very simple screen, besides), and the same is true here. Note that the two custom components are the same; they don't have a constructor passing props to the superclass constructor, and yet everything works as expected. But because React Native does things on your behalf, things you might not even realize, and given that at some point you may try to use a prop and find that things aren't working as you'd expect, it's always safer to have a constructor and, at a minimum, have it pass the props to the superclass constructor. You can often get away with not doing this, but you may face problems later that might be difficult to resolve, so I suggest getting in the habit of always doing the preceding.

After the constructor comes the render() method.

```
render() { return (

  <View style={styles.postChoiceScreenContainer}>

    <View><Text style={styles.postChoiceHeadline}>Enjoy your meal!</
    Text></View>

    <View style={styles.postChoiceDetailsContainer}>

      <View style={styles.postChoiceDetailsRowContainer}>
        <Text style={styles.postChoiceDetailsLabel}>Name:</Text>
        <Text style={styles.postChoiceDetailsValue}>{chosenRestaurant.
        name}</Text>
      </View>

      <View style={styles.postChoiceDetailsRowContainer}>
        <Text style={styles.postChoiceDetailsLabel}>Cuisine:</Text>
        <Text style={styles.postChoiceDetailsValue}>{chosenRestaurant.
        cuisine}</Text>
      </View>
      <View style={styles.postChoiceDetailsRowContainer}>
        <Text style={styles.postChoiceDetailsLabel}>Price:</Text>
        <Text style={styles.postChoiceDetailsValue}>
          {"$".repeat(chosenRestaurant.price)}
        </Text>
      </View>

      <View style={styles.postChoiceDetailsRowContainer}>
        <Text style={styles.postChoiceDetailsLabel}>Rating:</Text>
        <Text style={styles.postChoiceDetailsValue}>
          {"\u2605".repeat(chosenRestaurant.rating)}
        </Text>
      </View>

      <View style={styles.postChoiceDetailsRowContainer}>
        <Text style={styles.postChoiceDetailsLabel}>Phone:</Text>
```

```
        <Text style={styles.postChoiceDetailsValue}>{chosenRestaurant.
        phone}</Text>
      </View>
      <View style={styles.postChoiceDetailsRowContainer}>
        <Text style={styles.postChoiceDetailsLabel}>Address:</Text>
        <Text style={styles.postChoiceDetailsValue}>{chosenRestaurant.
        address}</Text>
      </View>

      <View style={styles.postChoiceDetailsRowContainer}>
        <Text style={styles.postChoiceDetailsLabel}>Web Site:</Text>
        <Text style={styles.postChoiceDetailsValue}>{chosenRestaurant.
      webSite}</Text>
      </View>

      <View style={styles.postChoiceDetailsRowContainer}>
        <Text style={styles.postChoiceDetailsLabel}>Delivery:</Text>
        <Text style={styles.postChoiceDetailsValue}>{chosenRestaurant.
        delivery}</Text>
      </View>

    </View>

    <View style={{ paddingTop:80}}>
    <Button title="All Done"
      onPress={ () => this.props.navigation.navigate("DecisionTimeScreen") }
    />
    </View>
  </View>

); }
```

Yep, this entire screen is, by and large, just a series of Text components, used to display the details about the restaurant. It starts out with a container View, as nearly every React Native component does, which has the following style applied:

```
postChoiceScreenContainer : { flex : 1, justifyContent : "center",
alignItems : "center",
  alignContent : "center" }
```

That should look very familiar to you now, because it's the same as what was used on the It's Decision Time screen, and for the same purpose: to fill the entire screen (flex:1) and center all the children horizontally and vertically.

The first child of this View is a Text component that is the title, or headline, of the screen, and it uses the following style:

```
postChoiceHeadline : { fontSize : 32, paddingBottom : 80 }
```

Obviously, the idea here is to make the text bigger and to ensure that there is some space below the headline, between it and the box that contains the restaurant details.

Speaking of that box, that's what the next View component after the headline is for, the one with the following style applied:

```
postChoiceDetailsContainer : { borderWidth : 2, borderColor : "#000000", padding : 10,
  width : "96%" }
```

This gives us a two-pixel solid black side border and ensures that there are ten pixels of padding between the border and whatever is inside the box. I also give it a width of not quite 100%, to ensure that there is space between the edges of the screen and the box, just because I think that looks better.

Within that View comes a series of other Views, each containing some information about the restaurant. The goal here is to ensure that the amount of space the field labels take up is consistent, regardless of the label itself. That sounds a lot like a layout in which there are multiple columns, two, to be more precise, with the first one containing the labels and the second containing the actual data. To achieve this, each of the View components has the following style:

```
postChoiceDetailsRowContainer : { flexDirection : "row", justifyContent : "flex-start",
  alignItems : "flex-start", alignContent : "flex-start" }
```

Setting flexDirection to row lays the children out in a row, which achieves the goal. Here, we want the content of each child to align to the left, so that all the labels line up (they would "float" if we centered them and look like they weren't lined up right), so that's why flex-start is used for justifyContent, alignItems, and alignContent.

Now, within each of these View components are two Text components, one for the label and one for the data for the field (restaurant name, cuisine type, etc.). The first Text component gets the following style:

```
postChoiceDetailsLabel : { width : 70, fontWeight : "bold", color : "#ff0000" }
```

This makes it so that the label column, so to speak, has a specific width of 70 pixels and that the label is red and bolded. The width is set this way so that regardless of the width of the actual label text, the data components after the labels will all line up properly. (Allowing the labels to size dynamically would make the data shift left and right and not line up correctly.)

Finally, we have the actual data Text components, with each referencing a property of the chosenRestaurant object that was previously populated to provide the value to display. These have a simple style applied.

```
postChoiceDetailsValue : { width : 300 }
```

That avoids potentially longer values wrapping. They'll just get cut off now. But this width is sufficient to allow for any "realistic" values I could think of, anyway.

Only one final piece of code exists in this source file, and it's the StackNavigator configuration.

```
const DecisionScreen = StackNavigator(
  { DecisionTimeScreen : { screen : DecisionTimeScreen },
    WhosGoingScreen : { screen : WhosGoingScreen },
    PreFiltersScreen : { screen : PreFiltersScreen },
    ChoiceScreen : { screen : ChoiceScreen },
    PostChoiceScreen : { screen : PostChoiceScreen }
  },
  { headerMode : "none" }
);
```

Just as you saw in the Restaurants screen's code, we have to tell StackNavigator what screens this stack controls and give it references to the components. Also, as with the Restaurants screen, we don't want a header, so, again, headerMode is set to none.

After that, we have to export the StackNavigator, because it's the top-level component.

```
exports.DecisionScreen = DecisionScreen;
```

And we're done! This screen doesn't require a componentDidMount() method either, so with that, Restaurant Chooser is now a complete app, and you've explored all the code it is made up of. Wasn't that fun?

Debugging and Troubleshooting

Writing code is, of course, only part of the equation. Debugging said code is the other big part and something I haven't talked much about yet. Oh, to be sure, you've seen that you can use `console.*` methods to output messages to the console on which you run the Expo server (most methods that you are probably familiar with from web development work the same with React Native), and indeed that can be beneficial. But, it's not the be-all, end-all of debugging facilities when working with React Native and Expo.

React Native automatically offers a developer menu inside your app. By default, this is accessed by shaking your device—but be careful! I don't want to hear about any reader shaking too vigorously and smashing an uber-expensive smartphone against a brick wall. You can change what triggers the menu in the Expo client app, but it's shaking by default. When you do so, you'll see the menu shown in Figure 4-3.

Figure 4-3. *The developer menu*

Here, you have several options. First, you can Reload the app from the Expo server. We'll skip the Debug JS Remotely option for just a moment and jump ahead to the Disable Live Reload. As you make changes to your code, assuming you have the app opened on a device, it will auto-reload (sometimes it takes a second or two), and this option allows you to disable that (it changes to Enable Live Reload, if you disable it, so it acts as a toggle). Similar to live reloading, but different, is Enable Hot Reloading. Hot reloading allows you to keep your app running as new versions of your files are injected into the JavaScript bundle automatically. This will allow you to persist the app's state through reloads.

The Toggle Inspector option is next, and tapping it leads to the screen(s) seen in Figure 4-4. (First, you'll see the screen on the left, then when you make a selection, you'll see the screen on the right.)

Figure 4-4. *The Inspector tool*

When you choose this option, you'll then be able to select an element in the app, as I've done here, for the clickable image on the starting page, indicated by it being highlighted. You'll see a bunch of information about it up top, including its place in the component hierarchy (the selected element is the one with the border). You can see things such as its box model and what file its code lives in. You can also select the tabs (Inspect, Perf, Network, and Touchables), to see more information about your app, including such things as performance statistics (Perf), requests going between the Expo app on the device and the Expo server on your development machine (Network), and touchable objects available at the time (Touchables). Note that you can also click the component names in the hierarchy at the top, to move up or down that hierarchy, as required.

Another tool available to you is the Perf Monitor, a tool for monitoring performance of your app. You can see that in Figure 4-5.

Figure 4-5. *The Perf Monitor tool*

This tool shows you the frame rate of your app, how many visual stutters there have been, etc. This is updated in real time, so you can monitor it as you navigate your app and find problem spots to investigate further.

Now, knowing about those tools is very good, but what happens when errors occur in your code? In that case, React Native has two ways to report problems: RedBox error pages and YellowBox warnings. See Figure 4-6 for an example of a RedBox error page.

Figure 4-6. *A RedBox error page*

Here, at the top of the page, you can see what triggered the error (in this case, I've tried to call a nonexistent method of the AsyncStorage API), and you can see stack trace information, to help you pinpoint the problem. At the bottom, you have some options. You can dismiss the error entirely, in which case your app may or may not function properly, of course, or you can reload the app. You can also copy the error information, if you need it elsewhere (StackOverflow time, perhaps?).

Warnings, on the other hand, are typically not critical enough to stop your app, but they are things you'll want to know about. Figure 4-7 shows what this looks like.

Figure 4-7. *A YellowBox warning*

You can then click on a warning, to see its full message in a full-screen YellowBox form, and you'll also have access to a stack trace there. You'll also have three buttons: Minimize (go back to the screen with the warning on the bottom), Dismiss the warning (it disappears), and Dismiss All (if there's more than one warning, as there is here). Note that these RedBox and YellowBox screens are disabled in release builds (which I'll be talking about in the next section).

The final topic related to debugging that I want to discuss is the option I skipped earlier when discussing the developer menu: Debug JS Remotely. This is where things get really cool! If you hit that option, assuming you have Google Chrome installed on your development machine, you should find that a new tab opens in the browser (any required configuration will have been done for you already by Expo), and on that tab, you can open Chrome Developer Tools and use it to debug your app running on your device. You can set breakpoints, inspect variables, and so on, just like debugging any other JavaScript code in Chrome. It's an elegant way to troubleshoot your code during development that should serve you well, and you'll get a little more detail about it in Chapter 8.

Tip   There are a few more debugging capabilities available to you as a React Native developer, but I consider the ones described here the primary means. If you'd like to see the others, however, look in the React Native docs here: `https://facebook.github.io/react-native/docs/debugging.html`.

Packaging It All Up

In Chapter 1, I showed you how to use Expo to develop an app, by starting the Expo server on your development machine and then using the Expo client to test the app. I hope that you did the same for the Components app in Chapter 2 and Restaurant Chooser. That's fantastic for development—being able to run an app on a real device that easily is awesome when you're hacking away at code. But what about when you want to show the app to others? If all you use is the Expo server, they will have to be able to reach the machine it's on, and that may not be terribly convenient, because you'll have to keep the Expo server running all the time.

Note   Interestingly, people can, in theory at least, reach your Expo server, even if they aren't on your local area network. Expo uses a unique domain, exp.direct, for tunneling. This allows anyone who knows the URL of the app (which is shown in the console when you start the Expo server) to reach you, even if you're behind a firewall on a virtual private network. I note that this is the case "in theory," because if you had to specify the packager URL as discussed in Chapter 1, this tunneling won't work. In addition, other things can go wrong that will make your machine unreachable. If it works, it's great, but my advice is not to count on it and, instead, look to publishing when and if you need to share your app with others.

And that doesn't even consider the next step: publishing the app to the Google Play Store or Apple App Store.

There are two paths you could take to get your app on other people's machines. First, you could publish the app via Expo, or you could build a native package for iOS and/or Android and then distribute it (or submit it to the stores). Let's talk about publishing first.

Publishing, in this context, means making the app public through the expo.io web site and, thereby, available to other people. Publishing is quite simple, but first, you'll have to create an account at expo.io and log in to the account by entering the following:

```
exp login
```

Once that's done, all you have to do to publish is run this command within your app's directory, just as when you start your app:

```
exp publish
```

This will trigger a process (this will take some time, so be patient) that will take your source code, minify it, and otherwise manipulate it, as necessary, and will produce two versions of your code, one for iOS and one for Android. At the end of the process, you'll be given a URL that can then be used in the Expo client app to launch your app, utterly independent of whether the Expo server is running on your machine.

However, your app won't be public at this point, which means someone will have to know the URL to access it. If you want to make it available for all the world, log in to your Expo account in a browser at expo.io and hit the View Profile link. There, you'll find a list of projects you've published and some options to manipulate each, including making one public.

Publishing is great for letting people see your work, but it requires that they have the Expo client app installed. That may be fine during development and testing, but, clearly, you wouldn't want to force users to have to use your app for real. No, you will almost certainly want them to go to app stores for iOS and Android as stand-alone apps. That, too, is extremely easy, thanks to Expo!

First, you'll have to ensure that the values in app.json are correct for building an app, which comes down to ensuring that you have values for bundleIdentifier, name, icon, version, slug, and sdkVersion. Any other options available are optional, but these are all required, as discussed in Chapter 3. Assuming you're good to go with that file, as Restaurant Chooser is, all you have to do is execute one of two commands, depending on what platform you want to build for. These are

```
exp build:android
```

or

```
exp build:ios
```

You'll be asked a question or two, which will vary, based on the platform you're targeting. For Android, you'll be asked if you want to upload your own keystore or use one provided by Expo (which is used to sign the final app package digitally). Unless you know what you're doing, I suggest letting Expo handle this for you. Don't worry, if you change your mind later, you can clear your current keystore by executing

```
exp build:android --clear-credentials
```

Then you'll be able to upload your own, if you wish.

For iOS, you'll be asked a similar question regarding credentials and distribution certificate (which serves the same fundamental purpose as the Android keystore), and you'll again have the choice of handling it yourself or letting Expo do the work for you.

After that, your code will be uploading to the Expo cloud infrastructure, which contains all the necessary tooling to build your app. Did you notice that at no point did I mention having to install any iOS or Android SDKs, no such IDEs as Xcode or Android Studio, and no requirements to do anything on one OS vs. another? None of that is necessary when you use Expo to do the builds for you. It's one of the ways using Expo that makes your life a lot easier as a developer.

Now, this build process will take a fair amount of time—15 minutes isn't unheard of, in my experience, but it'll usually take more like 5 or so. However long it takes, when it's done, you'll be shown a URL corresponding to either the iOS IPA file or the Android APK file, and you'll be able to download the file at those URLs. Alternatively, if you log in to your Expo account in a browser, you'll find that a link View IPA/APK builds where you can download them from (so you don't have to remember those URLs).

Note   For Windows users, you must have Windows Subsystem for Linux (WSL) installed, in order for builds to work. It's recommended that you install Ubuntu from the Windows store. Also, you must launch Ubuntu at least once, before attempting a build.

Now, downloading a file is only half the battle. After that, you have to get them onto a device (or perhaps an emulator or simulator on a development machine, because that's something you can totally do, if you want to). For Android, it's easy: you can copy the APK file to a device or emulator in whatever way you generally copy files to it. That might mean copying the APK to a network share and then accessing that share from a file manager on the device, or maybe sending it via Bluetooth, or perhaps using ADB (Android Developer Bridge) commands to install or push it. (ADB is part of the Android SDK, however, so you'd have to install it to use that method.) You can, of course, simply access the appropriate URL and download directly from it, or you could get old-fashioned and e-mail the file to yourself. Whatever the method, once the APK is on the device, you'll have to ensure that you have the developer option to allow installation of apps from unknown sources turned on. Where this option lives varies from device to device, but it's usually somewhere under a Security option in Settings—and, of course, Google is your friend. Once you find and set the option, you can "run" the file. That will trigger the usual Android installation procedure, and before long, the app will be ready to use.

Note   If you have an Android emulator set up, installing to that should be as easy as dragging and dropping the APK file onto it. If that doesn't work, you can always ADB install it (and if you have an emulator set up, then it's a good bet you've got the Android development tools set up and have ADB already).

For iOS, things are a bit trickier. If you happen to have Xcode installed, that means you have an iOS simulator ready to go. To run it on your iOS Simulator, first build your app, by adding a flag to the build command, like so:

```
exp build:ios -t simulator
```

Then, execute the following:

```
exp build:status
```

You can, in fact, run that anytime you want, and as many times as you want, to view the status of any builds you've submitted. Most important, in this case, is that, eventually, the output of this command will show a tarball available and a link to download it from. Do so, then unpack the `tar.gz` file by executing this command:

```
tar -xvzf your-app.tar.gz
```

Then you can run it, by starting an iOS Simulator instance and executing this command:

```
xcrun simctl install booted <app path>
```

followed by

```
xcrun simctl launch booted <app identifier>.
```

The other option, which you'll need to look into to run it on a real device, is Apple's TestFlight (`https://developer.apple.com/testflight`). This is similar conceptually to the Expo client but a little different (you don't have to launch it to launch an app installed with it, as you do the Expo client) and a bit more complicated (and also costly, because you'll require an Apple developer account to use it). The basic idea is that you download the IPA file that Expo built for you, upload it to TestFlight, add team members who can access the app, and then they'll be able to do so.

Note   Unfortunately, while installing and running an app on Android is very easy and doesn't require any special accounts, iOS is another story entirely. As mentioned, you'll need an Apple developer account (which costs $99/year); you'll have to set up that account; and you'll have to get set up on TestFlight. This procedure can become involved, so it's not detailed here. In addition to the TestFlight link, you'll want to access `https://developer.apple.com`, if you're going to run your app on iOS.

Once you're ready to submit your app to either the iOS or Android stores, you'll follow the procedures Google and Apple outline for app submission. That is left as an exercise for the reader, as it is beyond the scope of this book. However, I do want to point out this page in the Expo documentation: `https://docs.expo.io/versions/latest/distribution/app-stores.html`.

Here, you'll find some beneficial information that should be a starting point to make your journey as smooth as possible. Once you've read the information and are ready, you'll have to sign up for an Apple developer account, as previously described, and/or a Google developer account (at a flat fee of $25), and you'll be off to the races!

Summary

Whew, that was a ride, huh? In this chapter, in conjunction with Chapter 3, you thoroughly explored the code behind the Restaurant Chooser app, an app I hope provided a good learning experience *and* is useful in its own right. You learned many React Native concepts, including application structure, third-party components, layout, packaging, testing and debugging, Expo, and, of course, you were exposed to an excellent collection of React Native components and APIs in the process.

If this was all that this book had to offer, you would already have a good foundation from which to build your own apps. But that's not all there is. There's quite a bit yet to come.

In the next chapter, we'll build another complete app, one that will continue to make use of what you've learned thus far, but we'll also build on it, and I'll introduce more of React Native. So, grab a bite to eat (and don't forget to drink, because hydration is essential), then come right back, and we'll start to build another app together with React Native.

CHAPTER 5

React Native Trivia, Part 1

I hope, by this point, having read the first four chapters and having built a real app, that you're starting to see the power of React Native. No doubt, you can do a lot with it, all while just playing within the confines of a single mobile device.

But, in some ways, that isn't an accurate reflection of the computing world of today. It's becoming less and less frequent to find an app that exists and functions only on a single device. Today, most apps seem to have some degree of connectivity to other machines, whether to book a hotel, get directions, and maybe save some notes to a central server or connect two people in a friendly gaming competition.

React Native, naturally, can play in this connected arena as well, but how you do so presents myriad possibilities. Do you create a RESTful API on a server? Do you do some sort of direct socket connection? Maybe FTP or NNTP or any of a hundred other possible communication protocols?

In this chapter, we'll confront that very choice, in building the second of the three apps we'll create together in this book. In the process, you'll not only learn more about React Native, but you'll also learn some Node.js in the process, plus a somewhat newer method of client-server communication (Web Sockets), as this project will involve building a server component and connecting our React Native app to it. Let's kick things off, shall we?

What Are We Building?

In a word (err, that is, in *three* words), we're building React Native Trivia. No, wait, in *one* word, for real this time, we'll call it RNTrivia!

This app will allow us to run a trivia contest for a group of people. One person, the administrator (or "admin," for short), will be in control of when a new question is sent to the players. The players will then answer, and a leaderboard will be updated. When the admin chooses, the game can be ended. It's as simple as that!

© Frank Zammetti 2018
F. Zammetti, *Practical React Native*, https://doi.org/10.1007/978-1-4842-3939-1_5

This was an app I wrote when I gave a presentation on the Webix library in 2018, and I used it as a fun and exciting way to give swag away. I had a bunch of sci-fi trivia questions (which you'll see in the code download bundle), and the top three finishers got some free stuff. As such, I don't view this as a game, per se (a game project being reserved for Chapters 7 and 8); instead I see it as a tool, albeit a fun one, I hope.

RNTrivia consists of just a few screens, most of which you'll see in the next chapter, but the two main ones are the leaderboard screen (which can be thought of as a "game in progress, awaiting a question") and the question screen. The leaderboard screen, which you can see in Figure 5-1, is where the player waits until the admin triggers a new question to be sent to all the players.

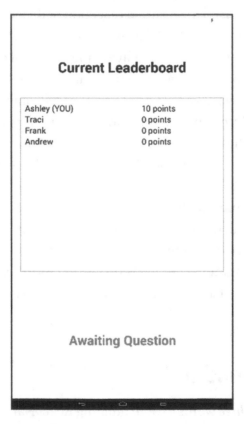

Figure 5-1. *The leaderboard ("game in progress, awaiting a question") screen*

Once a question is sent, the players find themselves on the question screen, as shown in Figure 5-2. Here, the player selects their answer and submits it.

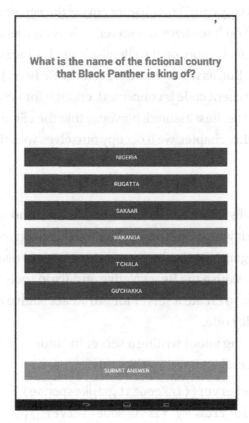

Figure 5-2. *The question screen*

All of this requires the client app, written with good 'ole React Native, and a server component, which we'll write using Node. The server acts as the intermediary between the admin and all the players, but how this communication occurs is quite interesting, I think, and I hope you will think so too. That's what we'll be spending all our time on in this chapter, reserving the client code for the next chapter. This server code will handle almost all the core logic of the game, including some logic that considers how long a player takes to answer a question in assigning points, so that not only is getting the correct answer critical but getting it as fast as possible also matters (it also ensures that a tie is virtually impossible).

Let's talk technical specifics now and get some prerequisites out of the way, so that we can get to the code.

The Client

How to divide this project between two chapters, which is the pattern I decided on for the book's three projects, was very easy. This chapter covers the server code, and Chapter 6 covers the client code. As you'll see here, the server code is neither very complicated nor voluminous. There is definitely more on the client side, including some new concepts, than there is on the server side. But, as we explore the server code here, I'll do my best to give you some context, as far as the client code is concerned, enough for you to understand what's happening in the server code. Rest assured, however, that the client code will be covered in detail in Chapter 6. Until that chapter, we'll occupy ourselves with the server code.

The Server

In Chapter 1, I talked briefly about Node, about installing it and about how to write some simple code and execute it with Node. Since then, you've been using Node little by little, and Node Package Manager (NPM), which goes along with it, even when you may not have realized you were, because the React Native and Expo tools use them both under the covers. Now, however, to create a server for our React Native app to talk to, we have to write some *actual* Node code.

If you do some searching about writing a server in Node, the first thing you're likely to encounter is code that looks something like this:

```
require("http").createServer((inRequest, inResponse) => {
  inResponse.end("Hello from my first Node server");
}).listen(80);
```

> **Note**   You will also almost certainly run into something called Express. That's a library that sits on top of Node and makes building non-trivial server applications much easier. The few lines of code here are fine and dandy, but as I'm sure you can guess, building something more robust quickly balloons into a fair bit of code. Express abstracts much of that away, saving you time and effort, while using a battle-tested library. Express doesn't fit our needs here, owing to what I'll discuss a few paragraphs from now, but I wanted to mention Express, so that if you run into it, you have some idea what it's about. It's not required for writing Node server code, which is the main point, although, if you ever have to, and what is used to build RNTrivia's server code doesn't fit the bill, definitely give Express a look.

That remarkedly small bit of code is all it takes in Node to write a server. If you execute that, then fire up your favorite web browser and access localhost, you'll get the reply "Hello from my first Node server." In short, the function passed to `createServer()` handles any incoming HTTP request. You can do anything you require there, including such things as

- Interrogate the incoming request to determine the HTTP method

- Parse the request path

- Examine header values

You can then perform some branching logic on any or all of these, perhaps access a database or other durable storage mechanism, and return an appropriate and fully dynamic response for the specific request. With just this little bit of code, you, in fact, know the basics of what you would require to write a server for RNTrivia.

However, if you think about what this RNTrivia app is, you should quickly notice a flaw: we must have the ability for the *server* to initiate *communication* with the client, our players. The server must send questions to the players. That's the exact opposite of how things usually work, and, indeed, the opposite of how this simple server example works. Here, it's the client, via his/her browser request, who initiates communication with the server, and that won't meet our needs. Surely there's an answer, right? Well, there's more than one, really, but the one we're going to use is something relatively new to web development, by way of a nifty little library: WebSocket and socket.io.

Note   If you've been doing web development for a while, you may recognize that you can achieve the stated goal by other means, one of which is polling, in which the client continually calls the server for a status update. While that would work for RNTrivia, the goal here is to have something more real-time (polling isn't, assuming you're using a reasonable poll interval) and also something that won't clog up the limited resources any server has, in terms of request handling capacity. Basically, we want something a little more forward-thinking than polling or any of the other "hack-y" techniques we could employ here.

Keeping the Lines of Communication Open: socket.io

The Web itself was initially conceived as a place where it was the client's responsibility to request information from a server, but that eliminates a host of interesting possibilities, or at least makes them more difficult and non-optimal.

For example, if you have a machine that provides stock prices to a client to display in a dashboard, the client must continuously request updated prices from the server. This is the typical polling approach. The downsides, primarily, are that it requires constant new requests from the client to server, and the prices will only be as fresh as the polling interval, which you typically don't want to make too frequent, for fear of overloading the server. The prices aren't real-time, something that can be very bad, if you're an investor.

With the advent of AJAX techniques, developers started to investigate ways to have bidirectional communication, in which the server could *push* new stock prices out to the client. One such method is long-polling. Sometimes called Comet, long-polling is a technique by which the client opens a connection with a server, as usual. But now, the server holds the request open, by never sending the HTTP response completion signal. Then, when the server has something to transmit to the client, the connection is already established. This is referred to as a "hanging-GET" or "pending-POST," depending on the HTTP method used to establish the connection.

This can be tricky to implement for many reasons, but probably the key one is that the connection processing thread is held on the server. Given that it's an HTTP connection, the overhead is not at all inconsequential. Before long, your server can be brought to its knees, without having all that many clients connected.

The WebSocket protocol was created to allow this sort of persistent connection without all the problems of long-polling, or other approaches. WebSocket is an Internet Engineering Task Force (IETF) standard that enables bidirectional communication between a client and a server. It does this by a special handshake when a regular HTTP connection is established. To do this, the client sends a request that looks something like this:

```
GET ws://websocket.apress.com/ HTTP/1.1
Origin: http://apress.com
Connection: Upgrade
Host: websocket.apress.com
Upgrade: websocket
```

Notice that Upgrade header value? That's the magic bit. When the server sees this, and assuming it supports WebSocket, it will respond with a reply such as this:

```
HTTP/1.1 101 WebSocket Protocol Handshake
Date: Mon, 21 Dec 2017 03:12:44 EDT
Connection: Upgrade
Upgrade: WebSocket
```

The server "agrees to the upgrade," in WebSocket parlance. Once this handshake completes, the HTTP request is torn down, but the underlying TCP/IP connection it rode in on remains. That's the persistent connection with which the client and server can communicate in real time, without having to reestablish a connection every time.

WebSocket also comes with a JavaScript API that you can use to establish connections and both send and receive messages (and messages is what we call data that is transmitted over a WebSocket connection, in either direction). However, I'm not going to go into that API, because rather than use it directly in RNTrivia, we're going to make use of a library that sits on top of it and makes it much easier to use, that library being socket.io. What you'll find is that this library exists for use in both Node-based server code and React Native–based client code and gives us a more straightforward and consistent API in both places.

In a tiny nutshell, using socket.io, beyond the import of the library, requires little more than a single function: io.on(). An app written with socket.io will have one or more such calls, one for each message that the app requires. It doesn't matter if the message comes from the client and goes to the server, or whether it starts on the server and goes to the client. io.on() is all it takes to handle the message on either side of the connection.

This method takes in two arguments. First, it takes the name of the message, which is an arbitrary string that you can make up to have meaning in your app. Second, it takes a callback function that handles that message. This callback is passed an object that is the data that was transmitted. You can then do whatever you have to do to handle that message. This could be nothing (an empty function), which is perfectly valid. And, there's nothing that says you *have* to have a handler at all for a given message. Nothing will break if you send a message that the receiver doesn't have a handler for.

If the message is updateStock and it is sent from the server, perhaps in your client code, you might write

```
io.on("updateStock", function(inData) {
  console.log(`Stock ${inData.tickerSymbol} price is now {inData.newPrice}`);
});
```

Now, whenever the server sends the updateStock price, which we term *emitting* the message, the client will output the new price to the console.

If you want to send a clearPreferences message from the client to the server, then on the server, you might write

```
io.on("clearPreferences", function(inData) {
  database.execute(`delete from user_preferences where userID=${inData.
  userID}`);
});
```

See? It looks the same whether on client or server.

Now, that's how you *handle* the message, but how do you *emit* them? Once again, it looks the same, regardless of where the message originates.

```
io.emit("updateStock", { tickerSymbol : database.getSymbol(), newPrice :
database.getPrice() });
```

Or

```
io.emit("clearPreferences", { userID : "fzammetti" });
```

As you can see, the socket.io API is incredibly simple but simultaneously extremely powerful. It also offers more advanced capabilities, such as namespaces and rooms, which allow you to segregate messages into logical groupings, to name a few. However, for what we're doing in RNTrivia, this is about all you'll need to know. There's only one small bit beyond this related to establishing the connection, but that will be easier to explain within the context of RNTrivia's code.

Getting Down to Business: Building the Server

Now it's time to dissect some server code. While it's true that this isn't a book about Node or socket.io or any of that, we naturally couldn't build an app like this without discussing the code, to get a holistic view of RNTrivia. You should keep in mind, however, that while I'm going to do my best to provide you with just enough information to understand this code, even if you have no previous Node experience, there is a lot more to Node than what you'll see here. So, if you find this exciting (and I hope that you do), then you'll definitely want to spend some time on your own diving in deeper.

That said, let's get to it!

A Non-Code Concern: questions.json

None of the code I'm about to discuss will do much if we don't have some questions to ask our players. Rather than hard-coding the questions into the server code, I chose to externalize them into their own file, which we'll read in later. The questions.json file is a simple list of questions, some of which you can see here:

```
{ "questions" : [
  { "question" : "What is the name of the Shadow's homeworld on Babylon 5?",
    "answer" : "Z'ha'dum",
    "decoys" : [ "Galifrey", "Hoth", "Arrakis", "Tagora", "Nihil", "Daxam",
    "Acheron", "Skaro", "Crematoria", "Qo'noS" ]
  },
  { "question" : "In Stargate SG-1, what galaxy is the lost city of
Atlantis discovered to reside in?",
    "answer" : "Pegasus",
    "decoys" : [ "Andromeda", "Seraphia", "Triangulum", "Krell", "Virgo",
    "Kaliem", "Ida", "Shi'ar", "Xeno", "Isop" ]
  },
...
] }
```

There are many more questions in which there are the ellipses, but this truncated bit gives you an idea. Each question is an object consisting of a question attribute that is the actual question, the correct answer, and an array of ten decoys (incorrect answers) for each question. Later, we'll chose six of the ten randomly to present to the players, just to provide a little variety to the proceedings.

Configuring the Server: package.json

While it's not required to write Node apps, whether server-based or not (something that should be apparent, given the previous simple Node code samples I've shown), it's very much standard to have a `package.json` file in the root of the app. In fact, if you're going to use third-party libraries, as we are in RNTrivia, this file becomes all but necessary. (It's not impossible to bring in dependencies without a `package.json` file, but it's pretty much unheard of.) Here's the `package.json` file for RNTrivia:

```
{
  "name": "com.etherient.rntrivia", "version": "1.0.0", "author": "Frank
  Zammetti",
  "description": "A trivia app written with React Native",
  "private": true, "license": "MIT", "main": "server.js",
  "dependencies": { "socket.io": "2.0.4", "lodash": "*" },
  "scripts": { "start": "node server.js" }
}
```

This isn't the first time you've seen such a file, of course, but it's the first time you've seen it in the context of a Node app. Most of it should be self-explanatory, and some of this is technically optional, but the attributes you see here are the required ones, and the ones you'll have to supply to avoid any warnings by NPM. Perhaps the most important things here are `main`, `dependencies`, and `scripts`.

The `main` attribute tells NPM and Node what the main JavaScript file is for our app. The `dependencies` attribute is, of course, the libraries our app depends on. As previously discussed, `socket.io` shouldn't be a surprise. The `lodash` library, in case you've never heard of it, is a general-purpose JavaScript utility library that provides a few generic and very useful functions, such as sorting helpers; helpers for iterating arrays, objects, and strings; helpers for manipulating and testing values; and helpers for creating composite functions, among many others. We'll be using it for small but critical functions later, but if this is your first encounter with lodash, then I highly recommend taking some time to see what it offers, because it's a very helpful library that is also very simple, small, and efficient, three attributes I very much like in my JavaScript libraries.

The script attribute sets up NPM commands. In other words, the configuration seen allows us to execute

```
npm start
```

With the configuration provided, NPM knows to execute

```
node.server.js
```

on our behalf. Why would you want to do this? Well, if all you're going to do is run a single JavaScript file with Node, then there's probably no significant benefit, but using NPM like this allows you to execute any arbitrary command(s) you like. Want to run Webpack on your code before executing it? No problem. Need to run the app under an alternate user account? You can do it with this. Plus, if you do this for all your Node apps, it means that you never have to think about how to run an app. It's always just npm start.

Note   Don't forget that you'll have to execute npm install before you can do npm start, because that's the way all the dependencies of the server-side code are installed. I'm sure you're well aware of this by now, but it never hurts to be reminded.

---

server.js Opening Volley: Imports and Variables

The main (and, in fact, *only*) source file for the server is the aptly named server.js, and this code begins as most Node code does, with some imports.

```
const fs = require("fs");
const lodash = require("lodash");
```

The fs variable will store a reference to the built-in Node File System API. We'll use this to read in the questions file seen earlier. The lodash import is, of course, the lodash library.

After the imports, it's time to build the server and hook socket.io to it. I've done that in this single line of code (something I wouldn't generally recommend, but variety is the spice of life, so here's a little spice for ya).

```
const io = require("socket.io")(require("http").createServer(function(){}).
listen(80));
```

If you parse this out, you'll see that it creates an HTTP server, just like you saw earlier in the simple server example. In this case, however, the server created will not be handling requests, but we still have to provide an empty function to fulfill the createServer() contract. That server is then passed to the socket.io constructor (which is anonymously imported, because, like the http import, it's not needed outside this line), which is what hooks socket.io to the server and makes it work. Essentially, socket.io piggybacks on the underlying HTTP server, extending it to handle WebSocket connections.

After that comes a series of variables that we'll need.

```
const players = { };
```

This stores objects, one representing each player participating. These are keyed by a unique playerID that will be generated when a player connects to the server.

```
let inProgress = false;
```

It is hoped that variable name is self-documenting. This is a flag that tells the code whether a game is currently in progress.

```
let questions = null;
let question = null;
let questionForPlayers = null;
```

These three variables store the questions read in from questions.json, the current question, and the question in a slightly different form for the players, respectively. Don't worry too much about these, and why the question is seemingly stored twice. That will all become clear before long.

```
let questionStartTime = null;
```

Remember that I said the interval a player takes to answer a question factors into his/her score? Well, this variable stores the time that the current question was sent to the players, and using it, the server can determine how long each player took to answer a question.

```
let numberAsked = 0;
```

Finally, numberAsked is how many questions out of the total number of questions have been asked. This will be used to tell the admin when there are no more questions left to be asked.

This small list of variables represents the sum total of the state the server code will require to do its work. Not many at all, right?

Utility Functions

In addition to that handful of variables, there are two utility functions we'll need in a couple of different places. These are the next bit of code you'll encounter as you examine this source file.

newGameData()

Anytime a new player connects, or a new game begins, we must reset some state for each player. This represents the data about what has transpired so far during the current game (for the most part). This is a simple object, a `gameData` object, as I call it, and the `newGameData()` function is used to create it.

```
function newGameData() {
  return { right : 0, wrong : 0, totalTime : 0, fastest : 999999999,
    slowest : 0, average : 0, points : 0, answered : 0, playerName : null
  };
}
```

The attributes of the constructed object should be pretty obvious: how many questions the player has gotten `right` and `wrong`, the `totalTime` taken to answer, the `fastest` and `slowest` the player has answered, the `average` time taken to answer, how many `points` the player has, and how many questions he/she has `answered`. The `playerName` is also stored here, even though it's conceptually not the same as the others, and that's done just to make it more readily accessible in some other places in the code later.

calculateLeaderboard()

Recall in the earlier screenshots that when the player is awaiting a question, they are on the leaderboard screen that shows the current players' points and ranking. A single function, `calculateLeaderboard()`, is responsible for generating the data behind that display.

```
function calculateLeaderboard() {

  const playersArray = [ ];
  for (const playerID in players) {
    if (players.hasOwnProperty(playerID)) {
      const player = players[playerID];
```

```
      playersArray.push({ playerID : playerID, playerName : player.playerName,
      points : player.points });
    }
  }

  playersArray.sort((inA, inB) => {
    const pointsA = inA.points;
    const pointsB = inB.points;
    if (pointsA > pointsB) { return -1; }
    else if (pointsA < pointsB) { return 1; }
    else { return 0; }
  });

  return playersArray;

}
```

The first block of code, the for loop, is responsible for taking the players object and generating an array from it. Because the leaderboard is a FlatList, and a FlatList gets backed by an array, that's what we need (players is an object, because it makes writing all the other code a snap, and this is the only time we need it as an array, so it made sense just to do a conversion here). However, as part of the transformation, we only need a few pieces of information to render the leaderboard, so rather than just pushing the existing object onto the array, a new minimal object is created instead.

The second chunk of code is a simple sort, based on points, so that the array is now in descending point order, exactly as you'd expect a list of standings to be.

Player Message Handlers

The next thing we have to do is to provide socket.io the functions that will handle the various messages that can be emitted to the server. And what are those messages, you ask? Here's the list:

- validatePlayer: Emitted when a player first connects to the server

- submitAnswer: Emitted when the player submits his/her answer to the current question

- adminNewGame: Emitted when the admin begins a new game

- adminNextQuestion: Emitted when the admin triggers the next question
- adminEndGame: Emitted when the admin ends the game

As you can see, there aren't many messages. Each is a function, and those functions must be provided to the io object inside a connection message handler. The connection message will be emitted automatically by the client when it connects to the server, and the socket.io API requires that all the message handlers be defined inside the handler for that message. So, we have this:

```
io.on("connection", io => {
...
});
```

and in place of the ellipses are five calls to io.on(), passing each the message name (from the preceding list) and then the function that handles that particular message.

But, even before those, there is one other statement you'll find inside the connection message handler:

```
io.emit("connected", { });
```

This emits a connected message back to the players. So, the sequence will be

- Player client app connects, emitting the connection message to the server. (This happens automatically when the socket.io object is created in the client code, as you'll see later.)

- The connection message handler emits a connected message to the player. (Note that, in general, it's not required to emit a message such as this. socket.io doesn't require it, but the flow of the RNTrivia app startup does, which will be explained in Chapter 6.)

- The connection message handler makes five io.on() calls to hook up handlers for each of the five messages required to make this whole mess work.

Once the connection message handler completes, the server is ready to handle all necessary messages from players.

Now, let's look at the handlers for each of the messages in turn.

validatePlayer

The first message to be handled is the validatePlayer message. This is triggered by the client handling the connected message emitted by the server in response to the automatic connection message to the server. This serves as something of a handshake: the client says "hello" when the socket.io object is created there, firing the connection message, then the server responds by saying "Oh, hello to you too!" by emitting the connected message, which the client then responds to by saying "Hey, can you please validate this player for me?" by emitting the validatePlayer message, which is handled by this code:

```
io.on("validatePlayer", inData => {

  try {

    const responseObject = { inProgress : inProgress,
      gameData : newGameData(), leaderboard : calculateLeaderboard(),
      asked : numberAsked
    };
    responseObject.gameData.playerName = inData.playerName;

    responseObject.playerID = `pi_${new Date().getTime()}`;
    for (const playerID in players) {
      if (players.hasOwnProperty(playerID)) {
        if (inData.playerName === players[playerID].playerName) {
          responseObject.gameData.playerName += `_${new Date().getTime()}`;
        }
      }
    }
    players[responseObject.playerID] = responseObject.gameData;
    io.emit("validatePlayer", responseObject);

  } catch (inException) {
    console.log(`${inException}`);
  }

});
```

First, you'll find that all the message handlers are wrapped in a try...catch block such as this. The goal is to ensure that the server keeps running, even if a problem occurs dealing with one player. No point taking the whole server down for everyone! But because this represents unexpected conditions, things the code can't reasonably handle, just logging the exception to the server console is all that's done.

The first thing is to construct an object that will be returned to the player. This will provide all the information required at this time. This includes whether a game is in progress (inProgress), a new gameData instance (which provided state for a new entry into the game), the current leaderboard standings, and the number of questions asked so far during this game. The playerName is also added to the gameData object at this time (as previously mentioned, this will make writing the client code a little easier, by making that name available more directly).

Next, a unique ID for this player is generated, which is merely the characters pi_ followed by the current time in milliseconds. Not the best way to produce a unique value, I grant you, but good enough for the needs of this app (meaning, it's unlikely two people will get the same ID, unless you've got a *vast* number of players all trying to get in at the same time).

After that, the "validate" part of validatePlayer() kicks in, by checking to see if the name that the client passed in as part of the inData argument is already in use. If it is, a new name is constructed, by appending the current time to the name. This just requires iterating over the attributes of the players object and checking the playerName attribute of each, looking for a match.

Then the gameData object that was earlier constructed is added to the players object, using the playerID as the key. This object contains all the pertinent information the server needs to retain about each player (remember that the unique ID, which is obviously also very pertinent, is the key to the attributes of the object). Finally, the validatePlayer message is emitted to the client. Note that there is no issue using the same message name here, because one is emitted by the client and one by the server, and the other responds to it (or ignores it, if there's no work to be done in response). I like the symmetry of seeing the same message name going in both directions when it's essentially a request-response model, as in the client sends validatePlayer, and something is expected in return (conceptually that is—messages never "return" values, per se, when dealing with socket.io), which happens to be the validatePlayer message, but from the server this time. Think of the whole cycle from client to server and back again as a method call, and I think it makes sense to name them the same. (But there is nothing beyond my own preference that says that must be the case. Just to be very clear, socket.io doesn't care, nor does Node.)

submitAnswer

The next message that can be emitted by the client and which must be handled by the
server is the submitAnswer message, which is transmitted when the user chooses an
answer to a question. This is probably the most complicated message handler of them
all, but it's relative to the others, so it's still not very complicated.

```
io.on("submitAnswer", inData => {

  try {

    const gameData = players[inData.playerID];
    let correct = false;
    gameData.answered++;

    if (question.answer === inData.answer) {

      players[inData.playerID].right++;
      players[inData.playerID].wrong--;

      const time = new Date().getTime() - questionStartTime;
      gameData.totalTime = gameData.totalTime + time;
      if (time > gameData.slowest) {
        gameData.slowest = time;
      }
      if (time < gameData.fastest) {
        gameData.fastest = time;
      }
      gameData.average = Math.trunc(gameData.totalTime / numberAsked);

      const maxTimeAllowed = 15;
      gameData.points = gameData.points + (maxTimeAllowed * 4);
      gameData.points = gameData.points - Math.min(Math.max(
        Math.trunc(time / 250), 0), (maxTimeAllowed * 4
      ));
      gameData.points = gameData.points + 10;
      correct = true;

    }
```

```
    io.emit("answerOutcome", { correct : correct, gameData : gameData,
       asked : numberAsked, leaderboard : calculateLeaderboard()
    });

  } catch (inException) {
    console.log(`${inException}`);
  }

});
```

The first step is to get the gameData object from the players collection for this player, using the playerID sent in as part of inData. Now we know which player we're dealing with. Next, the correct flag is set to false, as we assume the player got it wrong to begin with, until it's determined otherwise. The number of questions the player has answered is next bumped up on the gameData object for this player. Now the first bit of logic occurs, and it's precisely the critical bit: did she get the right answer? It's a simple comparison of what answer she sent in against the answer for the current question object.

If she did get it right, then the first step is to increment the count of the questions she got right and decrement the number she got wrong on gameData. Recall that when the question was sent, the number wrong was incremented. That way, if she doesn't answer by the time the next question is asked (or the game is ended), then this question is considered a wrong answer. But, we have to undo that here, because she *did* get it right, hence the decrement of wrong.

After that, it's time to see how long she took to answer. That's a simple matter of subtracting the time the question began from the current time. This is added to the player's totalTime, and then checks are done to see if this time was her fastest or slowest time, and this new time value is stored on gameData, if so. Finally, the average time is recalculated and updated on gameData.

Next, the number of points players get for this answer is calculated. The logic here is relatively straightforward and is designed to be as fair as possible for all players across knowledge levels. This logic is based on a maximum amount of time allowed to answer a question and a corresponding maximum number of points from which some number is subtracted, based on how much time the player took to respond. A correct answer starts off giving the player 60 points, because the maxTimeAllowed is 15, and that value is multiplied by 4. But then, for each quarter second taken to answer, we subtract 1 point, capping the loss at the max points the player could get. So, in the end, if he takes more than `maxTimeAllowed` seconds to answer, he'll get no points. Otherwise, he'll get something less than or equal to `maxTimeAllowed*4`. However, it seems a bit unfair to me to take *all* his points if he got the right answer, so at the end, we give him 10 points, regardless of how long he took to answer.

So, in the final analysis, all of this means that a player can get anywhere from 10–60 points for a correct answer, and it's the time it takes to answer that determines where in that range he falls. That gives less knowledgeable players a chance too, because if they get one or two questions that they know the answer to instantly, they can catch up with the players who may get more questions right overall but who take some time to answer each. It may not be a perfect algorithm, but it's reasonably equitable for what this app is.

Admin Message Handlers

The two messages discussed in the last section were the messages that players emit to get into the game and to submit answers, respectively. But, there's another set of messages that are only for the admin user to control the game.

When you first start the client app, you are prompted to enter your name via a modal, as you can see in Figure 5-3.

Figure 5-3. *The name prompt modal (Android version)*

You'll notice there's also a switch for indicating that you are the admin user. As you'll see in Chapter 6, when we look at the client code, the result of flipping this switch is that a different set of socket.io message handlers is engaged, ones specific to an admin, and the others that are for players are ignored. When that happens, the user sees a new screen, and only that screen, rather than the screens a player sees (all of which I'll cover in Chapter 6). This admin screen is not going to win any beauty pageants, but then it doesn't have to. Its purpose is just to give the user control over the game, so it's very simplistic, as Figure 5-4 shows.

Figure 5-4. *The not-at-all-impressive-bit-totally-gets-the-job-done admin screen*

Each of the buttons you see here triggers one of the following three messages to be emitted, so let's have a look at the server-side handlers for those messages.

adminNewGame

When the admin wants to start a new game, the uncreatively named `adminNewGame` message is emitted, to do all the work involved in setting up a new game.

```
io.on("adminNewGame", () => {

  try {

    question = null;
    questionForPlayers = null;
    numberAsked = 0;
    inProgress = true;
```

```
      questions = (JSON.parse(fs.readFileSync("questions.json", "utf8"))).
      questions;

      for (const playerID in players) {
        if (players.hasOwnProperty(playerID)) {
          const playerName = players[playerID].playerName;
          players[playerID] = newGameData();
          players[playerID].playerName = playerName;
        }
      }

      const responseObject = { inPongress : inProgress, question : null,
        playerID : null, gameData : newGameData(), asked : numberAsked,
        leaderboard : calculateLeaderboard()
      };
      const gd = newGameData();
      gd.asked = 0;

      io.broadcast.emit("newGame", responseObject);
      io.emit("adminMessage", { msg : "Game started" });

    } catch (inException) {
      console.log(`${inException}`);
    }

  });
```

First, all the "tracking" variables associated with the game are reset, so we start off with no current question (and questionForPlayers), zero numberAsked, and the inProgress flag set to true.

Next, the questions.json file is read in. This is where that Node File System API comes in, via the fs variable. This API provides a wide variety of methods, one of the simplest being readFileSync(). This will read in the specified file synchronously. (There's also a readFile() method that will do it asynchronously, but then you have to provide a callback and code accordingly, but in this case, speed isn't an issue, so holding up the thread with the synchronous version of the call is acceptable and makes the code more natural.) The file is read in and passed to JSON.parse(), to get an object from it, and a reference to it is stored in questions.

After that, all players currently known to the server must have their gameData object reset, because they may have participated in a previous game. That's a simple iteration over the keys of players and a call to newGameData() for each (plus adding the playerName to that gameData object).

Next, we have to tell all the connected clients about the new game. So, a responseObject is constructed, which you'll notice looks an awful lot like what is done when a player first connects. That's by design: the state of things after this should look very much like when a player first connects and enters the game, because, conceptually, they're both the same situation, as far as the server and client states go.

The final step is to emit the adminMessage message back to the client, to tell him or her that the game has started. The message passed as the payload of this message will be displayed on the screen, to confirm their new game request.

adminNextQuestion

The next function that an admin can perform is to trigger a question to be sent to the players. This emits an adminNextQuestion message, handled by this handler function:

```
io.on("adminNextQuestion", () => {

  try {

    if (!inProgress) {
      io.emit("adminMessage", { msg : "There is no game in progress" });
      return;
    }
    if (questions.length === 0) {
      io.emit("adminMessage", { msg : "There are no more questions" });
      return;
    }

    for (const playerID in players) {
      if (players.hasOwnProperty(playerID)) {
        players[playerID].wrong++;
      }
    }
```

```
    let choice = Math.floor(Math.random() * questions.length);
    question = questions.splice(choice, 1)[0];
    questionForPlayers = { question : question.question, answers : [ ] };

    const decoys = question.decoys.slice(0);
    for (let i = 0; i < 5; i++) {
      let choice = Math.floor(Math.random() * decoys.length);
      questionForPlayers.answers.push(decoys.splice(choice, 1)[0]);
    }

    questionForPlayers.answers.push(question.answer);
    questionForPlayers.answers = lodash.shuffle(questionForPlayers.
    answers);
    numberAsked++;
    questionStartTime = new Date().getTime();

    io.broadcast.emit("nextQuestion", questionForPlayers);
    io.emit("adminMessage", { msg : "Question in play" });

  } catch (inException) {
    console.log(`${inException}`);
  }

});
```

Next, we must perform two "idiot checks." First, if there isn't a game in progress, a suitable message is sent to the client, by emitting the adminMessage message. Similarly, if there are no more questions left to ask, the admin is informed of that as well. It's expected that the admin will emit the adminNewGame message in the first case and the adminEndGame message in the second, but that's entirely up to the admin.

Next, the wrong count is incremented for all players. As you saw previously, we start out assuming each player gets the question wrong until the server determines otherwise, and this count gets decremented if a player does get it right, but this default allows the server to treat no answer at all as a wrong answer.

Next, a question is chosen at random from the array of questions. That question is then removed from the array. This way, we don't have any unique code to keep track of what questions have and haven't been asked—if it's still in the array, it hasn't been asked yet. It's as simple as that. Because the questions.json file gets read anew every time a game is started, the questions array will be reconstituted at that time, so there's no need to worry about any sort of specific reset function for the next game either. As part of this choice, a new `questionForPlayers` object is constructed. That's because the objects in the `questions` array contain more information than the client app requires (including, critically, the correct answer). We don't want anyone trying to monitor the traffic between client and server and cheating by seeing the correct answer, after all. So, we'll construct a new object with only what the client *really* needs, rather than taking the lazy route of just returning the existing question object. (I could have deleted from the existing object what isn't required and sent that—six of one, half dozen of another, I suppose.)

The next task is to choose five of the ten decoy answers. The same sort of "pick one and then remove it" logic is going to be used, but in this case, I don't want to alter the original array, so it is first cloned with the `slice(0)` call. Then, six random choices are made, removing the decoy from the cloned array each time.

After the decoys are added to `questionForPlayers`, we have to add the correct answer too. Otherwise, this isn't going to be a compelling game. However, after `push()`ing it onto the `questionForPlayers.answers` array, it is, of course, the last answer, and will always be, so that's going to be pretty easy for the players to figure out. So, after that, that one lodash function I mentioned at the beginning that we needed is used: `shuffle()`. This simply randomizes the array, so the correct answer isn't always in the same slot, so to speak.

Now, we have a few more housekeeping tasks to take care of. First, the `numberAsked` variable is incremented, because determining this from the length of the `questions` array is a little tricky (we'd need to have kept track of how many questions there were to start, but it seemed more natural to me to just count off by one, each time a new question is chosen). Then the current time is stored, so that we can determine how long each player takes to answer.

The final step is to emit two messages, one for the players and one for the admin. The `nextQuestion` message goes to the players and triggers the client app to show the question screen. The `adminMessage` messages goes to the admin, obviously, and confirms to them that a question is now in play.

adminEndGame

The final server-side message handler to examine, and the final bit of code in `server.js`, in fact, is for dealing with the `adminEndGame` message that the admin user emits to end the current game.

```
io.on("adminEndGame", () => {

  try {

    if (!inProgress) {
      io.emit("adminMessage", { msg : "There is no game in progress" });
      return;
    }

    const leaderboard = calculateLeaderboard();
    io.broadcast.emit("endGame", { leaderboard : leaderboard });

    inProgress = false;
    questions = null;
    question = null;
    questionForPlayers = null;
    questionStartTime = null;
    numberAsked = 0;
    for (const playerID in players) {
      if (players.hasOwnProperty(playerID)) {
        const playerName = players[playerID].playerName;
        players[playerID] = newGameData();
        players[playerID].playerName = playerName;
      }
    }

    io.emit("adminMessage", { msg : "Game ended" });

  } catch (inException) {
    console.log(`${inException}`);
  }

});
```

First, an idiot check. Is there, in fact, a game in progress? If not, adminMessage is emitted to tell the admin user so. Next, the leaderboard is recalculated via a call to calculateLeaderboard(). This represents the final standings for the game, so this is sent to all the players as the payload for the endGame message that is emitted next.

After that, all the variables associated with the game state on the server are reset. This is mostly redundant (and also largely unnecessary), because most of this will be done again, if and when a new game begins. But, it's done here primarily so that if the admin user tries to send a new question or end the game again, the handlers will be able to inform them of that correctly. (I also like always having a known state, so I don't mind a little double resetting of things, to ensure that.) Part of that is resetting `gameData` for all the players as well, which is where the loop comes into play.

Finally, `adminMessage` is emitted, telling the admin that the game has ended, as confirmation.

And, with that, the server is complete!

Summary

In this chapter, we began building the RNTrivia app together. Specifically, we developed the server side of the equation. In the process, you got some exposure to Node, and you learned about Web Sockets and `socket.io`.

In the next chapter, we'll tackle the React Native–based client side of RNTrivia, hooking it up to the server and making this app do what it's supposed to do, from soup to nuts.

CHAPTER 6

React Native Trivia, Part 2

In the previous chapter, we built the server side of RNTrivia. React Native wasn't even involved in that task, but that's about to change. Now it's time to build the client side of the equation, our React Native RNTrivia app.

While there's more code to the app itself than there was the server, none of it is very complicated. That's because the server did most of the heavy lifting. However, one of the beautiful things about being relatively simple is that it provides me with an opportunity to introduce a few new concepts, without that being overwhelming.

Before we get to actual code, though, let's begin by looking at how the app is configured for React Native and Expo.

Application Structure and Overall Design

First, let's talk about the overall structure of RNTrivia. This comes in two forms: the layout of the source code on the file system (directory structure, primarily) and the design of the app, in terms of screens and such. I'll discuss the former first.

Source Layout

The server-side code had a straightforward structure: only a single source file (not counting "support" files, such as package.json) in a single directory. The structure of the client-side code is a bit more complex, however, as Figure 6-1 shows.

F. Zammetti, *Practical React Native*, https://doi.org/10.1007/978-1-4842-3939-1_6

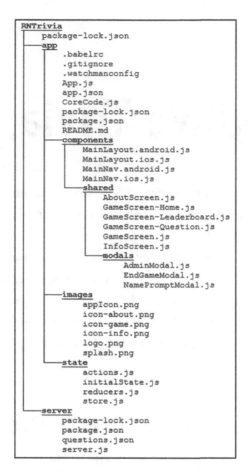

Figure 6-1. *The RNTrivia client app directory structure*

In the root directory, you have the usual suspects: App.js as the main entry point, app.json to describe the app to Expo, package.json (and its sibling package-lock.json) for dependency management (and configuration for NPM and packaging purposes), README.md (generated by react-native-create-app, though not important for our purposes here), and a couple of hidden files that carry configuration for various tools that Expo and React Native use. You'll also notice a CoreCode.js file, and as the name implies, that's where the "core" code of this application will live (as you'll see shortly, App.js is very sparse in this app, even more so than in Restaurant Chooser).

Beyond the root directory, you'll see that there are a number of subdirectories. The images directory, just as in Restaurant Chooser, is where any images the app requires are stored. For this app, I've put *all* the images there, including the app's icon and splash screen images. I recommend keeping your root directory as clean as possible, so this layout is, to my mind, better than that of Restaurant Chooser, which had that icon and splash screen images in it. You'll also find three icon images there for the tabs that will be our main navigation model (well, for iOS anyway, but I'm jumping ahead).

Then there is a components directory, again as in Restaurant Chooser, where all of the React Native component code is. However, unlike Restaurant Chooser, *all* the code is there. Screen components aren't split into their own directory, but there is a deeper directory structure at play here that we need to talk about now.

In Restaurant Chooser, you'll recall that there wasn't a lot of difference between iOS and Android—not a lot of code targeting either—and what *was* there was dealt with using the Platform API and some device info values provided by React Native and Expo. For a simple app, that will frequently be all you need, because it will almost entirely look, feel, and function the same on both platforms, so there's no need to branch any code. But, what if you want the layout of the app, and even, possibly, its functionality, to be more significantly different between the two platforms? If you suspect that it would get monotonous to have a whole bunch of conditional logic using the Platform API to branch between code paths, you would be quite right. Especially in the case of the app needing to have a different navigation model between the two (typically done to adhere to each platform's application design guidelines), you'll probably want a better way, and it turns out there is one.

Let's say you have a component, call it MyComponent, and it's in a file MyComponent. js. So, you

```
import MyComponent from "./MyComponent";
```

in some source file to use it. Now, let's say you must make MyComponent look very different on iOS than on Android. Rather than introduce any branching logic into that code, you can instead create a copy of MyComponent.js, name it MyComponent.android.js, then rename the original to MyComponent.ios.js, and guess what happens? When the React Native packager creates the JavaScript bundle for your app, it will select the appropriate file automatically, based on which platform your app is running on. Now, inside of those two files, you don't have to do anything special, you just write a component, as you would any other component, but specific to each platform. When the app is built, the correct version will be used. Pretty sweet, right?

Now, for RNTrivia, I decided early on that I wanted to use the same sort of tab navigation model as was used for Restaurant Chooser, but only for iOS. For Android, I wanted to use a navigation tray (that thing where you swipe in from the side of the screen to reveal a navigation menu), because that's more common on Android. While either navigation model can work on either OS, using the one that is more common on each provides a more native experience for the user, and this automatic choosing of source files is just the ticket to implementing that cleanly.

So, you'll find that there are four files in the `components` directory related to this: `MainLayout.android.js`, `MainLayout.ios.js`, `MainNav.android.js`, and `MainNav.ios.js`. We'll be looking at those later, but as a preview, the `MainLayout*` files will be the top-level component of the app, with some differences between each platform, and they will make use of the `MainNav*` files, with the packager ensuring the correct version of each is used, without us having to do anything other than name the files appropriately. You can use this switching mechanism as much or as little as you require, and all it "costs" is using specific file names (and note that the import does *not* specify a platform; that's the other vital part of it).

Now, once you introduce the notion of different components for different platforms, you'll probably then want to segregate those components that are shared between the two, and that's what I've done, by introducing the `shared` directory. Neither React Native nor Expo requires this, but it makes sense. In the case of RNTrivia, everything but the `MainLayout*` and `MainNav*` files are, in fact, shared, so the remainder of the app's code is in there. Then, within this `shared` directory, I essentially have two things: screen components and modal dialog components, so I've created a `modals` subdirectory in there where the code for the modals are found, and everything not in that directory is for a given screen, as the file names you see hint at.

The last directory you see off the root is `state`, and this is where you'll find some code, split across four files, related to application state. This is a broader conversation, however, one we'll be having a few sections from now. So, let's jump over to look at the first bit of source code, roughly speaking, right now.

App Navigation

The other consideration, strongly hinted at in the previous section, is how the user will navigate the app. In short, on iOS, he or she will navigate using a tabbed interface, as shown in Figure 6-2.

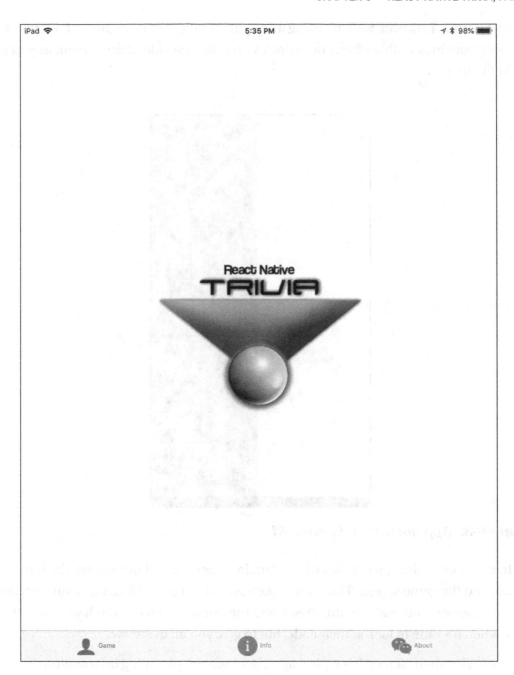

Figure 6-2. *App navigation in iOS*

In Android, however, we'll be using an application tray to navigate, a UI element that only becomes visible when you swipe in from the left side of the screen, as you can see in Figure 6-3.

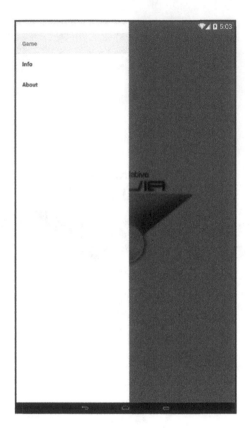

Figure 6-3. *App navigation in Android*

In either case, the app consists of three main screens: the about screen, the info screen, and the game screen. The game screen is further divided into three sub-screens: the home screen, the leaderboard screen, and the question screen. You'll see each of these when it's time to look at their code, but to give you an overview,

- The about screen is a typical app about screen, providing information about the app.

- The info screen shows information about the current game the player is participating in—things such as the score, right and wrong answer counts, and so on.

- The game ➤ home screen is the screen the user initially sees when the app is started, assuming there's no game in progress (in which case, the user would immediately see the game ➤ leaderboard screen instead). This home screen is nothing but an app logo.

- The game ➤ leaderboard screen is what the user sees when a game is in progress, and he or she is awaiting the next question. It shows the current standings for the game in progress.

- The game ➤ question screen is where the current question is shown, and the user submits his or her answer from. Note that this is the only screen that the user can interact with; everything else is read-only.

In addition to these screens and sub-screens, three modals can be shown in the app.

- The `NamePromptModal` is displayed when the app starts up and is used to get the user's name. This modal also has an element to allow the admin user to switch the app to admin mode.

- The `EndGameModal` is shown when the game ends and is used to tell the player the outcome of the game (what place he or she finished in).

- The `AdminModal` is, of course, where the admin controls are and is only seen by the admin user.

The user can freely move between the about, info, and game screens (via tabs in iOS or tray navigation links in Android), but movement between the game screen's sub-screens and display of the modals is controlled entirely by application logic and events.

Configuring the App

We won't spend too much time on the two configuration files, `package.json`, and `app.json`, because you've seen them already, and there's not a ton different in these, and they're mostly auto-generated for us anyway, but I don't want just to skip them entirely, so we'll take a quick peek now.

package.json

As you know, package.json provides information for NPM to use, and the most important thing to us as developers is the list of dependencies.

```
{
  "name": "rntrivia", "version": "0.1.0", "private": true,
  "devDependencies": {
    "react-native-scripts": "1.14.0",
    "jest-expo": "~27.0.0",
    "react-test-renderer": "16.3.1"
  },
  "main": "./node_modules/react-native-scripts/build/bin/crna-entry.js",
  "scripts": {
    "start": "react-native-scripts start",
    "eject": "react-native-scripts eject",
    "android": "react-native-scripts android",
    "ios": "react-native-scripts ios",
    "test": "jest"
  },
  "jest": { "preset": "jest-expo" },
  "dependencies": {
    "expo": "^27.0.1",
    "react": "16.3.1",
    "react-native": "~0.55.2",
    "react-navigation": "^2.5.5",
    "react-redux": "^5.0.7",
    "redux": "^4.0.0",
    "socket.io-client": "^2.1.1",
    "native-base": "^2.6.1"
  }
}
```

In this app, several dependencies beyond the defaults added automatically when the `create-react-native-app` is executed must be added. We have to add `react-navigation`, `react-redux`, `redux`, and `socket.io-client`. You know what `react-navigation` is already. React-redux and redux will be discussed shortly. `socket.io-client` is, of course, `socket.io`, as discussed in Chapter 5, but this is the client version of that library, as you'd expect given that we're writing a client app.

Note   The version of React Native, Expo, and NPM/Node you have installed will influence what you see here when you run `create-react-native-app`. Given that most of this is boilerplate stuff that you, as a developer, usually don't have to be concerned with, and also because what you see when you generate an app could be different, I haven't gone into detail about every element here. I'm only discussing the items that specifically matter within the context of this book, and I leave, as an exercise to you, exploring anything else, if and when it becomes relevant in your own development work.

---

app.json

The `app.json` file content is also just like that you've already seen in Restaurant Chooser, with only some name changes, for the most part.

```
{
  "expo": {
    "name": "RNTrivia", "description": "React Native Trivia",
    "icon": "images/appIcon.png",
    "splash" : { "image": "images/splash.png", "resizeMode": "cover" },
    "version": "1.0.0", "slug": "rntrivia", "sdkVersion": "27.0.0",
    "ios": { "bundleIdentifier": "com.etherient.rntrivia" },
    "android": { "package": "com.etherient.rntrivia" }
  }
}
```

Note that the `icon` and `splash` attributes now use relative paths to point to the images in the `images` directory, as discussed in the previous section.

Before We Begin, a Note on Imports

To keep this chapter from getting too long, in an effort to save some space, I've removed the imports from each of the source files. You've already seen many of them, and many are just code files from the app itself. But, I didn't want to leave you hanging, so here is the rundown of the imports you'll find in each of the files to be discussed and what each imported class is (and, of course, I'll explain the ones that you haven't seen before, as we encounter them):

- *Imported from* react: React

- *Imported from* react-native: Alert, Button, FlatList, Image, Modal, StyleSheet, Text, Vibration, View, WebView. Note that Text is aliased as RNText in one file (/components/shared/GameScreen-Question.js), to avoid a name conflict, but it's still the React Native Text component.

- *Imported from* native-base: Body, Button, Card, CardItem, Input, Item, Label, Root, Switch, Text, Toast

- *Imported from* react-navigation: createBottomTabNavigator, createDrawerNavigator, createSwitchNavigator

- *Imported from* redux: combineReducers, createStore

- *Imported from* react-redux: connect, provider

- *Imported from* socket.io-client: io

- *Imported from* /CoreCode.js: CoreCode

- *Imported from* /state/store.js: store

- *Imported from* /state/actions.js: answerButtonHighlight, resetAllButtons, setCurrentStatus, setEndGameMessage, setGameData, setIsAdmin, setPlayerID, setPlayerNamestate, setQuestion, showHideModal, updateAnswerButtonLabel, updateLeadboard, ANSWER_BUTTON_HIGHLIGHT, RESET_ALL_BUTTONS, SET_CURRENT_STATUS, SET_END_GAME_MESSAGE, SET_GAME_DATA, SET_IS_ADMIN, SET_PLAYER_ID, SET_PLAYER_NAME, SET_QUESTION, SHOW_HIDE_MODAL, UPDATE_ANSWER_BUTTON_LABEL, UPDATE_LEADERBOARD

- *Imported from* /state/initialState.js: initialState

- *Imported from* /state/reducers.js: gameDataReducer, leaderboardReducer, modalsReducer, playerInfoReducer, questionReducer

- *Imported from* /components/shared/modals/NamePromptModal.js: NamePromptModal

- *Imported from* /components/shared/modals/EndGameModal.js: EndGameModal

- *Imported from* /components/shared/modals/AdminModal.js: AdminModal

- *Imported from* /components/shared/MainLayout.<android|ios>. js: MainLayout

- *Imported from* /components/shared/MainNav.ios.js: Tabs

- *Imported from* /components/shared/MainNav.android.js: Drawer

- *Imported from* /components/shared/GameScreen.js: GameScreen

- *Imported from* /components/shared/GameScreen-Home.js: GameHomeScreen

- *Imported from* /components/shared/GameScreen-Leaderboard.js: GameLeaderboardScreen

- *Imported from* /components/shared/GameScreen-Question.js: GameQuestionScreen

- *Imported from* /components/shared/AboutScreen.js: AboutScreen

- *Imported from* /components/shared/InfoScreen.js: InfoScreen

The Starting Point (Or Lack Thereof?): App.js

As with any React Native app using Expo, our starting point is the App.js file. But, for RNTrivia, what you find in that file is, well, not very impressive.

```
export default class App extends React.Component {
```

```
constructor(inProps) {
  super(inProps);
}

render() {
  return (<Provider store={store}><Root><MainLayout/></Root></Provider>);
}

componentDidMount() {
  store.dispatch(showHideModal("namePrompt", true));
};

}
```

Besides imports, the top-level component defined here for the app renders little, because most of the work is delegated to other components. The `Root` component, as you saw in Restaurant Chooser, is the `NativeBase` component we have to wrap around some other component, to render `Toast` messages, which is how we'll be telling the user whether he or she answered a question right or wrong later on. Placing it here, at the highest level, means we can use those `Toast` messages from anywhere in the app and not have to remember to wrap some subcomponent in a `Root` component.

But what's the deal with that `Provider` component? That's one you haven't seen before. Well, to explain that, I have to talk about something called Redux first, and that's in the next section, so, for now, let's skip over it.

The `MainLayout` component, as I talked about not long ago, will be one of the components defined in either `MainLayout.android.js` or `MainLayout.ios.js`, depending on the platform. At the risk of stealing my own thunder, you'll find out shortly that the only difference between the two is which of the `MainNav*` files is used. Otherwise, they're the same. But, because they're split by platform like this, it's easy to extend the app later, to deal with any platform-specific problems that might arise. That's why it's done. Well, that, and so I could show you this platform-switching mechanism, of course.

In the `componentDidMount()` event handler, the `NamePromptModal` is shown. How it's shown, however, is something new, as is the `Provider` component that I suspiciously (but quite intentionally) skipped mentioning in the `render()` method. Both of these things are tied to something I mentioned earlier that I'd be discussing, namely, application state, and that's what I'm going to delve into right now.

The State of Things: Redux

If you've spent any time at all online researching React or React Native, doubtless you ran into something called Redux. In fact, you probably saw "React+Redux" many times, as if you *had* to use Redux with React and React Native (whatever it is). Before telling you what Redux is, I'll let you know that it is in no way required when working with either React or React Native (or Expo). However, it's true that a lot of developers find that they work great together, so well, in fact, that you can't always find tutorials and articles that *don't* use Redux! Ultimately, though, Redux is just another library that you may or may not want to use (and Redux is also far from the only option that does what it does, but it probably is the most popular by a pretty good margin, at least at the time of writing). In fact, you can even use Redux on its own, whether with another framework entirely or just on its own, but I digress.

What exactly *is* Redux and what does it do? Well, answering that is where we get into the notion of application state. You have, of course, seen that `React` components can have their own internal state when needed, for example, to provide data to a `FlatList` to display. Not all components require state, but many do. When the state is contained in the components themselves, however, you sometimes will find that writing your application becomes tricky, because, sometimes, components must work with the state of other components, or some outside code does.

You saw one way to approach this in Restaurant Chooser: keep the data that represents the state of a component external from the component but "feed it into the component," using the `data` attribute. Remember that list of participants, for example? That was stored in an array that was outside any one component, but then a few different components made use of it by referencing the array in the component's state (via the constructor copying a reference to the array inside the component) and then that `data` attribute, to use it in the component (or subcomponents). This is one way to go, and it works well enough, if the application is small and not very complex, because managing it isn't all that difficult.

But when an application starts to grow and becomes more complex, the story begins to change. Consider that state doesn't only mean the data your components are currently showing. It may also mean things such as server responses and various caches. There's also the consideration of ensuring the integrity of your application's state at all times (something you can't necessarily do with the state just sitting in some JavaScript variables that code anywhere could mutate). When the application gets large and complex, there are so many paths through the code that can mutate the state that it becomes challenging to reason about what's happening, and you can find your state changing in situations in which it's not even apparent how or why it is. Not great for debugging!

But, with all that said, you'll probably want your state to be accessible from almost anywhere in your code but safely so.

To accomplish all of that, you need a more robust mechanism than just plain JavaScript variables (though, hey, it'd be nice to have that sort of simplicity too), and that's precisely where Redux comes into the picture.

Redux is built on three fundamental principles.

- There is a canonical "single source of truth" for application state. This means that there is one store of data that everything in your app, all components, and all code, deals with. It's not spread out all over the place, and it's not sitting in "unmanaged" JavaScript variables that any code could change at any time. This has many benefits, some that may not be immediately apparent. For example, it becomes trivial to save the entire current state of your application and "rehydrate" it with that same state later. (It just becomes a save of the current state, maybe to Local Storage, then reloading it and passing it as the initial state when the store is created, something I'll talk about shortly.)

- State is read-only. This principle is a little bit of a misnomer, because, obviously, state wouldn't work if you *literally* couldn't change it. Imagine a `TextInput` component. If I want its state to be managed by Redux but it can't update state in some way, then Redux is useless to me. No, what this principle means is that there is only one way to mutate state, and it is highly controlled. As you'll see, with Redux, that means dispatching something called an action.

- Changes are made in the store using pure functions. This means that you can never directly touch the state data. Instead, a function (called a reducer in Redux) looks at the previous state, performs some action, and returns the new state.

Okay, that's all the theory behind Redux, but what does it look like in practice? Well, it all begins with creating a store.

```
const store = createStore(function(){}, {});
```

The two arguments to the createStore() function are a reducer function and an initial state, in that order. The initial state is a plain old JavaScript object that provides the data to be in the store initially. An empty object for the initial state isn't of much use, so let's give it something more interesting.

```
const initialState = {
  kid : { firstName : "Bart", lastName : "Simpson" }
};
const store = createStore(function(){}, initialState);
```

If you execute that code and then do a console.log(store), you'll see that the store is created, but you won't find the data in it. To get at the data, use the getState() method.

```
console.log(store.getstate());
```

However, even if you do that, you still won't see the data; you'll see undefined. What gives? To fix that, the currently empty reducer function must return something. That's because the reducer will be called by Redux when the store is created, and since it returns nothing right now, Redux treats things as if there is no initial state, even though we passed it into createStore().

Fortunately, fixing that is easy.

```
const store = createStore(function(inState) { return inState; }, initialState);
```

If you try the code now, you'll see the data in initialState echoed to the console. So far, so good! We've got a store, and we've got data in it. We can't yet *do* anything with this store, but it exists.

Now, let's talk about that reducer function. The job of that function is ultimately to make this line of code do something.

```
store.dispatch({ type : "update", payload : { firstName : "Lisa" } });
```

The dispatch() method is the one single way to mutate data in the store. This method takes a single argument: an object that is called an *action*. This object has a type attribute that tells the reducer what type of action to perform and a payload attribute that is an object with whatever data is to be updated.

Usually, you will see *action functions* being used, which are just functions that create action objects. This provides a level of abstraction and a way to better organize your code and makes use of actions more robust. So, here we'd write something like

```
const updateAction = function(inFirstName) {
  return { type : "update", payload : { firstName : inFirstName }};
};
```

And then, the `dispatch()` call would change to use it.

```
store.dispatch(updateAction("Lisa"));
```

That's great. Now we're telling the store that we want to perform an update action. Nothing will happen if we do that now, though, because we have to also provide a reducer function that actually *does something*.

```
const reducer = function(inState, inAction) {
  if (inAction.type === "update") {
    return inState.kid.firstName = inAction.payload.firstName;
  }
}
```

The `inState` argument will be the current state data, and the `inAction` argument is the action object passed to the `dispatch()` method (as created by the `updateAction()` function). Now, what you do inside the function has no real rules other than the output of the function must be the new state. How you get to that new state is up to you.

However, there is a significant problem in this code, in that the critical thing to remember about reducers is that you never touch the existing state in them. The current state (in `inState`) is never modified directly like is done here! Remember: Reducers are supposed to be "pure" functions, meaning they don't change their arguments or have any side effects.

Instead, you have to clone `inState` in some way, perhaps like this:

```
const reducer = function(inState, inAction) {
  const state = Object.assign({}, inState);
  state.kid.firstName = inAction.payload.firstName;
  return state;
}
```

That would work. A more modern way to do it, however, is with the spread operator, by replacing the `Object.assign()` call with this:

```
const state = { ...inState };
```

That "spreads" all the attributes from `inState` into a new object referenced by `state`. Alternatively, you could simply create a whole new object, if the payload contains all the data you need. That, too, is fine and is sometimes precisely what you'll want to do. Either way, never touch the existing state; that's the thing to remember.

It's also important to note that reducers can (and usually do, as you'll see later) handle more than one action type. Even though we're only defining one `update` action type here, we still need that `if` statement, because when Redux makes that initial call to the reducer, it will pass an internal action type that our code won't know how to handle. In that case, returning the existing state is what we want to do (which Redux will have set using `initialState`), so we still need the logic there, because without it, the code would overwrite that initial state data, trying to update it with an empty payload, and that would be a Very Bad Thing™.

That, very briefly, is what Redux is all about. Stores, actions, and reducers, a single source of truth that can only be modified with the `dispatch()` method. That's what it's all about. There's more to it when it comes time to hook React Native to a Redux store, but that will come later. For now, let's look at the actual code in RNTrivia that deals with Redux, which, as you'll see, is little more than building on the concepts just explained and, really, not even building on them all that much.

Note   The source code bundle contains this sample in an HTML file, so you just have to load it up in the browser of your choice (relatively modern browser, that is), and you'll see this in action.

---

initialState.js

So, with the discussion of what Redux is out of the way, now we can look at how it's used in RNTrivia. The first consideration is what the state of the app starts as, and the `initialState.js` file provides that.

```
export default initialState = {
```

```
leaderboard : { listData : [ ] },

gameData : {
  asked : "?????", answered : "?????", points : "?????", right : "?????",
  wrong : "?????",
  totalTime : "?????", fastest : "?????", slowest : "?????", average : "?????"
},

question : {
  answerButtonPrimary : [ true, true, true, true, true ],
  answerButtonDanger : [ false, false, false, false, false ],
  answerButtonLabels : [ null, null, null, null, null, null ],
  currentQuestion : null, selectedAnswer : -1
},

modals : {
  namePromptVisible : false, endGameVisible : false, adminVisible : false,
  endGameMessage : null, isAdmin : false, currentStatus : ""
},

playerInfo : { id : null, name : null }

};
```

As you can see, it's nothing but a JavaScript object. This data is made up of five "branches" of data:

- Leaderboard: This contains the data that the FlatList on the leaderboard screen displays (listData).

- gameData: This contains information about the current game for this player, including such things as her points, how many questions she's gotten right and wrong, and statistics about her speed in answering.

- Question: This contains data that is used on the game ➤ question screen. This includes two arrays (answerButtonPrimary and answerButtonDanger) that, you'll see later, are used to track and manipulate the state of the buttons (whether one is selected or not), the labels for the buttons (answerButtonLabels), as well as the currentQuestion, and which of the buttons the user has selected (selectedAnswer).

- modals: This contains flags used to determine what modal is showing. Aha! Remember that line in componentDidMount() in App.js? Don't worry, we'll come back to that later, but it's clearly related to this.

- playerInfo: This holds information about the player, namely his or her id and name.

Each of these branches will be controlled by a reducer. A reducer doesn't always have to deal with the entire state tree as the simple example from before does, and, in fact, a reducer almost never does deal with the entire state tree like that. Instead, you'll write multiple reducers, one for each logical chunk of state data. Each reducer will have one or more associated actions. You can start to see that all coming together in the next section when this initialState object is used.

Tip   If you work with Redux outside of React, you'll find that attributes of this object don't need to be objects, as they are here. For example, if you wanted playerInfo to be a Boolean (which wouldn't make sense, but work with me here), that would be fine. However, when you try to do it in React Native, you'll get an error saying that all attributes of state must be objects. It doesn't change anything here, because this structure is basically ideal anyway, but it's something I ran into and wanted to let you know about.

---

store.js

Once you have an initial state object defined, the next step is to create the store itself, which is done in the store.js file. Part of that creation is to tell it what reducer to use. However, it's prevalent to have more than one reducer in an app, as mentioned. So, given that the createStore() method accepts only a single reducer function, how do we handle that? Well, Redux provides a very handy combineReducers() function that you use like so:

```
const rootReducer = combineReducers({
  leaderboard : leaderboardReducer,
  question : questionReducer,
  modals : modalsReducer,
  playerInfo : playerInfoReducer,
  gameData : gameDataReducer
});
```

Now you've got a single `rootReducer`, but within it are five different reducers, each handling a different branch of the state object, based on the keys here. The `leaderboardReducer` works with the `leaderboard` branch, for instance, and so on. It's a little bit of black magic there, but Redux deals with that mapping under the covers. We only have to ensure that the keys match what's in the state object. Also, note that you'll get an error, if there is anything in state that does *not* have a reducer defined, so make sure you've got one for every branch in the state tree.

This `rootReducer` can then be used to create the store.

```
export default createStore(rootReducer, initialState);
```

Now we've got a Redux data store containing the initial state of our app. With that in place, it's time to build us some actions and reducers. We'll start with the actions.

actions.js

The `actions.js` file is where we find all the actions required throughout RNTrivia. Often, developers will have a separate source file for each action (as well as each reducer, which I'll cover in the next section), but there are no hard-and-fast rules about that. Use whatever organization makes the most sense to you. To me, a single file made sense, so that's what I went with. The first chunk of code in this file is defining some pseudo-constants that define action types.

```
exports.ANSWER_BUTTON_HIGHLIGHT = "abh";
exports.RESET_ALL_BUTTONS = "rab";
exports.SET_CURRENT_STATUS = "scs";
exports.SET_END_GAME_MESSAGE = "segm";
exports.SET_GAME_DATA = "sgd";
exports.SET_IS_ADMIN = "sia";
exports.SET_PLAYER_ID = "spi";
exports.SET_PLAYER_NAME = "spn";
exports.SET_QUESTION = "scq";
exports.SHOW_HIDE_MODAL = "shm";
exports.UPDATE_ANSWER_BUTTON_LABEL = "uabl";
exports.UPDATE_LEADERBOARD = "ul";
```

The values for these fields are completely arbitrary; they just need to be unique. I simply took the first letter of each in the action type as the value.

I'd be willing to bet that each of these is self-explanatory, but as we now look at the actions, you'll see what the meaning of each is. And, to help you grok what the actions are for, I've broken them down into logical groups, organized around what the actions at a high level are for.

Actions for Modals

First, we have actions related to working with modals. In this case, it's actually just a single action.

```
exports.showHideModal = (inModalName, inVisible) => {
  return { type : exports.SHOW_HIDE_MODAL,
    payload : { modalName : inModalName, visible : inVisible }
  };
};
```

This action is used to either hide or show one of the modals. As you can see, the name of the modal is passed in, and a flag saying whether it's visible or not and these become the payload, with the type being SHOW_HIDE_MODAL, one of the pseudo-constants from earlier.

This is the general form all the action functions will take: take in some arguments (or none, as is the case for one action) and return an object consisting of a type attribute, the value of which is one of the pseudo-constants, and a payload attribute (which might be an empty object). Nothing says you couldn't include some additional logic if it was necessary, and nothing says you couldn't create a single action function and use branching within it to return even the appropriate object. The bottom line, however, is that this function must return an object with those two attributes; that's what Redux requires (as part of the dispatch() call). In fact, given the commonality of this form, I won't be showing the code for the remainder of the actions; I'll just describe the functions. (I'll show the function name, the arguments it takes, the type associated with it and, of course, explain what it's for, though I suspect they're all abundantly obvious.) This will remove some redundancy from the conversation, I think.

If you go back now to the componentDidMount() method in the top-level component from App.js, you'll find the single line there:

```
store.dispatch(showHideModal("namePrompt", true));
```

That should make some sense now. The `dispatch()` method is how we always mutate state, and now you can see that the object passed to it is the result of calling the `showHideModal()` action function. It's the object returned by that function. This doesn't yet explain exactly how the `NamePromptModal` gets shown because of this call, but now you know that it is, somehow, controlled by the state maintained by Redux, and for the moment, that's sufficient. We'll get to the other part of the equation soon enough. Until then, let's move on to the other action functions.

Actions for Player Info

Two action functions exist for mutating the data in the `playerInfo` branch of state.

- `setPlayerID(inID)`: `SET_PLAYER_ID`: Used to mutate the `id` field only

- `setPlayerName(inName)`: `SET_PLAYER_NAME`: Used to mutate the `name` field only

Note that, in this case, I have two actions for mutating the two pieces of information in this branch of data individually. You'll see other cases in which the entire branch is mutated in one go. It's entirely dependent on your use case and which approach you use, neither is right or wrong, or better or worse. I didn't do it this way for any specific reason other than it made the code a little more straightforward, but primarily, it was just to demonstrate that you could do it this way vs. the all-at-once approach, which you can see in the next action function.

Actions for Game Data

Only a single action function exists for mutating the data in the `gameData` branch of state.

- `gameData(inGameData)`: `SET_GAME_DATA`: Used to mutate the entire `gameData` field

Actions for Question Data

We have four action functions that deal with manipulating data in the `question` branch.

- `answerButtonHighlight(inButtonNumber)`: `ANSWER_BUTTON_HIGHLIGHT`: Used to highlight a button when the user taps it (mutates the `answerButtonPrimary`, `answerButtonDanger`, and `selectedAnswer` fields)

- updateAnswerButtonLabel(inButtonNumber, inLabel): UPDATE_ANSWER_BUTTON_LABEL: Changes the label of a specified button (by number, 0–5), which is used when displaying the possible answers to the user (mutates the answerButtonLabels field)

- resetAllButtons(): RESET_ALL_BUTTONS: Used to reset all buttons to their default, non-selected state, which is done when a question is first shown (mutates the answerButtonPrimary and answerButtonDanger fields)

- setQuestion(inQuestion): SET_QUESTION: Used to mutate the currentQuestion field

Actions for Leaderboard Data

Two functions exist for dealing with the data in the leaderboard branch.

- setEndGameMessage(inMessage): SET_END_GAME_MESSAGE: Used to show the player a message when the game ends (mutates the endGameMessage field of the modals branch. Wait, what? Don't worry, I'll explain this.

- updateLeaderboard(inListData): UPDATE_LEADERBOARD: Used to update the data that the FlatList component on the game ➤ leaderboard screen displays (mutates the listData field)

Now, let's talk about that weirdness in setEndGameMessage(), namely, why it's touching anything outside the leaderboard branch of state data. It is indeed true that, generally speaking, action functions (and reducers, later) are "tied," in a sense, to a particular branch of state. However, there are no rules that say they can't mutate other data. It's purely a logical delineation. In this case, the message to be shown to the user is shown on the EndGameModal, so this function logically, perhaps, should have been in the modals group. But, on the other hand, the EndGameModal is only ever shown when on the game ➤ leaderboard screen at the end of the game, so it makes some sense to be in the leaderboard group too.

How do you decide? As with many other things in the world of React Native, the answer is whatever makes sense to you. However, I'll mention that there's a commonly accepted best practice to try and not tie your state to your UI. In other words, try not to have actions and reducers that are for a specific screen. Instead, design your state such that it's abstracted away from the UI itself. That being said, that's not always practical and not always necessarily the best design, and sometimes, if the state and UI aren't that complex, it just doesn't make very much difference either way. I think this is one of those cases in which there is no right or wrong or even "best" answer. But at least now you know what informed my thinking.

Actions for Admin Data

The final group of action functions are specific to the admin screen (which, of course, goes against the best practice I mentioned in the previous section!) and they actually mutate data in the modals branch (for the same basic reason, as I explained in that previous section, that is, these are only used from one specific modal).

- setIsAdmin(inIsAdmin): SET_IS_ADMIN: Used when the user flips the switch on the NamePromptModal (mutates isAdmin field)

- setCurrentStatus(inCurrentStatus): SET_CURRENT_STATUS: Used to display messages from the server to the admin used (mutates currentStatus field)

reducers.js

The reducers are the workhorse of Redux, as they are what react to the objects created by the action functions and mutate state. Well, to be more precise, they return new state; they do not mutate existing state. Well, to be even *more* precise, they return a new piece of state, which Redux then merges into the existing state object.

Whatever way you view it, the point is that they are responsible for getting the work done, at least as far as your own code goes. For RNTrivia, I've used the same overall organization for the reducers as I did for the action functions, that is, they are grouped according to which branch of state they deal with and are all in the same reducers.js file.

The Reducer for Modals

The first reducer is for the modals branch of state.

```
exports.modalsReducer = function(inState = {}, inAction) {

  switch (inAction.type) {
```

```
  case SET_CURRENT_STATUS : {
    const modalsNode = { ...inState };
    modalsNode.currentStatus = inAction.payload.currentStatus;
    return { ... inState, ...modalsNode };
  }

  case SET_END_GAME_MESSAGE : {
    const modalsNode = { ...inState };
    modalsNode.endGameMessage = inAction.payload.message;
    return { ... inState, ...modalsNode };
  }

  case SET_IS_ADMIN : {
    const modalsNode = { ...inState };
    modalsNode.isAdmin = inAction.payload.isAdmin;
    return { ... inState, ...modalsNode };
  }

  case SHOW_HIDE_MODAL : {
    const modalsNode = { ...inState };
    modalsNode[`${inAction.payload.modalName}Visible`] =
      inAction.payload.visible;
    return { ... inState, ...modalsNode };
  }

  default : { return inState; }

}

};
```

There's not really a standardized way to write a reducer and no definitive rules about how you break them down, but what you see here is typical. Each reducer (which typically is expected to handle more than one action type, assuming you *need* more than one action type to do the app's work) is a function with a switch statement, with each case of that switch being one of the types specified in actions.js. Each case does much the same thing: it gets the current object for the specified branch (or node, whichever term you prefer) via cloning, using the spread operator, and then sets whatever value(s) in it that must be changed. That way, we maintain whatever values are already in it and only change what we need to. Sometimes, we may replace the entire branch, sometimes, just specific attributes, such as is done here. You can do either. For the SET_CURRENT_STATUS type, for example, only the currentStatus attribute is updated on the modals node. You'll see two reducers later that replace the entire branch instead, but it's all a matter of what makes sense in your specific use case.

Note   When you have a single reducer, as in the simple example from earlier, that reducer will receive the entire state tree, but when you combine multiple reducers like this, each reducer will only receive the chunk of the state tree it's responsible for, based on the keys in the object passed to combineReducers().

Either way, what gets returned from the reducer is the new state, specifically, the branch the reducer deals with. In all the cases here, the spread operator is used to clone the inState object that was passed in (which, remember, is just the part of state this reducer deals with, not the entire state object) with the state object created by the code in each branch. Note that to avoid errors, we need a default value for inState, and an empty object suffices. You could, rather than passing an initial state to the createStore() call, create your state tree piecemeal, by specifying the default values in this manner. Similarly, the default case covers any situation that might not be covered by the reducer's switch block.

As was the case with the action functions, I'm not going to list every reducer here, because having seen the one for modals, you've in essence seen them all. I'll simply list what the reducers are, what types they handle, and any that may do something different than the one for modals.

The Reducer for Player Info

For the playerInfo branch, we have a corresponding playerInfoReducer() function. This function handles two types: SET_PLAYER_ID and SET_PLAYER_NAME. Its code is virtually identical to that of modalsReducer(), so there's nothing to see here.

The Reducer for Game Data

The reducer for the gameData branch is something a little different. Have a look.

```
exports.gameDataReducer = function(inState = {}, inAction) {

  switch (inAction.type) {

    case SET_GAME_DATA : {
      return { ...inState, ...inAction.payload.gameData };
    }

    default : { return inState; }

  }

};
```

Yep, this is one of those cases in which the entire branch is being mutated. The inAction.payload.gameData object contains all the data carried in this branch, so while it certainly would be possible to clone the branch, then copy each individual attribute over to it, it's more concise to do a simple merge with the spread operator like this and move on with our day.

The Reducer for the Question Data

For working with the question branch of state, we have to do some slightly different things. In all cases, we're still just cloning the existing branch, making changes and then merging it back, but the changes made are slightly more involved, at least in some cases, then the other reducers, as you can see for yourself.

```
exports.questionReducer = function(inState = {}, inAction) {

  switch (inAction.type) {

    case ANSWER_BUTTON_HIGHLIGHT : {
      const questionNode = { ...inState };
      questionNode.answerButtonPrimary = [ true, true, true, true, true ];
      questionNode.answerButtonDanger = [ false, false, false, false, false
];
```

```
      questionNode.selectedAnswer = inAction.payload.buttonNumber;
      if (inAction.payload.buttonNumber !== -1) {
        questionNode.answerButtonDanger[inAction.payload.buttonNumber] = true;
      }
      return { ...inState, ...questionNode };
    }

    case UPDATE_ANSWER_BUTTON_LABEL : {
      const questionNode = { ...inState };
      questionNode.answerButtonLabels[inAction.payload.buttonNumber] =
        inAction.payload.label;
      return { ...inState, ...questionNode };
    }

    case RESET_ALL_BUTTONS : {
      const questionNode = { ...inState };
      questionNode.answerButtonPrimary = [ true, true, true, true, true ];
      questionNode.answerButtonDanger = [ false, false, false, false, false
];
      return { ...inState, ...questionNode };
    }

    case SET_QUESTION : {
      const questionNode = { ...inState };
      questionNode.currentQuestion = inAction.payload.question;
      return { ...inState, ...questionNode };
    }

    default : { return inState; }

  }

};
```

The ANSWER_BUTTON_HIGHLIGHT is the first difference. First, the answerButtonPrimary
and answerButtonDanger arrays are reset to the initial values. As you'll see later, these
are used to determine what style (color, primarily) the buttons have, and this is used
to highlight a button when the user taps to select one. When a button is tapped, this

action type is dispatched, passing it the number of the button that was tapped. So, after resetting those arrays, and storing which button was tapped in the selectedAnswer attribute, we then have to highlight the specified button. If -1 is passed in, we don't do this, but, otherwise, the item in the answerButtonDanger array corresponding to the button has to be flipped to true. After that, it's again just a straightforward merge to complete handing for that type.

For the UPDATE_ANSWER_BUTTON_LABEL type, we only need to update the label for the specified button, so it's nothing but an update into the answerButtonLabels array, because the inAction.payload.buttonNumber value will be the index into the array for that button.

The RESET_ALL_BUTTONS type does the same sort of reset that ANSWER_BUTTON_ HIGHLIGHT does to the two button-related highlighting arrays, but that's it. There's no need to deal with the selected answer. This type will be dispatched when a question is shown to ensure all the buttons are in the correct starting state.

Finally, the SET_QUESTION type is dispatched when a question is shown to record the question in state, and there's nothing new in that case.

The Reducer for the Leaderboard Data

The reducer for the leaderboard branch is basically the same as that of the gameData branch, in that it replaces the entire branch in response to the UPDATE_LEADERBOARD action type. So, no need to examine it here. Let's get to a whole other new topic: a better way to deal with multi-platform development.

Cleaner Multi-Platform Development

When we looked at the overall application structure, I introduced you to the platform switch mechanism. Now it's time to look at the specific versions of the files that use this mechanism, beginning with the MainLayout* files.

The Android Version

The main layout defines the overall layout for the application, and the version for Android is, of course, named MainLayout.android.js, to take advantage of the platform switching mechanism.

MainLayout.android.js

We start out (after the imports that aren't shown, that is) with a very sparse StyleSheet definition.

```
const styles = StyleSheet.create({
  outerContainer : { flex : 1 }
});
```

Yep, that's all, and when you look at the component definition that follows, the reason for this style should be apparent.

```
export default class MainLayout extends React.Component {

  constructor(inProps) {
    super(inProps);
  }

  render() {
    return (
      <View style={styles.outerContainer}>
        <NamePromptModal />
        <EndGameModal />
        <AdminModal />
        <Drawer />
      </View>
    );
  }

}
```

A top-level View component using the style with flex:1 assures that the entire UI fills the screen. Inside that View are four custom components: the three modals, the code for which I'll get to later, and a Drawer component. The Drawer component represents the overall navigation model of the app, and that's where we're headed next.

MainNav.android.js

As with the `MainLayout.android.js` file, the overall navigation for the app is defined, for Android, in the `MainNav.android.js` file and, as previously mentioned, we'll be using a Drawer for this.

```
export default createDrawerNavigator(
  {
    GameScreen : {
      screen : GameScreen, navigationOptions: () => ({ title : "Game" }),
    },

    InfoScreen : {
      screen : InfoScreen, navigationOptions: () => ({ title : "Info" }),
    },

    AboutScreen : {
      screen : AboutScreen, navigationOptions: () => ({ title : "About" }),
    }
  },
  { initialRouteName : "GameScreen", backBehavior : "none" }
);
```

NativeBase provides the `Drawer` component via the `createDrawerNavigation()` function. The configuration passed to it as the first argument should look familiar, because it is very similar to the `TabNavigator` used in Restaurant Chooser. Each screen (route) is an entry in this config object, and the class for each is specified by the `screen` attribute. For `navigationOptions`, we only have to supply a `title`, because there are no icons on the `Drawer` (there can be, but I chose not to have them here, for no particular reason other than to make the configuration as simple as possible). The second argument to `createDrawerNavigation()` are the options for the navigator itself. Just as with the `TabNavigator`, the `initialRouteName` puts the user on the `GameScreen` by default, and the `backBehavior` option tells the navigator to do nothing when the hardware back button is pressed.

The iOS Version

Now we'll look at the iOS side of things, although in reality there's only one file to examine, and it holds no new concepts, so this won't take very long.

MainLayout.ios.js

See, here's the thing about the iOS version of the `MainLayout.ios.js` file: it's virtually the same as the Android version, save for two minimal differences.

- Rather than importing `Drawer` from `MainNav`, this version instead imports `Tabs` from `MainNav` (and notice that `MainNav` does not specify a platform—the React Native packager handles that for us).

- Instead of the `Drawer` component in the `render()` method, `Tabs` appears in its place.

That is, literally, all the changes necessary. So, let's not linger. Let's move on to the `MainNav.ios.js` file, which is indeed different than the `MainNav` file for Android.

MainNav.ios.js

Instead of a `Drawer`, for iOS, we'll use the same kind of `TabNavigator` as you saw in Restaurant Chooser. Here's the code, found in the `MainNav.ios.js` file:

```
export default createBottomTabNavigator(
  {
    GameScreen : {
      screen : GameScreen,
      navigationOptions : {
        tabBarLabel : "Game",
        tabBarIcon : ( {tintColor}) => (
          <Image source={ require("../images/icon-game.png") }
            style={[ styles.tabIcons, { tintColor : tintColor } ]}
          />
        )
      }
    },
```

```
InfoScreen : {
  screen : InfoScreen,
  navigationOptions : {
    tabBarLabel : "Info",
    tabBarIcon : ( {tintColor}) => (
      <Image source={ require("../images/icon-info.png") }
        style={[ styles.tabIcons, { tintColor : tintColor } ]}
      />
    )
  }
},
AboutScreen : {
  screen : AboutScreen,
  navigationOptions : {
    tabBarLabel : "About",
    tabBarIcon : ( {tintColor} ) => (
      <Image source={ require("../images/icon-about.png") }
        style={[ styles.tabIcons, { tintColor : tintColor } ]}
      />
    )
  }
},
{
  initialRouteName : "GameScreen", animationEnabled : true, swipeEnabled : true,
  backBehavior : "none", lazy : false, tabBarPosition : "bottom",
  tabBarOptions : { activeTintColor : "#ff0000", showIcon : true }
}
);
```

There's probably not much point rehashing this code, given that it is virtually identical to what you already parsed in looking at Restaurant Chooser. Of course, if you don't remember that discussion, then you may want to revisit it now and then compare that to this code, to see that aside from the screen names, there are no real changes. We can instead spend our time looking at the component and code specific to this application.

Shared Components

In the components directory, you find the source files that make use of the platform switching mechanism to define the high-level layout and navigation for the app. Everything else in the app is shared between both platforms, though, so all of that code is in the /components/shared directory (and, again, no rule says it has to be that way; it's just a structure that I thought made sense). We'll start exploring that code by looking at the three modals.

NamePromptModal.js

The first modal to look at also happens to be the first one the user sees, and one he or she will always see when the app starts up: NamePrompt Modal. This is the one in which the user enters his or her name or indicates he or she is the admin.

Note   You may notice that there is no control placed on who says they are the admin. Anyone and more than one person could. This was a conscious decision on my part, for two reasons. The first is that it decreases the complexity and helps keep an already long chapter from growing longer. The second reason is that this leaves open for you a great enhancement opportunity to test the knowledge you've gained. Maybe you should ask for a password, if a user says he or she is the admin and validate this on the server. Or, perhaps, make it so that once a user says he or she is the admin, the server won't let anyone else flip the switch (in fact, maybe hide the switch entirely). Either would work, although the latter would require a more significant change, and those aren't the only possibilities. Whatever direction you choose, plugging that hole serves as an excellent exercise.

The first bit of code in this NamePromptModal.js file, after the imports, is the StyleSheet definition. To save some space, I'll show you this code here, and rather than continually saying "and then this style is applied," you should refer back to this when you see one of the styles used in the component code, to understand how the styling is used. If there is any styling that I don't think is obvious or something you've seen before, I'll point it out specifically, but the clear majority of it will be basic flexbox and simple font styling, so you shouldn't by this point have any trouble parsing it, as most of it will be very familiar.

```
const styles = StyleSheet.create({
  outerContainer : { flex : 1, alignItems : "center", justifyContent : "center",
  margin : 20 },
  headingContainer : { height : 100, justifyContent : "center" },
  headingText : { fontSize : 20, fontWeight : "bold" },
  inputFieldContainer : { flex : 1, alignSelf : "stretch", justifyContent :
  "center" },
  switchContainer : { marginTop : 40, justifyContent : "center",
  flexDirection : "row" },
  buttonContainer : { height : 80, alignSelf : "stretch", justifyContent :
  "center" }
});
```

The one interesting bit here is the `alignSelf` set to `stretch` on the
`inputFieldContainer`, which is the container for the field in which the user enters his
or her name. This is necessary to ensure that the field stretches across the entire width
of the modal. `alignSelf` overrides the `alignItems` of the parent, which here would be
the `outerContainer` and its `center` setting. If that was in effect, the input field would
be centered, but it would, without specifying an explicit width, use some default value
that would be roughly half the width of the modal. Using `alignSelf` like this allows it
to expand to fit the space available to it, while not impacting the alignment of any other
items within that container.

Now we can look at the code for this component, which has one or two new and
exciting things to see.

```
class NamePromptModal extends React.Component {

  constructor(inProps) {
    super(inProps);
  }

  render() {

    return (
      <Modal
        presentationStyle={"formSheet"}
        visible={this.props.isVisible}
        animationType={"slide"}
        onRequestClose={ () => { } }>
```

```
        <View style={styles.outerContainer}>
          <View style={styles.headingContainer}>
            <Text style={styles.headingText}>Hello, new player!</Text>
          </View>
          <View style={styles.inputFieldContainer}>
            <Item floatingLabel>
              <Label>Please enter your name</Label>
              <Input
                onChangeText={
                  (inText) => store.dispatch(setPlayerName(inText))
                }
              />
            </Item>
            <View style={ styles.switchContainer}>
              <View>
                <Switch
                  value={this.props.isAdmin}
                  onValueChange={
                    (inValue) => store.dispatch(setIsAdmin(inValue))
                  }
                />
              </View>
              <View style={{ paddingLeft : 10 }}>
                <Text>I am the admin</Text>
              </View>
            </View>
          </View>
          <View style={styles.buttonContainer}>
            <Button block onPress={CoreCode.startup}><Text>Ok</Text></Button>
          </View>
        </View>
      </Modal>
    );

  }
}
```

Most of what you see here should be old hat by this point, because you've seen some modals before in Restaurant Chooser. Where things start to get interesting, though, is the Item component wrapping the Input component. These are components that you saw in Restaurant Chooser, but what's new is the floatingLabel prop on the Item component, and related to that, the Label component that is a child of the Item component. What these do, together, is provide a label inside the Input component that shrinks and moves out of the way when the Input gains focus. It's an excellent mechanism that makes efficient use of space while being informative to the user.

The other new component here is one from React Native itself, the Switch. This allows users to specify that they are the admin, and once they click the button, they'll be navigated to the AdminModal. The Switch is a nice widget for making a yes/no choice like this. I needed to have a label for this component as well, to let users know what it is, so the View that contains the Switch and the Text component for the label uses a flexDirection:row via the switchContainer style, so that they can be side by side. A little bit of padding on the left of the View containing the Text ensures that the label isn't smushed up against the Switch.

The other *very* interesting thing here is that this is the first time that you've seen Redux being tied into React Native components, and how that works goes back to the Provider component in the App.js file. That component is what allows us to tie Redux into the rest of the code. This component comes from a new package: react-redux. This package provides hooks into Redux specifically for React (and React Native by extension) with this Provider component being the biggie. What this does is make the store available to any "connected" components that are children of the Provider component.

And what does it mean to be a "connected" component, you ask? Well, that's where the next bit of code comes into play.

```
const mapStateToProps = (inState) => {
  return {
    isVisible : inState.modals.namePromptVisible,
    isAdmin : inState.modals.isAdmin
  };
};
```

Introducing state to a component is done through the component's props. In order to do that, we have to provide a function that takes in state (more precisely, some branch from the state tree) and maps data from it into props. Then, you wrap the component in a connect() function call, another thing provided by the react-redux package, like so:

```
export default connect(mapStateToProps)(NamePromptModal);
```

The result is that this component, which we now consider connected, will have two new props available to it, isVisible and isAdmin, which correspond to the modals. namePromptVisible and modals.isAdmin state attributes, respectively. You then use those props just like you would any other props, for example, as the value prop on the Switch, as you can see, or as the value of the visible prop of the modal itself. The values in state are used when rendering the component, no different than when using JavaScript variables not managed by Redux. Then, any change in the component transfers back to the state store. Well, more accurately, it *can* transfer back to state, *if* you write the appropriate code in an event handler to dispatch() an action, as you see on the Input component's onTextChange prop and the Switch's onValueChange prop.

And there you have the answer to a question from earlier in the chapter: how a modal gets shown or hidden. All three modals always, in fact, exist, thanks to them being children of the top-level component in the MainLayout* file, and they get displayed as a result of the corresponding attribute in the modals branch of the state tree being set to true, or hidden when they're set to false (which, you'll now notice, is the default in initialState.js). It's just a matter of dispatching an appropriate SHOW_HIDE_MODAL action, passing the name of the modal we want to show or hide and, of course, whether to actually show or hide it, and when Redux updates the state tree, the modals' visibility will be updated as well, without us having to do anything else, because the modal is a connected component.

Pretty cool, right?

Finally, note that the Button's onPress handler references the startup() method of some object called CoreCode. This is code we'll be looking at after all the code for the components, but the interesting thing here is that the value of the onPress prop isn't an anonymous function that has some code inside it that gets invoked right there. Instead, it's a reference to an existing function, and in this case, it's a reference to a method of an object. This is something you haven't seen before, but it is arguably a better way to write React Native code. Some developers advocate never having code inline in the components. For example, instead of having an anonymous function that calls dispatch() directly on the Input component, as you see here, embedded within it, they argue that you should reference some function, maybe updateInputValue(), somewhere (whether a method or an object) and reference it as the value of the onTextChange prop. The thinking is that it separates the action-performing code from the code that defines the component. However, some other developers argue that components are already independent, encapsulated things and, therefore, having the code embedded within them is right, proper, and correct. I leave the architectural/philosophical decision to you, but I wanted to demonstrate the two approaches regardless.

EndGameModal.js

The EndGameModal, found in the EndGameModal.js file, of course, is what the user sees when the game ends. It's a simple modal that tells the player what the outcome was. This component uses the following StyleSheet:

```
const styles = StyleSheet.create({
  outerContainer : { flex : 1, alignItems : "center", justifyContent :
  "center", margin : 20 },
  headingContainer : { height : 100, justifyContent : "center" },
  headingText : { fontSize : 20, fontWeight : "bold" },
  messageContainer : { flex : 1, alignSelf : "center", justifyContent :
  "center" },
  buttonContainer : { height : 80, alignSelf : "stretch", justifyContent :
  "center" },
  buttonText : { fontWeight : "bold", color : "white" }
});
```

The code for the component is as follows:

```
class EndGameModal extends React.Component {

  constructor(inProps) {
    super(inProps);
  }

  render() {

    return (
      <Modal
```

```
        presentationStyle={"formSheet"}
        visible={this.props.isVisible}
        animationType={"slide"}
        onRequestClose={ () => { } }
    >
        <View style={styles.outerContainer}>
          <View style={styles.headingContainer}>
            <Text style={styles.headingText}>Game over</Text>
          </View>
          <View style={styles.messageContainer}>>
            <Text>{this.props.message}</Text>
          </View>
          <View style={styles.buttonContainer}>
            <Button block onPress={ () => { } }>
              <Text style={ styles.buttonText }>Ok</Text>
            </Button>
          </View>
        </View>
      </Modal>
    );

  }

}
```

Within the top-level View component, which has some margin styling to put space all around it, there's a View that contains the heading. This View has a set height to help ensure proper spacing. After that is another View that then includes a Text component. The text displayed there is pulled from the message prop, which comes from the Redux-controlled state. Finally, a View containing a Button component finishes things up. Note that the onPress prop is an empty function. The onPress prop is required by React Native, but there's no actual work to do; the modal will be dismissed when the Button is tapped automatically, hence the empty function.

This component is also connected, so it has a mapStateToProps() function and uses the connect() function. The prop mappings are isVisible maps to modals.endGameVisible and message maps to modals.endGameMessage.

AdminModal.js

Like the `EndGameModal`, the `AdminModal` is also quite simple, although because there are some interactive elements, there's a little more to see. Beginning with the `StyleSheet` in the `AdminModal.js` file, we have

```
const styles = StyleSheet.create({
  outerContainer : { flex : 1, margin : 50, justifyContent : "center",
alignItems : "center" },
  headingText : { fontSize : 40, fontWeight : "bold", margin : 50 },
  buttonContainer : { margin : 50 },
  currentStatusContainer : { margin : 50 },
  currentStatusText : { fontSize : 20, fontWeight : "bold", color : "red" }
});
```

As with `EndGameModal`, all are simple, basic styles. After that is the actual code of the component, as you can see here:

```
class AdminModal extends React.Component {

  constructor(inProps) {
    super(inProps);
  }

  render() {

    return (
      <Modal
        presentationStyle={"fullScreen"}
        visible={this.props.isVisible}
        animationType={"slide"}
        onRequestClose={ () => { } }
      >
        <View style={styles.outerContainer}>
          <Text style={styles.headingText}>Admin</Text>
          <View style={styles.buttonContainer}>
            <Button title="New Game"
              onPress={ () => {
```

```
              CoreCode.io.emit("adminNewGame", {});
          } }
        />
      </View>
      <View style={styles.buttonContainer}>
        <Button title="Next Question"
          onPress={ () => {
            CoreCode.io.emit("adminNextQuestion", {});
          } }
        />
      </View>
      <View style={styles.buttonContainer}>
        <Button title="End Game"
          onPress={ () => {
            CoreCode.io.emit("adminEndGame", {});
          } }
        />
      </View>
      <View style={styles.currentStatusContainer}>
        <Text style={styles.currentStatusText}>
          Current Status: {this.props.currentStatus}
        </Text>
      </View>
    </View>
  </Modal>
);

}

}
```

In essence, this modal is nothing but a Text component for a heading, followed by
three Buttons, each inside a View, styled to ensure consistent spacing between them.
(We wouldn't want any accidental taps just because the buttons are too close together.)
Each button emits a socket.io message to the server, none of which requires any
payload. After the buttons is another View with a Text component inside of it. This is
where any message returned from the server will be displayed. You can see here another

example of how the Text component uses a value from state by way of the `this.props.currentStatus` reference, all courtesy of that `redux-react` package tying things together with the store.

This component is also connected, so it has a `mapStateToProps()` function and uses the `connect()` function. The prop mappings are `isVisible` maps to `modals.adminVisible` and `currentStatus` maps to `modals.currentStatus`.

AboutScreen.js

With the three modals discussed, we now come to the screens of the app, beginning with probably the simplest, the AboutScreen. As with the modals, we'll look at the StyleSheet first, in the AboutScreen.js file.

```
const styles = StyleSheet.create({
  outerContainer : { flex : 1, alignItems : "center", justifyContent : "center" },
  spacer : { flex : .2 },
  textContainer : { flex : .15, justifyContent : "center", alignItems : "center" },
  textTitle : { fontWeight : "bold", fontSize : 20 },
  textVersion : { fontWeight : "bold", fontSize : 18 },
  textSource : { fontWeight : "bold", fontSize : 16 },
  textAuthor : { fontWeight : "bold", fontSize : 14 }
});
```

One thing of note here: when you see the code for the component, you'll understand that there are six View components involved that are children of the View with outerContainer applied. There is one for each of the four pieces of information to display (title, version, source, and author), and then there are two that contain no content at all. You'll find that those two have the spacer style applied. When you add up the flex values for those six Views (.2 + .15 + .15 + .15 + .15 + 2), you'll see that they total up to 1, as expected. Doing it this way, with flex, rather than padding or margin or static heights, means that the content of this screen will stretch or contract according to screen size. To be sure, most of the other screens you've seen in either Restaurant Chooser or this app will do that to some degree as well, but this is the first time you've seen one that will expand or contract *completely*, based on screen size. It's an entirely responsive layout, in other words. It isn't always feasible or even advisable to do a layout like this. More often than not, you'll have some combination of flexible items and fixed-size items, but when you can do it, as with this screen, it's not a bad thing.

That out of the way, let's look at the code.

```
export default class AboutScreen extends React.Component {

  constructor(inProps) {
    super(inProps);
  }

  render() {

    return (
      <View style={styles.outerContainer}>
        <View style={styles.spacer} />
        <View style={styles.textContainer}>
          <Text style={styles.textTitle}>RNTrivia (React Native Trivia)</Text>
        </View>
        <View style={styles.textContainer}>
          <Text style={styles.textVersion}>v1.0</Text>
        </View>
        <View style={styles.textContainer}>
          <Text style={styles.textSource}>Published in the Apress book</Text>
          <Text style={styles.textSource}>Practical React Native Projects</Text>
          <Text style={styles.textSource}>in 2018</Text>
        </View>
        <View style={styles.textContainer}>
          <Text style={styles.textAuthor}>By Frank W. Zammetti</Text>
        </View>
        <View style={styles.spacer} />
      </View>
    );

  }

}
```

Yep, as promised, it's little more than an outer container View with six child View components. Except for the first and last one, which are the spacer Views, each has one or more Y components inside it. All the information shown is hard-coded. Nothing here needs to be in state, so it's about as clean-cut as you can get. This screen doesn't even have to be connected, so this is the full extent of the code this time.

InfoScreen.js

Next up is the InfoScreen, shown in Figure 6-4 and housed in the InfoScreen.js file, naturally enough.

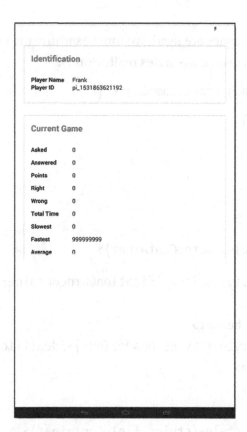

Identification

| Player Name | Frank |
| Player ID | pi_1531863621192 |

Current Game

Asked	0
Answered	0
Points	0
Right	0
Wrong	0
Total Time	0
Slowest	0
Fastest	999999999
Average	0

Figure 6-4. *The game info screen*

This is another rather simple one, like the AboutScreen, starting with a StyleSheet, as always.

```
const styles = StyleSheet.create({
  outerContainer :
    { justifyContent : "center", marginTop : 50, marginLeft : 20,
    marginRight : 20 },
  identificationCardContainer : { height : 150, marginBottom : 20 },
  currentGameCardContainer : { height : 360 },
```

```
  headerText : { fontWeight : "bold", fontSize : 20, color : "red" },
  fieldContainer : { flexDirection : "row" },
  fieldLabel : { width : 100, fontWeight : "bold" },
  fieldSpacing : { marginBottom : 12 }
});
```

And, to see how these styles are used, we must examine the component code (which has a few new things in it, even if the styles really don't).

```
class InfoScreen extends React.Component {

  constructor(inProps) {
    super(inProps);
  }

  render() {

    return (
      <View style={styles.outerContainer}>

        <View style={styles.identificationCardContainer}>
          <Card>
            <CardItem header>
              <Text style={styles.headerText}>Identification</Text>
            </CardItem>
            <CardItem>
              <Body>
                <View style={styles.fieldContainer}>
                  <Text style={styles.fieldLabel}>Player Name</Text>
                  <Text>{this.props.playerName}</Text>
                </View>
                <View style={styles.fieldContainer}>
                  <Text style={styles.fieldLabel}>Player ID</Text>
                  <Text>{this.props.playerID}</Text>
                </View>
              </Body>
            </CardItem>
          </Card>
        </View>
```

Rather than dump all the code in one big listing, I'll break it up a bit, pausing here, so I can talk about what's new. NativeBase, as you've seen, provides many slick components on top of what React Native offers out of the box. Some of them take inspiration from one mobile platform or another, although they work across all platforms. On this modal, we have something taken from the Android playbook: the Card component.

The Card metaphor is common on Android as a way to delineate one set of content from another. Ultimately, it's just a robust container for content; it doesn't do anything on its own. The NativeBase Card component is a flexible and extensible content container that includes options for headers and footers, a wide variety of content (virtually anything, in fact), contextual background colors (optionally), and a robust set of display options.

However, all that said, in its purest form, it's mainly just a box, but a box with a shadow, so that it stands off the screen a little, and it also ensures proper spacing between other cards, if any, without you having to account for it. That's all without using any options available to it, which is how it's used in RNTrivia on this screen.

It all starts with a Card component, and nested inside of it will be at least one CardItem components. If there is only one CardItem, then it's the content for the Card. If there is more than one, then one of them should have the header prop on it, making it the header element. Likewise, you can have a CardItem with the footer prop, making it the footer. You can still put virtually any content you like in a header or footer CardItem, but the card component will render them on the top and bottom, respectively, befitting their names.

As you can see from this first Card, which is the identification card, we have information that identifies the player, his/her playerName, and playerID. Each is contained in a View with the fieldContainer style applied to activate a row-based flex layout, so that the two Text components, one for the field label and one for the value, are displayed next to each other. The value Text components reference some props (playerName and playerID) that are added to the component via a mapStateToProps() function, so the values from the Redux state store are what is shown in them.

Now, I can talk about the rest of the code, which really is just a repeat of what was just explained, with a few more fields involved.

```
<View style={styles.currentGameCardContainer}>
  <Card>
    <CardItem header>
      <Text style={styles.headerText}>Current Game</Text>
```

```
        </CardItem>
        <CardItem>
          <Body>
            <View style={[ styles.fieldContainer, styles.fieldSpacing ]}>
              <Text style={styles.fieldLabel}>Asked</Text>
              <Text>{this.props.asked}</Text>
            </View>
            <View style={[ styles.fieldContainer, styles.fieldSpacing ]}>
              <Text style={styles.fieldLabel}>Answered</Text>
              <Text>{this.props.answered}</Text>
            </View>
            <View style={[ styles.fieldContainer, styles.fieldSpacing ]}>
              <Text style={styles.fieldLabel}>Points</Text>
              <Text>{this.props.points}</Text>
            </View>
            <View style={[ styles.fieldContainer, styles.fieldSpacing ]}>
              <Text style={styles.fieldLabel}>Right</Text>
              <Text>{this.props.right}</Text>
            </View>
            <View style={[ styles.fieldContainer, styles.fieldSpacing ]}>
              <Text style={styles.fieldLabel}>Wrong</Text>
              <Text>{this.props.wrong}</Text>
            </View>
            <View style={[ styles.fieldContainer, styles.fieldSpacing ]}>
              <Text style={styles.fieldLabel}>Total Time</Text>
              <Text>{this.props.totalTime}</Text>
            </View>
            <View style={[ styles.fieldContainer, styles.fieldSpacing ]}>
              <Text style={styles.fieldLabel}>Slowest</Text>
              <Text>{this.props.slowest}</Text>
            </View>
            <View style={[ styles.fieldContainer, styles.fieldSpacing ]}>
              <Text style={styles.fieldLabel}>Fastest</Text>
              <Text>{this.props.fastest}</Text>
            </View>
```

```
      <View style={ styles.fieldContainer }>
        <Text style={styles.fieldLabel}>Average</Text>
        <Text>{this.props.average}</Text>
      </View>
    </Body>
  </CardItem>
</Card>
</View>

</View>
);

}

}
```

See? It's just another Card, this time, with nine fields, all data that comes from the gameData branch of the state tree and conveys to the user information about the current game.

Note how multiple styles are applied to the field containers, the fieldContainer style, as expected, and also the fieldSpacing style on all but the last one. Look at the fieldSpacing style. It just has a marginBottom specification. So, applying it to each field gives us some space between the fields, but, of course, that's not necessary on the last field.

This component is also connected, so it has a mapStateToProps() function and uses the connect() function. The prop mappings are playerName maps to playerInfo.name, playerID maps to playerInfo.id, asked maps to gameData.asked, answered maps to gameData.answered, points maps to gameData.points, right maps to gameData.right, wrong maps to gameData.wrong, totalTime maps to gameData.totalTime, slowest maps to gameData.slowest, fastest maps to gameData.fastest, and average maps to gameData.average.

GameScreen.js

Now it's time to move on to the last of the three screens, which, you'll recall, is made up of three sub-screens, so to speak. The GameScreen.js is the parent of those three, however, and the source found there is extremely tiny.

```
export default createSwitchNavigator(
  {
    GameHomeScreen : { screen : GameHomeScreen },
    GameLeaderboardScreen : { screen : GameLeaderboardScreen },
    GameQuestionScreen : { screen : GameQuestionScreen }
  },
  { headerMode : "none", initialRouteName : "GameHomeScreen" }
);
```

Here, we encounter a new React Navigation navigator. The SwitchNavigator is in most respects just like the StackNavigator, in that it's for managing a collection of screens where only one is visible at a time. The primary difference between the two is that with StackNavigator, every transition to a new screen places that screen on the top of the stack, but the history of how the user navigated through the screens is maintained. That way, they can go back easily by the StackNavigator internally, just popping each screen off the stack. Of course, if you disable the back button, as I did in Restaurant Chooser, the difference between the two becomes basically nothing. The SwitchNavigator doesn't maintain a stack like that, so there is no navigation history to back through.

Aside from that difference, they function the same and, more important, are configured the same, as the code here should indicate, because it looks almost identical to the configuration of the StackNavigator in Restaurant Chooser. Note that the initialRouteName specifies that the GameHomeScreen, one of the three sub-screens, is the one initially shown, and that's the code up next for review.

GameScreen-Home.js

The GameHomeScreen in the GameScreen-Home.js file is a very simple screen that is just a logo, a landing pad, if you will, for the user, when the app first starts up (if a game is in progress, however, they will immediately be navigated to the leaderboard screen, but that's for a little later). The code begins with a single style.

```
const styles = StyleSheet.create({
  outerContainer : { flex : 1, alignItems : "center", justifyContent :
  "center" }
});
```

The only goal is to ensure that the children of the container this style is applied to are centered both vertically and horizontally and, as has become our custom, that this container fills the screen.

The component code after that is straightforward.

```
export default class GameHomeScreen extends React.Component {

  constructor(inProps) {
    super(inProps);
    CoreCode.mainNavigator = inProps.navigation;
  }

  render() {
    return (
      <View style={styles.outerContainer}>
        <Image source={require("../../images/logo.png")} />
      </View>
    );
  }

}
```

In the constructor, aside from the usual super(), we have something that we'll need later, namely, storing a reference to the navigator managing this screen. This will become important when the code has to navigate from one screen to another automatically. This is only possible if you have a reference to the navigator, but you just have a reference to the navigator from within the component code, because it's automatically passed as the navigation prop by React Navigation. So, a reference to it is stored on the CoreCode object, which will be the last bit of code we look at in this chapter, thus making it available outside of the component code, which is precisely what it needed, as you'll see.

Aside from that, as stated earlier, this screen is merely a logo inside a View container, with the outerContainer style applied. Don't you just love when the code *actually* turns out to be as simple as the explanation of it says it will be? I know I do.

GameScreen-Leaderboard.js

The leaderboard screen, found in the GameScreen-Leaderboard.js file, is the second of the three game screen sub-screens, and it kicks off with a StyleSheet, as usual.

```
const styles = StyleSheet.create({
  outerContainer :
    { flex : 1, alignItems : "stretch", justifyContent : "center",
    marginTop : 50 },
  headingContainer : { height : 150, justifyContent : "center", alignSelf :
  "center" },
  headingText : { fontSize : 34, fontWeight : "bold" },
  listContainer : { flex : .6, marginLeft : 20, marginRight : 20,
  marginBottom : 40,
    borderColor : "silver", borderWidth : 2, padding : 10 },
  awaitingQuestionContainer : { flex : .4 },
  awaitingQuestionWebView : { backgroundColor : "transparent" }
});
```

The overall structure of this screen is that there are three main sections: the header section, the list section (where the leaderboard itself is displayed), and a section with some text that tells the player that he or she is awaiting a question. That's where headingContainer, listContainer, and awaitingQuestionContainer styles come into play, as those are the styles for the container View components of those three sections, and you can see that their flex values add up to 1 (with headingContainer having a static height). The awaitingQuestionWebView with backgroundColor set to transparent is something I'll come back to after we look at the component code (again, because I think it'll make more sense putting it in this order).

There's a chunk of code that comes after the StyleSheet and before the component code, but I'm going to come back to that, because I think it'll make more sense if you see the component code first.

```
class GameLeaderboardScreen extends React.Component {

  constructor(inProps) {
    super(inProps);
  }

  render() {
```

```
  return (
    <View style={styles.outerContainer}>
      <View style={styles.headingContainer}>
        <Text style={styles.headingText}>Current Leaderboard</Text>
      </View>
      <View style={styles.listContainer}>
        <FlatList
          data={this.props.listData}
          keyExtractor={ (inItem) => inItem.playerID }
          renderItem={ ({item}) => {
            return (
              <View style={{ flex : 1, flexDirection : "row" }}>
                <View style={{ flex : .6 }}>
                  <Text style={{ fontSize : 20 }}>{item.playerName}
                    {store.getState().playerInfo.id === item.playerID ? "
                    (YOU)" : ""}</Text>
                </View>
                <View style={{ flex : .4 }}>
                  <Text style={{ fontSize : 20 }}>{item.points} points</Text>
                </View>
              </View>
            );
          } }
        />
      </View>
      <View style={styles.awaitingQuestionContainer}>
        <WebView
          style={styles.awaitingQuestionWebView}
          source={{ html : awaitingQuestionHTML }}
        />
      </View>
    </View>
  );
}
}
```

Okay, so we see the outer View with the outerContainer style applied, as usual. Then we have a View with headingContainer applied, so that's the first of the three sections, and inside it is a Text component with headingText applied. Simple so far.

After that is a View container for the FlatList that is the leaderboard itself. The data comes from our Redux store, transferred into the listData prop by the mapStateToProps() function that comes later. Note that the keyExtractor prop is used and employs the playerID as the unique key for each item in the list, which avoids React Native yelling at us about missing keys, even though we don't need keys here. The renderItem prop renders a View that stretches across the screen for each item in the list, and inside that View are two more View components, one for the player's name and one for their current points. If the player happens to be you, as one of them obviously will be, then the "(You)" text is appended to the player's name. Note how store.getState().playerInfo.id is referenced directly to do this check. I did it this way just to show that you can, but, in practice, it would be better form to map that to a prop and access it that way.

After the list, we have the third of the three View containers, this one containing a WebView component. This component is one we can use to display arbitrary HTML, and the reason it's used here is so that I can show the message to the user, telling her she is awaiting a question and have it spinning. With a WebView, you can load content from the network, or off the file system, or you can feed HTML into it directly, as is done here, and the HTML fed in is this:

```
const awaitingQuestionHTML = `
<style>${awaitingQuestionSpinStyles}</style>
<div class="spinText">Awaiting Question</div>
`;
```

As you can see, it's really just an HTML fragment, a <style> section that has the awaitingQuestionSpinStyles inserted into it using string interpolation, and then a <div> with the actual text in it and the spinText style class applied. That style class is this:

```
const awaitingQuestionSpinStyles = `
.spinText {
  animation-name : spin, depth;
  animation-timing-function : linear;
  animation-iteration-count : infinite;
  animation-duration : 3s;
  text-align : center;
```

```
      font-weight : bold;
      color : red;
      font-size : 24pt;
      padding-top : 100px;
    }
@keyframes spin {
    from { transform : rotateY(0deg); }
    to { transform : rotateY(-360deg); }
}
@keyframes depth {
    0 { text-shadow : 0 0 black; }
    25% { text-shadow : 1px 0 black, 2px 0 black, 3px 0 black, 4px 0 black,
    5px 0 black; }
    50% { text-shadow : 0 0 black; }
    75% { text-shadow : -1px 0 black, -2px 0 black, -3px 0 black, -4px 0
    black, -5px 0 black; }
    100% { text-shadow : 0 0 black; }
}
`;
```

The result of all of this is that you have a WebView, with the awaitingQuestionWebView
style applied, thus making its background transparent, which effectively means that
all you'll see is the content inside of it. (Without that style applied, the WebView would
occlude what's underneath it, which looks ugly and not at all seamless.) Then the HTML
displayed inside it uses some CSS animation and transformations to spin the text.

This may not be the only way to have accomplished this, possibly not even the best,
but it does demonstrate how you can use the WebView component in an interesting way.
If you're ever working with React Native and feel like what you're trying to accomplish
is giving you trouble, but that it would be easy to do in plain HTML, this is one way you
can go right ahead and mix plain HTML into your app and open up the full power of
HTML and CSS. Of course, you have to remember that anything you do there is necessarily
a separate view, sort of like an <iframe> tag in HTML, so you have to recognize the
limitations (such things as the content within the WebView not being aware of React Native
and vice-versa) and, as always, performance. But, for something like this, it works great.

This component is also connected, so it has a mapStateToProps() function and uses the connect() function. The prop mappings are listData maps to leaderboard. listData and, actually, that's it for this component.

GameScreen-Question.js

The last of the three game screen sub-screens is the question screen, where the player sees the current question and answers it. This code is housed in the GameScreen-Question.js file and begins with a StyleSheet definition.

```
const styles = StyleSheet.create({
  outerContainer : { flex : 1, alignItems : "stretch", justifyContent : "center",
    marginTop : 50, marginLeft : 20, marginRight : 20 },
  questionContainer : { flex : .2, justifyContent : "center", alignSelf :
  "center" },
  answerButtonsContainer : { flex : .8, alignItems : "center", justifyContent :
  "center" },
  submitButtonContainer : { justifyContent : "center", height : 140 },
  question : { fontWeight : "bold", fontSize : 26, color : "red", textAlign :
  "center" },
  answerButton : { marginTop : 20 },
  buttonText : { fontWeight : "bold", color : "white" }
});
```

On this screen, we've got three main sections: the View where the question is shown (styled with questionContainer), the View where the six answer buttons are (styled with answerButtonsContainer), and the Submit Answer at the bottom (styled with submitButtonContainer). The first two View containers use a flex of .2 and .8, respectively, with the container for the button being a static height.

Now for the component code, and I'm going to break this up a bit to better explain it, beginning with this:

```
class GameQuestionScreen extends React.Component {

  constructor(inProps) {
    super(inProps);
  }

  render() {
```

```
return (
  <View style={styles.outerContainer}>
    <View style={styles.questionContainer}>
      <RNText style={styles.question}>{this.props.question}</RNText>
    </View>
    <View style={styles.answerButtonsContainer}>
      <Button
        full
        style={styles.answerButton}
        primary={this.props.answerButtonPrimary[0]}
        danger={this.props.answerButtonDanger[0]}
        onPress={ () => { store.dispatch(answerButtonHighlight(0)) } }>
        <Text style={styles.buttonText}>
          {this.props.answerButtonLabels[0]}
        </Text>
      </Button>
      ...
```

First up is the View with outerContainer applied, as always. Inside it is the View for the question. Note that RNText is used. As mentioned earlier, this is just a React Native Text component, but because this component is also going to use the NativeBase Text component, there would be a name conflict if one wasn't aliased, so I chose to alias the React Native version for no particular reason. The question, of course, is stored in the question prop, mapped from the state store.

After the question View is the View that contains the six answer buttons, and I've cut out the other five, because they're identical to this first one, except for the array indexes used (they just go up by one with each button) and the argument passed to the answerButtonHighlight() action function. Each button, which is a NativeBase Button, not a React Native Button (because the NativeBase version provides some useful additional features), uses the full prop, to ensure that the button stretches across its parent, which, in this case, makes it spread across the screen. Each button has the answerButton style applied, which puts some space above each button, to keep it separated nicely.

Now it gets interesting. Each button has a primary and a danger prop. Those props determine the look of the button. When primary is true, the button has a blue background. When danger is true, the button has a red background. Note how the values for those props come from the answerButtonPrimary and answerButtonDanger props, which you saw are arrays in state that these props map to. The reason this is done is that when the user taps one of the buttons, we want that button to be red, while all the others are blue. What that means is that we want all the elements in the answerButtonPrimary array to be true, and all but the one associated with the tapped button to be false, in the answerButtonDanger array. Because these props are tied to state, it means that when we alter the values in state, the look of the buttons on the screen will change. You can see that the onPress prop dispatches a message that you can presume alters the arrays according to that logic, and you'll see that later in the section on the CoreCode.

The Text components inside the Button components are NativeBase Text components this time, and the reason they are used rather than the React Native Text components is that the NativeBase documentation says we should always use this component with the Button component. (No reason is given for this in the documentation, but who am I to argue?)

After the six buttons is the Submit Answer button.

```
<View style={styles.submitButtonContainer}>
  <Button
    block
    success
    onPress={
      () => {
        if (store.getState().question.selectedAnswer === -1) {
          Alert.alert("D'oh!", "Please select an answer",
            [ { text : "OK" } ], { cancelable : false }
          );
        } else {
          CoreCode.io.emit("submitAnswer", {
            playerID : store.getState().playerInfo.id,
            answer : store.getState().question.answerButtonLabels[
              store.getState().question.selectedAnswer
            ]
          });
```

```
          }
        }
      }
    >
      <Text style={styles.buttonText}>Submit Answer</Text>
    </Button>
  </View>
</View>
);

  }

}
```

For this one, I used the `block` prop, to give the button a slightly different look than the answer buttons, and the `success` prop, to make the button green. The `onPress` handler first checks to see if the `question.selectedAnswer` state attribute, which will be set as part of the `dispatch()` call in the answer button `onPress` handlers, has a value other than -1, which is our "no selected answer" value. If so, an `Alert` message is shown. Otherwise, the `submitAnswer` message is emitted to the server, to indicate the selected answer. The `playerID` is sent to the server, along with the selected answer, and note that it's the textual answer itself that is sent, not the number stored in `selectedAnswer`, so we get that via the `question.answerButtonLabels` array in state.

This component is also connected, so it has a `mapStateToProps()` function and uses the `connect()` function. The prop mappings are `answerButtonPrimary` maps to `question.answerButtonPrimary`, `answerButtonDanger` maps to `question.answerButtonDanger`, `answerButtonLabels` maps to `question.answerButtonLabel`, and `question` maps to `question.currentQuestion`.

Getting Down to the Core of Things: CoreCode.js

Let's talk architecture for a moment. When I started writing this app, it quickly became apparent that there would be some code that shouldn't (or perhaps even couldn't) live inside individual React Native components. I had a choice to make: do I put all the code in some common place and just have the components call it, or do I spread the love around a bit, having some in a central location and some in the components?

261

For example, when I have a `Button` component, it's going to have an `onPress` event handler. (Otherwise, it's not much of a `Button`, is it?) Where does the code that gets executed in response to that event go? So far, you've seen it go directly into the component, "inlined" with the `onPress` prop, in other words. Some developers say this is precisely the right place for it, because React Native, like React, is component-based, and components are supposed to be self-contained, stand-alone things. Other developers say that you should be trying to separate your presentation code from your action code, so, instead, you should have some object that has a method, and then the `onPress` prop references that method.

There's a middle ground that says that because a component is a JavaScript module, you should put a "naked" function in the same source file, but not inline with the component markup, and reference it in the component markup. The point is that all these approaches work and have pluses and minuses. A central location gives you that clean separation that, before the world of components, was something to strive for. Now that we're in a world of components, maybe that's no longer a valid goal. Isn't architecture fun?

Ultimately, however, the way I organized the code is based on the understanding that, conceptually, there are two types of code: code that responds to user interaction and code that doesn't. It's a bit of an oversimplification, and some cases will straddle the line, certainly, but as an overarching design principle, it works. Given that principle, the decision becomes relatively easy. Any code that represents a user interaction goes into the component code (and, as a rule, I *tend* to prefer it be inline with the component markup, *unless* I know it's code that will be shared, in which case, I'll make it a stand-alone function within the module). Any code that I can't classify as a user interaction will go into a central object that I call `CoreCode`.

This `CoreCode` object is just a JavaScript object, and since I know that there will always be just one canonical instance of it, I use the singleton approach, rather than making it a class. It begins, innocently enough, with some properties.

```
const CoreCode = {

  serverIP : "127.0.0.1",
  io : null,
  mainNavigator : null,
```

The serverIP is the IP address of the server. You'll want to update this for your environment appropriately (and the 127.0.0.1 loopback address won't work, unless you somehow get the React Native app to run on the same machine natively, which, if you figure out how to do that, let me know 'cause it would be *awesome*). The io property is a reference to the socket.io client object, and that will get created later. The mainNavigator is the reference to the main navigator for the app, and you saw this reference get populated in the constructor of the game screen's home sub-screen.

The first function we run into in this object is startup(), which, you'll recall, is the function referenced by the onPress prop of the Button on the NamePromptModal. (So, here's one example of where I, in a sense, broke my own organization rules, but only because this is one case in which the code really did straddle the line.)

```
startup : () => {
  if (!store.getState().modals.isAdmin &&
    (store.getState().playerInfo.name == null ||
    store.getState().playerInfo.name.trim() === "" ||
    store.getState().playerInfo.name.length === 1)
  ) {
    return;
  }
  store.dispatch(showHideModal("namePrompt", false));
  CoreCode.io = io(`http://${CoreCode.serverIP}`);
  if (store.getState().modals.isAdmin) {
    CoreCode.io.on("connected", function() { console.log("ADMIN CONNECTED"); });
    CoreCode.io.on("adminMessage", CoreCode.adminMessage);
    store.dispatch(showHideModal("admin", true));
  } else {
    CoreCode.io.on("connected", CoreCode.connected);
    CoreCode.io.on("validatePlayer", CoreCode.validatePlayer);
    CoreCode.io.on("newGame", CoreCode.newGame);
    CoreCode.io.on("nextQuestion", CoreCode.nextQuestion);
    CoreCode.io.on("answerOutcome", CoreCode.answerOutcome);
    CoreCode.io.on("endGame", CoreCode.endGame);
  }
},
```

The job here is, first, to make sure, if the user didn't indicate he or she is the admin that they entered a name and that it's more than one character long. Ed was about the shortest real name I could think of, so, if anyone looking at this happens to have a name that's only one letter long, I apologize, but I'm going to have to see your birth certificate before I believe it.

Once that confirmation is done, the NamePromptModal is hidden, by dispatching the message returned by the showHideModal() action function.

With that out of the way, it's time create the socket.io object referenced by the io property. That requires the serverIP address from before, and note that you must specify the protocol as well, making this a proper URL, or the connection won't work. Once that object is created, it's time to hook up message handler functions, but which ones get hooked up depends on whether the user is an admin or not. If she is, then the only concerns are the connected message and the adminMessage. For players, the code will have to respond to connected, validatePlayer, newGame, nextQuestion, answerOutcome, and endGame messages. All the handler functions are just methods of the CoreCode object, so the remainder of this section will be looking at those functions, starting with connected.

```
connected : function(inData) {
  CoreCode.io.emit("validatePlayer", {
    playerName : store.getState().playerInfo.name
  });
},
```

Once the client and server connect, the server emits the connected message, at which point the client emits the validatePlayer message, passing the server the player's name. The server then does the validation, as you saw in the last chapter, and emits the validatePlayer message to the client, which is handled like this:

```
validatePlayer : function(inData) {
  store.dispatch(setPlayerID(inData.playerID));
  if (inData.inProgress) {
    inData.gameData.asked = inData.asked;
    store.dispatch(setGameData(inData.gameData));
    store.dispatch(updateLeadboard(inData.leaderboard));
    CoreCode.mainNavigator.navigate("GameLeaderboardScreen");
  }
},
```

First, the playerID returned by the server is stored in state, and then a check is done, whether a game is in progress. If no game is in progress, the user would currently be seeing the game ➤ home screen, waiting for a new game to start. (Remember: That's the default route for the SwitchNavigator, which is why it's visible at this point.) If a game is in progress, the count of asked questions is transferred into the gameData object on the inData object, because we'll need it there for display on the info screen, but it won't be there at this point, and the game data is dispatched to the store, as is the current leaderboard data that the server will have sent. Finally, you can see why getting a reference to the main navigator was necessary: so that a call to navigate() can be made, sending the user to the game ➤ leaderboard screen.

At this point, the app is in whatever starting state it needs to be. The rest of the message handler functions deal with the other messages that can come at any time, beginning with the newGame message handler.

```
newGame : function(inData) {
  store.dispatch(showHideModal("endGame", false));
  inData.gameData.asked = inData.asked;
  store.dispatch(setGameData(inData.gameData));
  store.dispatch(updateLeadboard(inData.leaderboard));
  CoreCode.mainNavigator.navigate("GameLeaderboardScreen");
},
```

When a new game starts, we know that the user is either on the game ➤ home screen or the game ➤ leaderboard screen, and if she's on the latter, the end game modal might be showing. So, we first dispatch a state update to hide that modal. Next, the count of asked gets transferred, as was done in validatePlayer (although we know it's going to be zero in this case). Then we have to set the game data and starting leaderboard data in the store, so two dispatch() calls take care of that. Finally, the game ➤ leaderboard screen has to be shown. A call to navigate() on the mainNavigator reference is done to accomplish that. The user is now where she needs to be, with state all nice and fresh, awaiting a question.

When the admin indicates that it's time for a new question, the server emits the nextQuestion message, which is handled by this method:

```
nextQuestion : function(inData) {
  store.dispatch(answerButtonHighlight(-1));
  store.dispatch(setQuestion(inData.question));
```

```
for (let i = 0; i < 6; i++) {
  store.dispatch(updateAnswerButtonLabel(i, inData.answers[i]));
}
store.dispatch(resetAllButtons());
CoreCode.mainNavigator.navigate("GameQuestionScreen");
},
```

When this message is received, the app has to display the question and the six possible answers, and it also has to ensure that the state of the buttons is set correctly (meaning none is highlighted). Then the game ➤ question screen has to be shown. So, we begin by dispatching two updates to state, the first using the answerButtonHighlight() action function and passing it a value of -1. As you saw earlier, that's a special value that tells the reducer that no button should be highlighted, so it takes care of setting all the answerButtonPrimary array elements to true and all those in the answerButtonDanger array to false. Then the labels for each of the buttons is updated. This requires dispatching the updateAnswerButtonLabel() action, sending it the index of the button to update and the label to give it. After that, the resetAllButtons() action is dispatched. This will, if you're paying attention, seem very odd, because if you compare what the reducers associated with these actions do, you'll see that they're essentially the same. The problem I encountered is that the labels on the buttons would not update on the screen, unless I updated the type of all the buttons a second time. Honestly, I'm not sure why this is, and it may well just be a bug in NativeBase. The simple answer is just to do it twice, but rather than use answerButtonHighlight() again, I thought it made more sense to create a separate action for it. That way, if an update causes it to work as I expected it to in the first place, I can just remove this hack-y dispatch action and associated case in the reducer and not touch anything else.

In any case, the next message the code has to handle is the answerOutcome message, which the server emits after the client sends his answer to the current question.

```
answerOutcome : function(inData) {
  let msg = "Sorry!  That's not correct :(";
  let type = "danger";
  if (inData.correct) {
    msg = "Hooray!  You got it right :)";
    type = "success";
  }
```

```
    inData.gameData.asked = inData.asked;
    store.dispatch(setGameData(inData.gameData));
    store.dispatch(updateLeadboard(inData.leaderboard));
    CoreCode.mainNavigator.navigate("GameLeaderboardScreen");
    Toast.show({ text: msg, buttonText : "Ok", type : type, duration : 3000
});
    Vibration.vibrate(1000);
  },
```

It begins by assuming the user got it wrong, because good code tends to be pessimistic. But then, if inData.correct comes back from the server true, the message is changed, as is the type. As with all the other messages, asked is copied over into the gameData, and the game data (shown on the info screen) and the leaderboard data (shown on the game ➤ leaderboard screen) are dispatched to the store. Then the game ➤ leaderboard screen is navigated to. Next, the Toast component from NativeBase is used, to show a toast message with the right or wrong message and employing the type to make it either green (correct) or red (wrong). Finally, the React Native Vibration API is used to vibrate the device.

We're down to only two methods left to examine, and only one more related to players, and that's the very next one, associated with the endGame message.

```
endGame : function(inData) {
  inData.gameData.asked = inData.asked;
  store.dispatch(setGameData(inData.gameData));
  store.dispatch(updateLeadboard(inData.leaderboard));
  CoreCode.mainNavigator.navigate("GameLeaderboardScreen");
  if (inData.leaderboard[0].playerID === store.getState().playerInfo.id) {
    store.dispatch(setEndGameMessage("Congratulations! You were the
    winner!"));
    store.dispatch(showHideModal("endGame", true));
  } else {
    let place = "";
    let index = inData.leaderboard.findIndex((inPlayer) =>
      inPlayer.playerID === CoreCode.playerID);
    index++;
    const j = index % 10;
```

```
        const k = index % 100;
        if (j === 1 && k !== 11) {
          place = `${index}st`;
        } else if (j === 2 && k !== 12) {
          place = `${index}nd`;
        } else if (j === 3 && k !== 13) {
          place = `${index}rd`;
        } else {
          place = `${index}th`;
        }
        store.dispatch(setEndGameMessage(
          `Sorry, you didn't win. You finished in ${place} place.`)
        );
        store.dispatch(showHideModal("endGame", true));
      }
    },
```

When the game ends, we have two primary tasks: show the final game data and leaderboard and tell the user if he won (and if not, what position he finished in). The first four lines are just like what you've seen in previous handlers, culminating in the user being navigated to the game ➤ leaderboard screen with the final leaderboard data shown. After that, we see if the first player in the leaderboard data is the current player, based on ID. If so, we show the EndGameModal, with an appropriate congratulations message in it.

If a player didn't win, then we have to show him a message saying what place he finished in. His index in the array is his finishing position, and based on that, we want to attach a suitable suffix, either "st," "nd," "rd," or "th," whichever is appropriate for the value. When that's determined, the EndGameModal is shown, but with the "sorry" message this time.

With all the player-related message handlers examined, there's only a single method on the CoreCode object, and it's for handling the adminMessage message.

```
adminMessage : function(inData) {
  store.dispatch(setCurrentStatus(inData.msg));
}
```

Yep, that's it! The message returned by the server gets dispatched to the store, where it's used as the value of the `Text` component at the bottom of the `AdminModal`.

And with that, we've completed our dissection of the second of the three apps. I hope you learned a lot from this one and had some fun doing so.

Summary

In this chapter, and in Chapter 5, we built a neat little app together that demonstrated several new concepts, including platform switching; a few new components from React Native, NativeBase, and React Navigation; state management with Redux; and, of course, communicating with a server in real time.

Although I used the word *game* quite a lot throughout these two chapters, I don't consider this app a game, per se, even though it is supposed to be fun to use. That said, React Native is perfectly suited for writing actual games, and that's what the next two chapters will cover. Get ready 'cause fun time is coming!

CHAPTER 7

Time for Some Fun: A React Native Game, Part 1

Writing books isn't my day job. My regular job is as an architect (who, thankfully, still gets to hack code a lot) for a large financial firm, and in that capacity, I also do a lot of mentoring of more junior developers. In that role, every so often, I am asked by developers what they can do to improve their skills. My answer is always immediate: make a game! Game programming is, I've found, a unique endeavor, because it forces you to confront so many different problems, and it touches on a great many computer science topics, many in subtle ways that you don't even realize at first. I've found that few other types of projects are as good an educational experience as game programming, and that's why I think all developers should make games.

Plus, games are, by their nature, fun. That's the goal of a game, after all, and making a game tends, likewise, to be fun (even when the inevitable frustrations of things not working as expected come up). Now, in the previous chapter, we did, in a sense, make a game. However, I would argue that it wasn't a game, per se (that certainly wasn't the objective when I wrote the original Webix version); it was more of an app that happened to have an element of fun to it.

In this chapter and the next, however, we're going to create a straight-up game with React Native. In the process, we'll have to confront some new problems and find some interesting solutions to them that will offer insights into React Native that you may not have gained in developing more traditional apps. Part of game programming tends to be finding ingenious solutions to problems, to make things work just the way you want, and that's no less true when making a game with React Native, which offers you the opportunity to see things a little differently than you have to this point.

© Frank Zammetti 2018
F. Zammetti, *Practical React Native*, https://doi.org/10.1007/978-1-4842-3939-1_7

So, let's jump right in and talk about what kind of game we're going to build. Make no mistake, this won't be the next Fortnite or Halo or Angry Birds. It's not going to make anyone a million bucks on the app store, but, as a learning experience, it'll get the job done.

What Are We Building?

As a kid, did you ever have one of those sliding puzzle games? You know, a plastic square with a bunch of numbered plastic tiles on it that you can slide around, the goal being to put the tiles in order. Well, that, in a nutshell, is what we'll be building. In Figure 7-1, you can see what it looks like. It's not a complex concept, to be sure, but it's a proper game nonetheless.

Figure 7-1. *The FunTime game*

Playing is as easy as can be: the player taps a tile, and if it's beside the blank space, the tile slides into the blank space. That's literally it for game mechanics. If and when the player gets all the tiles into the right order, he or she will be rewarded, such as it is, with some pretty colors. I'll show you the You Won! screen later, when we're looking at the code for it. But, of course, if you're reading this in a physical book, you won't see the colors, so I recommend grabbing the download bundle for this book, building the app, and playing it for a few minutes, to see it for yourself (assuming you can solve the puzzle, that is).

There will also be a "control" menu that will give the player some options, including the ability to start a new game and the ability to control the number of tiles on the board. This will allow the player to increase the difficulty, by having more tiles to try and put in order. A bit later, I'll show you this screen as well, when we're looking at the code for it.

As I said, this is by no means a complicated game, but you'll find that some new concepts and interesting approaches are present in the related code. Before we look at that code, however, let's talk about overall structure and architecture, because this app is a little bit different.

Directory and Code Structure

With this project, I took a somewhat different approach than with the previous two apps. I wouldn't say it's better or worse, just different. The directory structure you see in Figure 7-2 begins to hint at this structure.

```
FunTime

    .babelrc
    .gitignore
    .watchmanconfig
    App.js
    app.json
    FunTime.iml
    package-lock.json
    package.json
    README.md
    state.js

├──functions
        alterMatrixSize.js
        buildMatrix.js
        determineOutcome.js
        generateSolvableLayout.js
        tilePress.js

└──images
        appIcon.png
        splash.png
        won.png
```

Figure 7-2. *The FunTime directory structure*

By this point, I would hope I could ignore the boilerplate, generated files, and directories that React Native and Expo introduce when scaffolding out the skeleton app, so let's talk about what's specific to this app.

First, you'll see two directories, one new and one you've seen before. The image directory is again where any images the app requires are put. For this app, it might surprise you to learn that there's only a single image required: won.png. This is a background image that the player will see if and when he or she wins the game. It's just a large color gradient with the words *You Won!* over it. We'll come back to that later.

The other directory is named functions, and it's precisely what the name implies: a directory in which you'll find JavaScript functions. Each of the JavaScript files you see in this directory houses one complete function that is needed for the game. These are

- alterMatrixSize.js: This will be used from the control menu when the player wants to alter the size of the tile matrix, meaning how many tiles there are to move around.

- `buildMatrix.js`: This contains the function that is responsible for drawing the tiles on the screen.

- `determineOutcome.js`: Anytime a tile is moved, some code has to check to see if the tiles are now in order and the player won. That function is here.

- `generateSolvableLayout.js`: As you'll learn later, there's more to a sliding puzzle game then just randomly putting the tiles anywhere to start. This function ensures that the random layout at the start is solvable and won't lead to a dead-end game.

- `tilePress.js`: I'm sure you're guessing that this is a function that will be called anytime the player taps on a tile, and you're right about that.

We will be looking at each of these functions in turn, but why break it down this way? Why have individual functions in their own source files? The reason is that, as I built this app, I realized there isn't all that much code that goes into it. Yes, it's *interesting* code, to be sure, but there's not all that much of it. The first thought you may have is to just put it all in one single `App.js` file (which, of course, is here, too, as it's our starting point and where the high-level app structure is built), but then you wind up with a source file that's a little unwieldy. So, do you break it down into components, as we've done before? Well, this app, in a sense, doesn't really require components, or at least not many, and, in fact, because I wanted to demonstrate some other concepts that are easier to show without components, that would have been counterproductive.

So, my thinking was "well, each of these functions represents a discrete unit of work, something I might want to look at in isolation," thus you can make an argument that each should be in its own source file, so that's what I did. To be clear, I'm not presenting this as the right way to do things, just *another* way to do things. I think that being exposed to alternatives is always useful for a developer, and given that games, as I mentioned earlier, often make you think a little outside the box, I figured this structure is in line with that thinking as well.

That's about all there is to the overall structure. It's a pretty straightforward app. So, let's start tearing into that code now and see what makes FunTime tick.

package.json

Beginning, as we generally have thus far, with the package.json file reveals no surprises.

```json
{
  "name": "FunTime",
  "version": "0.1.0",
  "private": true,
  "devDependencies": {
    "jest-expo": "~27.0.0",
    "react-native-scripts": "1.14.0",
    "react-test-renderer": "^16.4.1"
  },
  "main": "./node_modules/react-native-scripts/build/bin/crna-entry.js",
  "scripts": {
    "start": "react-native-scripts start",
    "eject": "react-native-scripts eject",
    "android": "react-native-scripts android",
    "ios": "react-native-scripts ios",
    "test": "jest"
  },
  "jest": {
    "preset": "jest-expo"
  },
  "dependencies": {
    "expo": "^27.1.0",
    "lodash": "*",
    "react": "16.3.1",
    "react-native": "~0.55.2",
    "prop-types": "latest"
  }
}
```

In fact, it's all boilerplate, except for the addition of lodash to the dependencies. This project, aside from lodash, is written with pure React Native and Expo—no React Navigation or NativeBase or anything else.

app.json

The other configuration file, of course, is app.json and, like package.json before it, there are no surprises here either.

```
{
  "expo": {
    "name": "FunTime",
    "description": "A React Native Game",
    "icon": "images/appIcon.png",
    "splash" : {
      "image": "images/splash.png",
      "resizeMode": "cover"
    },
    "version": "1.0.0",
    "slug": "funTime",
    "sdkVersion": "27.0.0",
    "ios": {
      "bundleIdentifier": "com.etherient.funTime"
    },
    "android": {
      "package": "com.etherient.funTime"
    }
  }
}
```

Yep, again, this is all boilerplate and stuff you've seen before. So, let's get to some actual code.

App.js

Our main entry point, as always, is in the App.js file, and the start of it is, of course, our import statements, all but one of which you've seen before.

```
import React from "react";
import { Button, Image, Platform, Slider, Text, View } from "react-native";
import state from "./state";
import { Constants } from "expo";
```

Application State (state.js)

The one new import is state. The short and sweet explanation for this is that I've taken the initial definition of state for the top-level React Native component and moved it out into a separate file. Why? Because I can! And because I'll have to use it a few different times throughout the code. If you look back on our previous projects, or, indeed, in most examples online, you'll see that the object containing state is most typically built up in the constructor of a component. This works well, because you only require that object definition in that one place, so there's no real benefit to externalizing it from the constructor. However, as you'll see here, sometimes you may need it in a few different places in the code. In those cases, it makes sense to pull the object definition out of the constructor. But then you must decide where to put it. If the multiple places you need it happen to be in the same module, you can make it a global in the module. But if it's in multiple modules, you have to think about something such as a global scope (or perhaps Redux, but that seemed like overkill to me in this instance). But, a better option, in my opinion, anyway, is to make state its own module. In this case, that module, which is in the state.js file, looks like this:

```
import { Dimensions } from "react-native";
```

We're going to need the dimensions of the screen later on, so it's imported first.

```
const controlAreaHeight = 80;
```

If you look back on the screenshot of the game, you'll see the Control Menu Button at the top. The controlAreaHeight variable defines how tall the area that button lives in is, a fact for which we'll have to do some sizing calculations later, and because it will be required more than once, it must be a separate variable (or we'd just be repeating a magic value in a few places, both of which are Very Bad Things™). This will be necessary later, as the tiles are built.

```
const { height, width } = Dimensions.get("window");
```

Here, a destructuring assignment is used to get the width and height of the screen into some separate variables.

Next, it's time to define and export the object that contains the state for this application.

```
module.exports = {
  tiles : [],
  numberOfTilesAcross : 3,
```

```
numberOfTilesDown : 3,
screenUsableWidth : width,
screenUsableHeight : height - controlAreaHeight,
refs : {},
virtualTiles : null,
tileWidth : null,
tileHeight : null,
controlAreaHeight : controlAreaHeight,
controlMenuVisible : false,
controlMenuWidth : 380,
controlMenuHeight : 480,
controlMenuButtonDisabled : false,
wonVisible : false,
moveCount : 0,
startTime : new Date().getTime()
};
```

As I said, it's just a plain old JavaScript object, very much like what we'd normally see directly in a constructor of a component. Here's a rundown of what each of the state attributes are:

- tiles: The array of tile View components. Each tile will be its own React Native View component, with some other components inside, as you'll see.

- numberOfTilesAcross: The default number of tiles across the matrix. This will be changeable by the user.

- numberOfTilesDown: The default number of tiles down the matrix. This will be changeable by the user.

- screenUsableWidth: The "usable" space for the tiles across the screen. We'll use this to figure out how wide each tile is.

- screenUsableHeight: The "usable" space for the tiles down the screen (This just leaves some space at the top of the Control Menu Button). We'll use this to determine how tall each tile is.

- refs: References to the individual tile View components. This will take some explanation later, because on the surface, it probably seems like this is redundant, given the tiles attribute, but, trust me, it's not, and we'll get to why before long.

- virtualTiles: The array of virtual tile objects. Like refs, this will require some explanation, so hold tight.

- tileWidth: The width of an individual tile

- tileHeight: The height of an individual tile (This and tileWidth are calculated later in the buildMatrix() method.)

- controlAreaHeight: The space the Control Menu Button takes up. The control menu is what the user sees when he or she taps the Control Menu Button, obviously, and it's where the user will be able to alter the number of tiles or start a new game.

- controlMenuVisible: true to show the control menu, false to hide it

- controlMenuWidth: The width of the control menu

- controlMenuHeight: The height of the control menu

- controlMenuButtonDisabled: true if the Control Menu Button is disabled, false if it's enabled. The button gets disabled when the control menu is shown.

- wonVisible: Is the You Won! screen visible?

- moveCount: The number of moves the player has made in this game

- startTime: The time the current game began. This will be used to tell the user how long it took him or her to win.

"Global" Imports

Next up, we have a few more imports.

```
global.alterMatrixSize = require("./functions/alterMatrixSize");
global.buildMatrix = require("./functions/buildMatrix");
global.determineOutcome = require("./functions/determineOutcome");
```

```
global.generateSolvableLayout = require("./functions/
generateSolvableLayout");
global.tilePress = require("./functions/tilePress");
```

One thing you haven't seen yet is a true global scope. In general, global scope is to be avoided, to prevent any possible naming conflicts. It also tends to make your code better behaved, because, with things in global scope, they could be changed from unexpected places in the code, making it harder to debug problems. But there are indeed times when global scope makes total sense. But how do you even do it in a React Native app? Every JavaScript file you load is a separate module, and while you can have variables defined in them that are global within the module, meaning any code can access them within that module, there's no way to make something global to code in disparate modules. Well, not without creating a module to hold global information and then importing that module everywhere you need it, as you saw in previous apps, but that's not *quite* the same thing.

React Native does offer another way to do this, however, and that's through the global object. This is nothing but a JavaScript object that is automatically available to code in all modules. You can attach anything you like to this object, and it will be available everywhere. Here, what we have are five different functions, each housed in its own module. I need these to be accessible from several different places throughout the code base, and while it's certainly true that I could just have imported them into each module I need them in, I did it this way, to demonstrate the use of the global object.

As it happens, this winds up presenting a bit of a problem, but that gets solved in the constructor of the top-level App component, the code for which is here:

```
export default class App extends React.Component {

  constructor(inProps) {

    super(inProps);

    this.state = state;

    global.alterMatrixSize = global.alterMatrixSize.bind(this);
    global.buildMatrix = global.buildMatrix.bind(this);
    global.determineOutcome = global.determineOutcome.bind(this);
    global.generateSolvableLayout = global.generateSolvableLayout.bind(this);
    global.tilePress = global.tilePress.bind(this);

  }
```

Two interesting things can be seen here. First, the component's state is set to the state object that was imported earlier. Beyond that, though, is bind() being called on each of the functions I imported earlier. This is owing to that one little problem I hinted at earlier: when these functions execute, they have to do so within the context of the top-level component being constructed here; otherwise, the this keyword won't point to the right thing. We could write the code in these functions to not use this, but it turns out that would make things more difficult and would make the code less clear and concise. So, instead, I want to ensure they all have the right context, which means having to bind them to the component being constructed. As long as none of these functions is called before this component is built—which none is—then binding them in the constructor like this is perfect and will make everything very tidy and work as expected later.

render(): The Control Menu

Now, we can move on to the render() method. There are definitely some new things to see here, and while it's not conceptually very complicated, there *is* a fair bit of code to examine, so I'm going to break it down into chunks, beginning with this one:

```
render() {

  let controlMenu = null;
  if (this.state.controlMenuVisible) {
    controlMenu = (
      <View style={{ padding : 20, position : "absolute", zIndex : 9999,
      flex : 1,
        alignItems : "stretch", justifyContent : "center", borderRadius : 20,
        backgroundColor : "rgba(100, 64, 255, 0.95)",
        width : this.state.controlMenuWidth, height : this.state.
        controlMenuHeight,
        left : (this.state.screenUsableWidth - this.state.controlMenuWidth) / 2,
        top : (this.state.screenUsableHeight - this.state.
        controlMenuHeight) / 2
      }}>
        <View style={{ alignSelf : "center", paddingBottom : 40}}>
          <Text style={{color:"#ffffff", fontSize:24,
          fontWeight:"bold"}}>Control Menu</Text>
        </View>
```

```
  <View style={{ paddingBottom : 40, alignSelf : "center" }}>
    <Button title="Start A New Game" style={{ width : 150 }}
      onPress={ () => {
        state.numberOfTilesAcross = this.state.numberOfTilesAcross;
        state.numberOfTilesDown = this.state.numberOfTilesDown;
        this.setState(state, buildMatrix);
      }}
    />
  </View>
  <Text style={{ color : "#ffffff" }}>Tiles Across</Text>
  <Slider minimumValue={3} maximumValue={6} value={3} step={1}
    maximumTrackTintColor="white"
    onSlidingComplete={ (inValue) => global.
    alterMatrixSize("across", inValue) }
  />
  <Text style={{ color : "#ffffff", paddingTop : 40 }}>Tiles Down</Text>
  <Slider minimumValue={3} maximumValue={6} value={3} step={1}
    maximumTrackTintColor="white"
    onSlidingComplete={ (inValue) => global.alterMatrixSize("down",
    inValue) }
  />
  <View style={{ paddingTop : 40 }}><Text style={{ color : "#ffffff" }}>
    Warning: changing the grid size will automatically begin a new game!
  </Text></View>
  <View style={{ paddingTop : 40, alignSelf : "center" }}>
    <Button title="Done" style={{ width : 150 }}
      onPress={ () => this.setState({
        controlMenuVisible : false, controlMenuButtonDisabled : false
      }) }
    />
  </View>
</View>
);
}
```

As previously mentioned, the control menu is what the user gets when he or she clicks the `Control Menu Button`, naturally enough. The resultant screen is what you see in Figure 7-3.

Figure 7-3. *The control menu*

Now, the first thing to notice is that this screen is really just some content overlaid on top of the screen. There's no navigation to a new screen, as you've seen in other apps. You can still see the tiles behind it. Before we get to how that's done, let's talk about the way the code is written.

Here, you see an example of what's known as conditional rendering, which is pretty common in React and React Native apps. The problem we're concerned with here is how to hide and show elements dynamically, such as this control menu when the button is tapped. With many other UI toolkits, you could somehow get a reference to the control menu, perhaps through some `getComponent()` function, and then call a `hide()` or `show()` method on it. In the world of React Native, however, that's not really possible. (Well, it *sort of* is, as you'll see later, but as a general rule, it's not, and even if it is possible, it's definitely not the way you're *supposed* to do it.) If there's no way to hide and show a component directly, how do you do it? Clearly, it must be possible, or React Native wouldn't be of any use to us.

The answer is that you exploit the nature of React itself, mainly the fact that when there's a change in state, the framework will intelligently re-render any part of the screen that has to be updated. Most important, that means that the render() method of the component will get called again. Given that fact, if we have a way to alter what gets rendered, then perhaps we can simply not render part of the component hierarchy. That certainly would hide content, in effect.

As it happens, that's exactly what we do here. The controlMenuVisible state attribute is checked in the if statement. If it's true, then the variable controlMenu will contain the component to render. (Remember that JSX here will be interpreted, and the resultant content will be the value of that variable.) If the controlMenuVisible attribute is false, the controlMenu variable will have a value of null. That means that anytime we want to show the control menu, all we have to do is:

```
this.setState({ controlMenuVisible : true });
```

To hide it, we do the same but give it a value of false. The change in state will cause React Native to call the render() method, which will now use that logic to give the controlMenu variable a value of null, when hidden, or the component configuration, with a value of true. You saw this same concept in the previous app using Redux when hiding and showing modal dialogs, and it's conceptually no different here, just without Redux in the mix.

Hold on to this fact for a little while, because we're going to come back to it shortly, to see the other piece of the puzzle that makes this work. Before we get to that, however, let's talk about the actual code for the control menu. The basic structure is a View component that is positioned absolutely on the screen. Yes, that's something you can totally do. It's the first time you've seen it, but, in fact, this entire app is based on absolute positioning, which works just like it always does with CSS. The width and height are taken from the state.controlMenuWidth and state.controlMenuHeight attributes, and the left and top style attributes responsible for positioning the View are calculated using that width and height of the control menu itself, along with the width and height available on the screen. (Subtracting the width of the menu from the width of the screen and dividing by two, and doing the same for the height, centers the View.) The control menu is given rounded corners with the borderRadius style attribute, and it's given a semitransparent purple color using the backgroundColor attribute and the rgba()

function (specifying a color in red, green, blue, alpha components). The rest of the styles set up our typical flex layout, with children centered horizontally and vertically.

Within the parent View, we first find another View with a Text component inside it. This is the Control Menu heading text, bolded and in white and a larger font size.

After that is another View, this one with a Button component inside it. This is the Start a New Game button. When tapped, the first thing that's done is to copy the current value of the numberOfTilesAcross and the numberOfTilesDown attributes from the current state object into the canonical state object. If we didn't do this, the tile size the user selected would be overridden when the next line executes, which sets the state to that state object that was imported earlier (which, remember, has the default matrix size values in it).

Here, too, we have something new: notice how the setState() call has two arguments? That's something you've never seen before. Previously, all setState() calls had a single argument, an object with the attributes that should change in state. That's still true here. The first argument is indeed an object, and it happens to be the starting state object (with those two attributes for how many tiles across and down updated), but now there's a second argument. If you notice, it's one of the functions imported earlier, namely the buildMatrix() function. What's happening here?

Well, as it happens, a call to setState() is *always* asynchronous. It is effectively a request, not a directive per se, to React Native to update state. It's like saying "Hey, React Native, do me a favor and update state when you get around to it, m'kay?" But it may not happen immediately, indeed not by the time the next line of code executes. Most of the time, that doesn't matter, because it happens so quickly that it's rarely a problem. But if you have a situation in which the code that executes right after a call to setState() does, you can run into a problem, in that the code that follows the setState() call may read state and see the old values, not the new ones. In this particular instance, the buildMatrix() function, which we'll look at later, very much depends on state being updated. That's where the second argument comes into play: it's a function that React Native will call once the setState() call is done. That ensures that buildMatrix() won't execute until setState() finishes, which guarantees seeing the new values, just as we need.

After that come two groups of a Text component and a Slider component. The Text component is just a label for a Slider component, and the Slider components allow the user to change the matrix size, that is, the number of tiles across (using the first Slider) and the number of tiles down (using the second Slider). Each dimension can have a value of 3, 4, 5, or 6, as defined by the minimumValue, maximumValue, and step props. Each is given an initial value of 3. I also set the color of the track to the right of the knob to white, using the maximumTrackTintColor, so that it shows up better. For each Slider, remember that we, as the programmer, are responsible for updating state, so that's done in the onSlidingComplete handler prop, which fires only when the user lifts a finger off the knob. (You could also use onValueChange, but that fires every time the value changes, which isn't really necessary in this case.) However, it's not a simple matter of updating a state attribute, because I want the tiles to be redrawn whenever a change is made. Therefore, a call to alterMatrixSize() is made, passing the direction that was changed (across or down) and the new value. We'll look at what that function does later, but in short, it redraws the tiles.

In addition to the two Sliders and labels is another View with a child Text component, this one just gives a warning that changing the Slider values will start a new game.

Finally, we have another View with a Button inside it for dismissing the control menu. When tapped, the controlMenuVisible state attribute is set to false, which you'll remember will cause the render() method to fire again and, thanks to the conditional rendering, result in the control menu not being rendered this time, in effect, hiding it. At this point, the Control Menu button will be disabled, because, as you'll see very soon, that is disabled when the control menu is shown, so that the user can't trigger it twice. Therefore, the controlMenuButtonDisabled state attribute has to be flipped back to false, to re-enable the button.

render(): the You Won! Screen

With the control menu out of the way, we have another of these pseudo-overlays to consider, and that's the screen that the user will see when (and if!) he or she wins the game. This, again, is a situation in which we have to hide and show something dynamically, so we'll use the same conditional rendering trick as with the control menu.

```
let wonScreen = null;
if (this.state.wonVisible) {
  const elapsedTime = Math.round(
    (new Date().getTime() - this.state.startTime) / 1000
  );
  wonScreen = (
    <View style={{
      zIndex : 9998,
      position : "absolute",
```

```
        left : 0,
        top : this.state.controlAreaHeight,
        width : this.state.screenUsableWidth,
        height : this.state.screenUsableHeight
      }}>
        <Image source={require("./images/won.png")}
          resizeMode="stretch" fadeDuration={0}
          style={{
            width : this.state.screenUsableWidth,
            height : this.state.screenUsableHeight
          }}
        />
        <View style={{
          alignItems : "center",
          justifyContent : "center",
          position : "absolute",
          width : "100%",
          left : 0,
          zIndex : 9999,
          top : this.state.screenUsableHeight - 240
        }}>
          <Text style={{ fontSize : 20, fontWeight : "bold" }}>
            You took {this.state.moveCount} moves to win
          </Text>
          <Text style={{
            fontSize : 20, fontWeight : "bold", paddingBottom : 40
          }}>
            Game lasted {elapsedTime} seconds
          </Text>
          <Button title="Start A New Game"
            onPress={ () => {
              state.numberOfTilesAcross = this.state.numberOfTilesAcross;
              state.numberOfTilesDown = this.state.numberOfTilesDown;
              this.setState(state, buildMatrix);
```

```
        }}
      />
    </View>
  </View>
);
}
```

While seeing this You Won! screen on a physical device is much better, owing to the colors, I'll show it here, regardless, in Figure 7-4.

Figure 7-4. *The You Won! screen (It looks better in all its colorful glory on a physical device)*

Inside the `if` statement that checks the value of the `wonVisible` state attribute (which, remember, is how this conditional rendering works) is first a line that determines how long the game took the player to win. As you'll see, when a game begins, the `startTime` attribute of state is set to the current time, so it's just a simple matter of subtracting that from the current time to determine the elapsed time.

After that comes the component definition, beginning with an enclosing `View` that is, as with the control menu, absolutely positioned. Because I want this overlay to appear below the `Control Menu Button`, the top style attribute uses the value of the `controlAreaHeight` state attribute, as that's how far down it must be to avoid the button.

Inside that `View` is, first, an `Image` component that displays the `won.png` image from the `images` directory. Three things are of note here. First, the `resizeMode` prop is set to `stretch`, which will ensure that the image is stretched to fill the screen in both directions, regardless of the physical size of a device's screen. Second, the `fadeDuration` prop is set to zero. This is necessary because on Android devices, by default, the image will fade into view (but not on iOS). This looks very nice, but it presents a problem: the text that tells players how long they took and how many moves they took, plus the button, don't fade in. What happens is players see these elements, and *then* the gradient, which also includes the "You Won!" text, fades in. Frankly, it just looks bad! There are three possible ways to solve that problem. You could fade those elements in along with the `Image`, or you could not show them until the fade completes, or you could make the `Image` not fade at all. The first option is complicated to achieve, because the fade is controlled by React Native, so there's no way to hook into the fade. You would have to figure out the time the fade takes and have a parallel fade animation running, so that both complete at about the same time. That's doable theoretically, but tricky. The second option is similarly difficult to do, because there's no callback hook when the `Image`'s fade completes, so no way for our code to be informed, when it's done, to then show those elements. In the end, setting `fadeDuration` to zero achieves the third option and sidesteps the problem entirely. The third thing to notice is that the `width` and `height` style attributes are set to the size of the screen. This should make the `resizeMode` setting irrelevant, but doing both absolutely ensures proper sizing of the Image.

After the Image is another child of the outer `View`, this one itself a `View`. This is a `View` that will contain the two `Text` elements for number of moves and game length, as well as the Start a New Game button. This is done for one specific reason. See the `top` style attribute setting? The position of this `View` is relative to the bottom of the screen. This ensures that this `View` is a reasonable distance away from the "You Won!" text, regardless of how high the screen is. Essentially, the space between that text and this View can flex, depending on the physical size of the screen, but this View will always be 240 pixels away from the bottom of the screen, which is enough space to display its content, no matter the size of the screen.

Within this View, as mentioned, are three things: two Text components and a Button component. I think they're straightforward, so there's no need to dissect them in detail, except for the onPress handler of the Button. In this case, we again need to set the current number of tiles across and down, because, otherwise, they would be overwritten, as previously described. It applies here as well, so we have to take care of that here too.

Finally, the Basic App Layout

To this point, you'll notice that we haven't returned anything from this render() method. All we have are two variables, controlMenu and wonScreen, that have values of either null (if they aren't currently visible) or React Native components. We haven't actually *used* them yet. We haven't defined and returned the main application layout yet. Well, that's exactly what the next chunk of code does, and it's here that you can finally see the missing piece of the puzzle, in terms of conditional rendering.

```
return (
  <View style={{
    flex : 1,
    alignItems : "stretch",
    backgroundColor : "#000000"
  }}>
    <View style={{
      position : "absolute",
      left : 0,
      width : "100%",
      top : Platform.OS.toLowerCase() === "android" ?
        Constants.statusBarHeight + 10 : 0
    }}>
      <Button title="Control Menu"
        disabled={this.state.controlMenuButtonDisabled}
        onPress={ () => { this.setState({
```

```
                controlMenuButtonDisabled : true, controlMenuVisible : true
          }) }}
        />
      </View>
      {wonScreen}
      {controlMenu}
      {this.state.tiles}
    </View>
  )
```

It starts out simply enough: a single View, as is almost always the case with a React Native app, to contain the layout of our app. Also, as usual, it's got a flex of 1, to ensure it fills the screen. This time, however, alignItems is set to stretch, so that the children stretch to fill the width. This is done for the Control Menu Button, so that it stretches across the entire screen (the tiles themselves will have defined widths, so that they won't stretch; defining a child's width will always override a stretch such as this). I also set a backgroundColor of black, rather than the default white, because that just looks better to my eyes.

Inside the parent View is another View, and this one houses the Control Menu Button. Notice that it's positioned absolutely and set to 100% of the width of the screen. The top position takes into account the height of the status bar on an Android device, as you've seen before. Inside the View comes the Control Menu Button. It can be disabled, based on the value of the controlMenuButtonDisabled state attribute. You saw where it gets enabled earlier, and you'll see where it gets disabled, well, right now. The onPress handler does this, while also showing the control menu, by setting controlMenuVisible to true in state. Remember that both of these state changes will trigger re-rendering, which means the render() method will execute again, and this time, the conditional rendering will kick in to show the control menu (and the Control Menu Button will be disabled, by virtue of its disabled prop being set to the value of controlMenuButtonDisabled in state).

After the inner View come three JSX values, seemingly floating out there on their own. You should recognize the first two right off the bat—the two conditional rendering variables. Here's the magic that makes conditional rendering work: if these variables are null, React Native simply skips them and does nothing. If they are component definitions, however, they get inserted as if their code was right there, thereby, in essence, *conditionally* rendering them. Neat, right?

The last such "free-floating" value is this.state.tiles, and if you're guessing that's where the tiles themselves are, then you'd be absolutely correct. We have to build up those tiles, though, which is done in the aptly named buildMatrix() function, which is what we're going to look at next. In fact, you can see where it's called from, in the componentDidMount() method.

```
componentDidMount() {

  this.setState(state, buildMatrix);

}
```

Once again, we have a situation in which we must ensure that the setState() call completes before we try to build the tiles, so we use the callback of setState() here and the callback function is the buildMatrix() function itself.

Functions, Part 1

As previously discussed, I decided to break down the code in this app into individual functions and have each be its own module. I felt that was a logical way to structure things and make it easy to know which source file to load when working on the code. I'm going to discuss two functions in this chapter, and the remainder will be covered in the next, so let's begin with the one briefly discussed in the previous section, namely, buildMatrix().

buildMatrix()

I'm using the term *matrix* to describe the grid of tiles you see on the screen and the code that produces that matrix. The tiles in it are in the buildMatrix.js file in the functions directory. Being a typical JavaScript module, it begins with a few imports.

```
import React from "react";
import { Animated, Text, TouchableWithoutFeedback, View } from "react-native";
```

We don't require very much from React or React Native to make this work, but given that the tiles will slide around the screen, we'll need the Animated API for this. You've seen the other components before, of course, so nothing's new here.

After that, we begin our code by setting `module.exports` to a function, because that's all we want to export in this case (and, in fact, in all the function modules).

```
module.exports = function() {

  const screenUsableWidth = this.state.screenUsableWidth;
  const screenUsableHeight = this.state.screenUsableHeight;
  const numberOfTilesAcross = this.state.numberOfTilesAcross;
  const numberOfTilesDown = this.state.numberOfTilesDown;
```

In order to construct our tiles and get them arranged in a grid, we're going to have to know a few things, namely, the screen's width and height and how many tiles there will be across and down the grid. Fortunately, that information is all in state, so we'll just grab them into some local variables for speed, and we're good to go.

The next thing to determine is how wide and tall each tile is.

```
const tileWidth = Math.floor(screenUsableWidth / numberOfTilesAcross);
const tileHeight = Math.floor(screenUsableHeight / numberOfTilesDown);
```

Using the size of the screen allows us to size the tiles so that they will fill the screen. It would be easier if the tiles were always fixed sizes, of course, but on a large screen device, you'd have a lot of empty space if they were too small. So, dynamically calculating the size makes a lot more sense. There can, of course, be some leftover space, and we'll want to know that, so we can center the tiles. We'll calculate that space now.

```
const spaceLeft =
  Math.floor((screenUsableWidth - (numberOfTilesAcross * tileWidth)) / 2);
const spaceTop =
  Math.floor((screenUsableHeight - (numberOfTilesDown * tileHeight)) / 2);
```

Now we know how much space is on the left of our tiles and above our tiles, which also tells us how much is on the right and below, because it's symmetrical, which will make it look centered and attractive onscreen.

Next, we have to determine the random order of the tiles on the screen. If we have a 3 × 3 matrix, then, of course, we have tiles numbers 1–8, with one empty space. We need these tiles to be randomized, but there's a problem. It turns out that not every random layout of tiles is solvable. Sometimes, the initial ordering can make it impossible for the game to be won. While I like a challenging game as much as anyone, one I literally can't win isn't very much fun. So, we have a function to call.

```
let tileNumbers = global.generateSolvableLayout();
```

We're going to look at the generateSolvableLayout() function when we're done with buildMatrix(), but for now, it's enough to know that it does exactly what its name implies: it returns an array of tile numbers in a random order that is guaranteed to be solvable.

With that array in hand, we can start building the tiles. Each tile is ultimately a React Native View component that is absolutely positioned.

```
const tiles = [];
const virtualTiles = [];
let tileCount = 0;
```

The tiles array will contain those View components, and tileCount is just a counter variable that will be used to determine when we've built all the tiles. All that's left is the blank one, because that has to be handled a little differently.

The virtualTiles array is where it gets interesting. The basic idea is that we need an easy way to determine when the tiles are in the right order, meaning the player won. However, if we're creating View components and throwing them into the tiles array, which is precisely what we'll be doing here, those tiles will be physically moving around the screen, which means that the View component referenced by tiles[0] might be the fifth tile physically on the screen. Therefore, we can't just look into the tiles array and ensure that the tile numbers ascend in perfect order. No, we need a way to track the *logical* position of tiles separately from their *physical* positions. This logical position is in a sense a *virtual* position, hence the variable name. As tiles move around the screen, what we'll do is move them around in this virtualTiles array. So, if the first tile on the screen has tile number 1 on it, and the second tile on the screen has tile number 2 on it, that means that virtualTiles[0] has a tile number of 1 and virtualTiles[1] has a tile number of 2. If they were to swap positions, owing to a player move, then we just have to swap the pointers in virtualTiles[0] and virtualTiles[1]. We can then just iterate over virtualTiles after the move, to see if the tile numbers are 1–8, and if so, the player has won. Of course, tiles can't swap like that. They can only move into the blank space, but the concept is still the same.

Note   My original approach was to have an additional attribute on each of the `View` components that specified its tile number. That way, rather than swapping pointers in a separate array, I could just swap the tile numbers when two tiles change positions. This, in theory, would have worked, but, frankly, it wound up being more difficult to conceptualize and manage, so I went with a separate array. I've been making games for the better part of 40 years, but even with all that experience, sometimes you just don't know what's going to work or what's going to work best, until you just get in there and try it, which, I guess, is true of any type of programming, come to think of it.

So, because we're building a matrix of tiles, that means we're dealing with rows and columns, and that means our code should be in the form of two loops, which is precisely what you see following:

```
for (let row = 0; row < numberOfTilesDown; row++) {

  const rowArray = [];
  virtualTiles.push(rowArray);
```

The `virtualTiles` array is, in fact, an array of arrays, each element being a row in the matrix, so with each iteration of the outer `row` loop, a new array is pushed into `virtualTiles`.

```
  for (let col = 0; col < numberOfTilesAcross; col++) {

    const tileNum = tileNumbers[tileCount];
    const refID = `refID_${tileCount}`;
    const left = spaceLeft + (col * tileWidth);
    const top = this.state.controlAreaHeight + spaceTop + (row * tileHeight);
```

It's inside the inner `col` loop where the tiles are actually created. First, we grab the next tile number from the `tileNumbers` array that `generateSolvableLayout()` provided for us. This tells us what the number on the tile is. Next, we must construct a unique ID for the tile, and why we do this will be explained next, so let's skip it for now. We also must figure out the physical location of the tile. This means calculating the `left` and `top` style attributes. The `left` attribute is calculated by multiplying the column number by the width of the tile and then adding that `spaceLeft` value we determined earlier.

For top, it's a bit more complicated, but only slightly: we multiply the row number by the height of a tile, and then we have to add the spaceTop value, just like spaceLeft, and we also must add the controlAreaHeight from state to it, so that all the tiles wind up below the Control Menu Button.

Next, we have to do a bit of logic: if the tileCount variable, which keeps track of how many tiles we've built, is one less than the total number of tiles in the matrix, it's time to render the empty tile. We actually do need a View component for that to work, but it will have a lot less content than a regular tile, as I'm sure you'd logically conclude.

```
if (tileCount === (numberOfTilesAcross * numberOfTilesDown) - 1) {

  rowArray.push({ refID : refID, tileNum : 0 });

  tiles.push(
    <View key={tileCount}
      ref={ (inRef) => {
        const refs = this.state.refs;
        refs[refID] = inRef;
        this.setState({ refs : refs });
      }}
    />
  );
```

Yes, indeed, there's not much there. First, a new element is pushed into the rowArray array, which contains the refID value as well as the actual number of the file, its "face value," so to speak. In this case, because this is our blank tile, it has a special value of zero. All of this is building up our virtualTiles array of arrays. After that, we must create an actual tile, and that's where the View component pushed into the tiles array comes into play.

As part of that component definition, however, there is something new and exciting, and it goes back to that refID you saw created earlier. As you're going to see in Chapter 8, I've painted myself into a bit of a corner with the approach of breaking things down by function. Essentially, I'm going to have to have access to the individual tiles when they're tapped, but I won't (well, not *easily*, at least). I'm going to require another way to do so, and it turns out that React Native offers such an alternative. Up until now, throughout this book, if you've been paying attention, you'll notice that you've never seen code similar to the following:

```
document.getElementById("<some_id>").doSomething();
```

In other words, you've never seen code that gets a reference to a component and then does something with it. That's because, for the most part, you can't! And, that's very much by design. In React Native, and React generally, you're meant to do everything through state. This is what you often hear referred to as one-way data flow. This means that the parent component contains the state for itself and all its child components, then elements of that state get passed down to child components via props only. If a child has to communicate with a parent in some way, that's done strictly through state updates. In other words, data flows down the component hierarchy only. (Setting values in state in a sub-component from the parent is data flowing, but only in one way, hence the designation one-directional, or unidirectional, as it's sometimes described.)

This concept extends even further to how you work with components, in the sense that, generally, you only have references to the component code it is contained in (via the `this` reference), and you can't (usually) simply go off and grab a reference to another component in the hierarchy by ID. It makes sense, given unidirectional data flow. If you can easily get references to other components and mutate them, then data can flow in all sorts of directions and won't always be managed by React, which makes things more complicated and error-prone.

There are times, however, when you really do need to just reach out and touch someone, as it were, meaning fire a function on a component or read a prop or whatever else. React Native provides a mechanism for that called refs, short for "references," of course. The way it works is simple enough and can be seen in the `View` created in the `if` branch here. The `ref` prop is a function that is passed a reference to the component being built. You can then do whatever you want with it, but the most typical thing developers do is store that reference somewhere for later. In this case, it gets stored inside the `refs` attribute of the `state` object. The `refs` attribute is just an object in which the keys are the `refID` values that are constructed in the form `refID_<tileCount>`. That way, each tile has a unique ID, and we can just grab the value associated with a given key in the `refs` object, and we'll then have a reference to that `View` component. Once we add the reference, it's simply a matter of calling `setState()`, handing it the updated `refs` object, and we're good to go.

In Chapter 8, you'll see how and why those refs are used, but for now, just keep in mind that these references exist and will allow us to get at tiles by an ID, because that's going to matter.

Now, that was the if branch of the check that determines if we're building a real tile or the special empty tile. The else branch, as I'm sure you guessed, is where we build a real tile.

```
    } else {

      rowArray.push({ refID : refID, tileNum : tileNum });

      tiles.push(
        <Animated.View key={tileCount}
          ref={ (inRef) => {
            const refs = this.state.refs;
            refs[refID] = inRef;
            this.setState({ refs : refs });
          }}
          style={[
            {
              position : "absolute",
              backgroundColor : "#d08080",
              flex : 1,
              alignItems : "center",
              justifyContent : "center",
              borderWidth : 10,
              borderTopColor : "#80a080",
              borderLeftColor : "#80a080",
              borderBottomColor : "#c0f0c0",
              borderRightColor : "#c0f0c0",
              borderStyle : "solid",
              borderRadius : 20
            },
            {
              left : new Animated.Value(left),
              top : new Animated.Value(top),
              width : tileWidth - 4, height : tileHeight - 4
            }
          ]}
        >
```

```
          <TouchableWithoutFeedback onPress={ ()=> global.tilePress(refID) }>
            <View style={{ width : tileWidth, height : tileHeight,
              alignItems : "center", justifyContent : "center"
            }}>
              <Text style={{
                fontWeight : "bold", fontSize : 24
              }}>{tileNum}</Text>
            </View>
          </TouchableWithoutFeedback>
        </Animated.View>
      );
    }

    tileCount = tileCount + 1;

  }

}
```

First, a virtual tile is pushed into `rowArray`, just as in the `if` branch, but this time, the tile number is taken dynamically from the `tileNumbers` array via the `tileNum` variable, so that the face value of the tile is determined by the order returned by `generateSolvableLayout()`.

Next, the physical tile's `View` component is defined. Because we want tiles to slide around the screen, the `Animated` API comes into play. To be able to use this API, the component being animated must support the API. Only a handful of components support it, but most important is the `View` component itself, or, more specifically, the `Animated.View` component. So, that's the top-level component defined here.

Because the tiles are part of a collection, React Native will require each to have a key prop, even though we don't need it for our purposes here, so the value of `tileCount` is used, which is just a counter variable.

As with the empty tile, we must capture a reference to this tile in `state.refs`, so that is done, same as before.

The `style` for the `View` is mostly just some visual niceties, such as rounded corners and some coloring, but the critical piece is that the tile is positioned absolutely. That, of course, is the key to all of this, because we'll want to be able to move individual tiles around on our own. Note that the `width` and `height` attributes have four pixels shaven off, which introduces a few pixels of padding around each tile. I felt this looked better than letting them bump up against each other.

Another requirement of using the `Animated` API is that `style` attributes that are to be animated must use an "animatable" value. To make an attribute's value animatable with the `Animated` API, we can't just set "naked" values. Instead, we must wrap them using the `Animated.value()` function—the object it returns, to be more precise. Here, the `left` and `top` style attributes wrap the values previously calculated for them, using this function. Failing to do so will cause our animations not to work later.

Then, inside this `Animated.View` component is a `TouchableWithoutFeedback` component. This is just a wrapper that reacts to touch events and does not provide any system-specific visual feedback. The visual feedback, in this case, is the tile moving around, so there's no need for Android or iOS to do whatever they would normally do. The `onPress` prop of this component calls the `tilePress()` function in `global` scope, and note that it passes the `refID` to it. We'll come back to this in the next chapter, but it's why we needed to do all this ref stuff in the first place. (Well, that, and it gave me an opportunity to introduce the refs concept, which is just as good as having a *real* technical reason for it, I suppose!) Note, too, that this `TouchableWithoutFeedback` component has a `width` and `height` that is the size of a tile, as previously calculated. That way, touch events will react anywhere on the tile, not just some small area in the middle.

Finally, inside the `TouchableWithoutFeedback` is a regular old `View` that contains a regular old `Text` component, centered, that includes the tile's face value. After that, `tileCount` is bumped up, and the next loop iteration fires.

Once both the loops conclude, the only thing left to do is to update state with everything we just did.

```
this.setState({
  tiles : tiles, virtualTiles : virtualTiles,
  tileWidth : tileWidth, tileHeight : tileHeight
});
```

Now, we have a populated collection of tile `View` objects (`tiles`), a collection of `virtualTiles` with objects that contain reference IDs and tile number (face values), as well as the calculated width and height of a tile, information we'll need later (in Chapter 8), to animate the tile movements.

And with that, we have a grid of tiles on the screen! But, there's a part still left out of the equation, and that's the `generateSolvableLayout()` function that I said we'd come back to. Well, here it comes.

generateSolvableLayout( )

Remember earlier when I said that if you just randomly order the tiles, you will sometimes wind up with an arrangement that won't be solvable? The generateSolvableLayout() function is responsible for ensuring that doesn't happen (thereby ensuring that no angry gamers come after us for frustrating them needlessly). Before we even look at the code, let's talk about the logic behind it more generally.

Whether one of these puzzles can be solved in its current arrangement is based on the concept of *inversions*. An inversion is merely a pair of tiles whose face value is in the opposite of what it should be in the end. In other words, if you have tile two next to tile one, that's an inversion (tile one next to tile two would *not* be an inversion). Pairs of tiles mean tiles that are right next to each other, and this includes considering the edges too. In other words, if you have a row of tiles numbered three, one, and two in a 3 × 3 matrix, you have two inversions: three and one and also three and two. The three and one inversion is apparent, but the three and two inversion isn't, but it is an inversion, because you have to consider the tile all the way on the opposite side of that row ("considering the edges," in other words).

With that information in hand, the rule becomes simple if you reason it out: if the total number of inversions for the current arrangement of tiles is odd, this arrangement cannot be solved. If it's even, it can be.

Now that we know the rule to determine solvability, let's look at the code that implements it, beginning with a single import in the module.

```
const lodash = require("lodash");
```

We're going to use lodash to randomize an array, because it's good at that and it'll save us some time and effort. After the import, a single variable is defined:

```
const testWin = false;
```

The problem is that I'm not as good at these sliding puzzles as I was as a kid. I used to be able to blast through them quickly and easily, but while developing this app, I needed to solve the puzzle numerous times as I developed the You Won! screen. Rather than struggle for maybe a few minutes each time, I introduced this variable instead. When set to true, the array returned by the generateSolvableLayout() function will be in winning order immediately. That means that all I need to do to test is slide the last tile into the blank space and then back, which triggers the logic that determines that I won.

Now, on to the function itself, and I'll break this down to make it easier to follow.

```
module.exports = function() {

  const numberOfTilesAcross = this.state.numberOfTilesAcross;
  const numberOfTilesDown = this.state.numberOfTilesDown;
```

Naturally, we have to know the number of tiles across and down. The logic to determine solvability doesn't change based on the number of tiles, but the logic, of course, has to know this information.

```
  let tileNumbers = [];
  for (let i = 1; i < numberOfTilesAcross * numberOfTilesDown; i++) {
    tileNumbers.push(i);
  }
```

The first step is to generate an ordered array of values. We'll be shuffling this and testing whether the resultant array is solvable, and that all happens within a while loop.

```
  let isSolvable = false;
  while (!isSolvable) {

    tileNumbers = lodash.shuffle(tileNumbers);
    if (testWin) {
      tileNumbers = [ 1, 2, 3, 4, 5, 6, 7, 8, 0 ];
      isSolvable = true;
      continue;
    }
```

Inside the loop, we shuffle the array of numbers we just generated, using the `lodash.shuffle()` function, because we're supposed to be generating a random arrangement here, of course. Now, if the `testWin` flag is set to `true`, that means we want the special test case, so `tileNumbers` is overridden in correct, defined order. Note that this test will only work for a 3 × 3 matrix, because there are nine elements in `tileNumbers`. (Of course, you can just extend the array to test larger matrix sizes, but there's no real point. If all the win logic works with a 3 × 3 matrix, it's going to work with any size matrix.) Finally, the `isSolvable` flag is set to `true` so that we won't get another iteration of the loop after the continues, and that effectively ends the loop.

If we're not dealing with a test scenario, however, it's time to get down to counting inversions.

```
const numberOfTiles = numberOfTilesAcross * numberOfTilesDown;
let inversionCount = 0;
for (let i = 0; i < numberOfTiles - 1; i++) {
  for (let j = 1; j < numberOfTiles; j++) {
    if (tileNumbers[j] && tileNumbers[i] &&
      tileNumbers[i] > tileNumbers[j]
    ) {
      inversionCount = inversionCount +1;
    }
  }
}
isSolvable = (inversionCount % 2 === 0);
}
return tileNumbers;
};
```

We need to loop over rows and columns and check the tile next to each tile (when there is a tile next to it, because, remember, we could hit edge cases at the start and end of each row, which would break the logic). Anytime we encounter an inversion, we bump the `inversionCount` variable, and at the end, we set `isSolvable` to the result of seeing if `inversionCount` is odd or even. If it's odd, we generate another random arrangement and try again. Otherwise, `tileNumbers` is returned to the caller, and it now knows that it has a solvable random arrangement of tiles to work with.

Summary

In this chapter, we began building our React Native FunTime sliding puzzle game. In the process, you saw some new and interesting things, including global variables; refs; a different way to organize your code, based on functions; absolute layout; and digging into the guts of components to meet our needs.

In Chapter 8, the final chapter of this book, we'll finish looking at the code that makes up FunTime and at a few more new and useful tricks to make your React Native development more flexible. We'll do this while continuing to think a bit outside the box, so as to afford you the opportunity to expand your view of React Native and what you can do with it.

Time for Some Fun: A React Native Game, Part 2

In the previous chapter, we began the process of building FunTime, a little React Native slide tile puzzle game. You saw the overall architecture, how the interface was laid out using absolute positioning, and how the grid of tiles was built.

The one thing you *didn't* see is an actual game! What I mean by that is that seeing how the tiles are built and put on the screen is great, and seeing how the control menu works is great, but none of that makes a game. It just makes, well, a tile drawing app.

So, in this chapter, we're going to look at the two functions that make this a game, and we're going to look at one other function that's required to make the control menu work. By the end, you'll have a holistic picture of how this game works.

Functions, Part 2

There are just three functions left, two that make the game work (the `tilePress()` and `determineOutcome()` functions) and another (the `alterMatrixSize()` function) that implements the control menu's ability to change the matrix size. The first two functions are somewhat lengthy, but not unbearably so, while the last is quite short and sweet.

Let's start with probably the longest and, arguably, most important one— `tilePress()`.

© Frank Zammetti 2018
F. Zammetti, *Practical React Native*, https://doi.org/10.1007/978-1-4842-3939-1_8

tilePress()

As you'll recall from the previous chapter, each of the tiles, as part of it, has a TouchableWithoutFeedback component, and this is what allows the tiles to react to touch events. When tapped, the tilePress() function is called and is passed the ID of the tile. The tilePress() function is in the tilePress.js file, naturally, and begins as follows:

```
import { Animated } from "react-native";
```

Because the main task of this code is essentially to move tiles around when touched (assuming one tile is next to a blank tile), it makes sense that we would need the Animated API here. You'll see how that's used a little later, but first, we have to begin the actual function.

```
module.exports = function(inRefID) {

  if (this.state.controlMenuVisible) { return; }
```

We're exporting a single function here, as you've seen in other cases, so the module. exports reference points to the function. After that, we have some quick "short-circuiting" logic: if the control menu is visible, then tiles should not react to touches. Without this, the user can actually slide tiles around when the control menu is visible, which just seems wrong. More important, it could actually lead to some breakage, or at least some peculiar situations, because if the user happens to win the game while the control menu is visible, the logic associated with that event would kick in, and we'd have a situation that really shouldn't be allowed.

Next, we have a variable definition.

```
const tile = this.state.refs[inRefID];
```

The tile's ID is passed into the function, and that's done so that we can get a reference to the tile itself, meaning the containing Animated.View component, and you'll recall in Chapter 7 that we used the refs mechanism to capture that reference and store it in the refs object in state, keyed by the ID. Now, we can work with the tile object directly, without the difficulty involved in attaching this function to each tile instance.

The task now is to find this tile in our collection of virtual tile objects and record its location within the matrix. This will be necessary to examine the tiles around this one to see if one is the blank, because only then will the tile move. So, to begin, a few variables must be set up to do the work to follow.

```
const virtualTiles = this.state.virtualTiles;
let virtualTile = null;
let tileLoc = null;
const numberOfTilesAcross = this.state.numberOfTilesAcross;
const numberOfTilesDown = this.state.numberOfTilesDown;
```

A reference to `virtualTiles` in `state` is grabbed, just for performance purposes. It's always a good idea, especially in game programming and especially in loops (which is exactly what's coming), to avoid extended scope lookups. So, getting a reference in local scope will help, even if it's not going to make a big difference.

The `virtualTile` and `tileLoc` variables will be used to reference the tile once it's found and stores its x and y locations within the matrix, respectively.

Finally, `numberOfTilesAcross` and `numberOfTilesDown` is, as with `virtualTiles`, grabbed into local scope, because they will be used inside loops.

Speaking of loops, the first one we encounter—the first two actually—are used to find the tile:

```
for (let row = 0; row < numberOfTilesDown; row++) {
  const rowArray = virtualTiles[row];
  for (let col = 0; col < numberOfTilesAcross; col++) {
    const vt = rowArray[col];
    if (vt.refID === inRefID) {
      virtualTile = vt;
      tileLoc = { row : row, col : col };
      break;
    }
  }
}
```

We iterate over the rows and columns in the `virtualTiles` array of arrays, looking for the tile with the `refID` matching the one passed in. Remember that at this point, while we have a reference to the `Animated.View` that contains all the tile's content, we don't have a reference to the tile in `virtualTiles`, because that's not a simple map structure, that's an array of arrays. So, in order to find it, we have to go look for it. We must find it, because it's virtualTiles that has the information we need to determine first if this tile can move (if the blank space is next to it), as well as whether the move results in a win (because virtualTiles has objects in it that each has the tileNum attribute, specifying the tile's face value). Once the tile is found, we store a reference to it in virtualTile, and we also create an object, referenced by tileLoc, that tells us what row and column (col) the tile is in.

Next, we must get a reference to the tile above, below, to the left, and to the right of the tile:

```
let virtualTileLeft = null;
let virtualTileRight = null;
let virtualTileAbove = null;
let virtualTileBelow = null;
```

These four variables will reference those tiles, and the code to actually get the references follows:

```
try {
  virtualTileLeft = virtualTiles[tileLoc.row][tileLoc.col - 1];
} catch (e) { }
try {
  virtualTileRight = virtualTiles[tileLoc.row][tileLoc.col + 1];
} catch (e) { }
try {
  virtualTileAbove = virtualTiles[tileLoc.row - 1][tileLoc.col];
} catch (e) { }
try {
  virtualTileBelow = virtualTiles[tileLoc.row + 1][tileLoc.col];
} catch (e) { }
```

Why wrap them in try...catch you ask, especially when the catch block does nothing? Well, what happens if the tile that was touched is the first one, in row 1, column 1? That would mean that when we try to get a reference to the tile above and to the left of it, we'll be out of bounds on at least one array, and we'll throw an exception. Now, throwing an exception doesn't represent a problem situation here, because we know these edge conditions can occur, and it just means there's no tile to check in that direction. So, in those cases, the associated variable will be null, and we can check for that later when it's time to check the actual files.

But, before checking the actual files, there's a few other pieces of information we need.

```
const tileWidth = this.state.tileWidth;
const tileHeight = this.state.tileHeight;

let moveTile = false;
```

We're going to have to know how wide and how high a tile is when it comes time to move the tile (if we wind up moving it at all, that is), and it happens that information is in state, so some local references are grabbed. The moveTile variable is also declared and set to false. The logic that follows will be simply that the tile does not move unless the blank tile is next to it, and that logic is coming up next, but one last detail is needed before that.

```
let toLeftValue = tile.props.style[1].left.__getValue();
let toTopValue = tile.props.style[1].top.__getValue();
```

Now here, I'm doing something very naughty. Notice how the __getValue() method has two underscores before it? That indicates that this is a private method that you aren't meant to use directly. Further, notice the way I'm digging down into the props of the component? You're also not really supposed to do that. These sorts of internals are generally meant for React Native use only, not your application code (and, generally, these things won't even appear in the docs; I had to dig around in the code itself to find them). You generally should avoid things like this, if for no other reason than these sorts of internals may change in future versions, and you'd find yourself with a breakage in your app, all of a sudden. But this is a "practical" book after all, which means getting things done by hook or by crook. Knowing the rules also means knowing when and how to bend them. If nothing else, this sort of thing gives you some insight into the inner working of React Native, which isn't bad to have. All that said, I'll tell you, dear reader, the same thing I say to my kids: "Do as I say, not as I do."

Nevertheless, continuing, the situation here is that to move the tile, we're going to need to know its current absolute x and y coordinates (left and top style attributes) on the screen. Because that information isn't stored somewhere, such as in virtualTiles perhaps, we need a way to get it directly from the component. So, I've dug down into its props and into its style attribute.

If you go back and look at the definition of a tile's `Animated.View`, which you'll find in the `buildMatrix()` function, you'll see that it's an array of style objects. You'll also notice that `left` and `top` are defined in the second one, which is why `tile.props.style[1]` is used. That gets us a reference to that second style object in the array. However, we can't directly read the `left` and `top` attribute values, because, you'll recall, they are of type `Animated.Value`. In order to read the underlying value that we need, the private `__getValue()` function has to be used.

Now, once all that ickiness is out of the way, we now have all the information we need to determine if the tapped tile should move or not. Remember that a tile can only move up, down, left, or right and only into the blank space, so we must check each of those four adjacent tiles with logic like this:

```
if (virtualTileLeft && parseInt(virtualTileLeft.tileNum) === 0) {
  toLeftValue = toLeftValue - tileWidth;
  moveTile = true;
  virtualTiles[tileLoc.row][tileLoc.col] = virtualTileLeft;
  virtualTiles[tileLoc.row][tileLoc.col - 1] = virtualTile;
}
```

If there is a tile to the left of the tapped one (remember that there may not be, because of the conditions on the edges), and if the face value of the file is 0, which indicates the blank tile, the tile can move. To do so, we're going to animate the tile's `left` style property, moving it a number of pixels equal to the `width` of a tile. The `moveTile` flag gets set to `true`, to indicate that the tile will move, and, finally, we have to deal with the `virtualTiles` entries. All we have to do is swap the two tiles—the one tapped and the blank one.

For the other three tiles, it's the same exact logic, but, of course, getting the face value from the appropriate variables and using height instead of width, where appropriate, and different offset values into the arrays when swapping tiles.

```
if (virtualTileRight && parseInt(virtualTileRight.tileNum) === 0) {
  toLeftValue = toLeftValue + tileWidth;
  moveTile = true;
  virtualTiles[tileLoc.row][tileLoc.col] = virtualTileRight;
  virtualTiles[tileLoc.row][tileLoc.col + 1] = virtualTile;
}
```

```
if (virtualTileAbove && parseInt(virtualTileAbove.tileNum) === 0) {
  toTopValue = toTopValue - tileHeight;
  moveTile = true;
  virtualTiles[tileLoc.row][tileLoc.col] = virtualTileAbove;
  virtualTiles[tileLoc.row - 1][tileLoc.col] = virtualTile;
}

if (virtualTileBelow && parseInt(virtualTileBelow.tileNum) === 0) {
  toTopValue = toTopValue + tileHeight;
  moveTile = true;
  virtualTiles[tileLoc.row][tileLoc.col] = virtualTileBelow;
  virtualTiles[tileLoc.row + 1][tileLoc.col] = virtualTile;
}
```

You may have noticed that, at this point, the tile hasn't actually moved anywhere. All we know is that it *should* move, because moveTile is set to true. It has moved in virtualTiles by virtue of the swap, but not on the screen. That's what the next bit of code is responsible for.

```
let moveCount = this.state.moveCount;
if (moveTile) {
  moveCount = moveCount + 1;
  const moveDuration = 250;
  Animated.parallel([
    Animated.timing(
      tile.props.style[1].left,
      { toValue : toLeftValue, duration : moveDuration }
    ),
    Animated.timing(
      tile.props.style[1].top,
      { toValue : toTopValue, duration : moveDuration }
    )
  ]).start(global.determineOutcome);
}
```

First, the number of moves made in this game so far is pulled from state and incremented. Note that we have to do this outside the `if` statement, because `moveCount` is used in the line of code that follows the `if` statement. Next, the duration of the tile move animation is defined. This way, as a separate value, not only is it good form to not use magic values, but the time the slide takes can be changed in one spot, if we want.

Next, we use the `Animated` API's `parallel()` method. This allows us to have multiple animations run simultaneously. The reason I did it this way is to avoid a few lines of code. Right now, we only know that the tile should move; we don't know which direction it should move. In the previous logic blocks, the `left` and `top` values are altered and stored in `toLeftValue` and `toTopValue`, respectively, but only one of those will be different from the tile's current `left` or `top` value, never both (which is why we needed to retrieve the current `left` and `top` values in the first place). Now, we can either do an `if` check, to figure out which changed, and then only do the one animation that we really need to, or we can save ourselves some typing and go ahead and animate both style attributes, regardless of whether the value has changed, because that does no harm.

So, we fire off two `Animated.timing()` method calls, which animate a given property over a given period of time. The first argument passed to it is a reference to the style attribute we want to animate, which drills down into the tile's `props` again to get at the second `StyleSheet` object, and eventually, the `left` and `top` attributes. Then, the second argument is an object that configures the animation. In this case, we just have to give it a `toValue`, which is the value the attribute is animating to, and `duration`, which is how long it takes. The object returned by the `Animated.parallel()` method contains a `start()` method, which we call to begin both animations.

Now, when the animations complete, we're going to have to see if this tile move results in the player winning, and, fortunately for us, the `start()` method accepts a callback function to call when the animations complete. We have a function named `determineOutcome()` that we're going to want to execute (and which we'll be looking at next), so that's what is passed to it.

With the animations now running, the last task to complete in the `tilePress()` function is to update state. The `virtualTiles`, since we swapped those, have to be updated, as does the `moveCount`.

```
this.setState({ virtualTiles : virtualTiles, moveCount : moveCount });
```

And that takes care of what happens when the player presses a tile.

determineOutcome()

Now that the player can move tiles around, half of what makes this a game is complete. The other half is to check to see if a player won, which is done after each tile move, once the animations have completed. The determineOutcome function, in the determineOutcome.js file, starts out with a single import.

```
const lodash = require("lodash");
```

We're going to need one function from lodash again, but a different one than before, as you can see here, in the opening of the function itself:

```
module.exports = function() {

  const virtualTiles = lodash.flattenDeep(this.state.virtualTiles);
```

As with the other functions in the other files, this one becomes the value of module. exports. Inside the function, the task that needs to be accomplished is to look at all the tiles and see if they are in the correct order. The virtualTiles array has the information we need, namely, the face value of each tile, but you'll recall that virtualTiles is a multidimensional array, an array of arrays in other words. While it's certainly not too difficult to do a loop nested inside another to iterate over the tiles, a pattern used in other parts of the code, wouldn't it be a lot easier if we had a regular old single-dimension "flat" array? In fact, it would be, and rather than have to write that code, we can take advantage of the lodash flattenDeep() method. This method recursively flattens the array, meaning it'll keep digging down into each element of the top-level array, and then into each element that is itself an array, and so on, as far as it has to, and grab each non-array element and stick it into a regular array. So, if you have

```
[ [ 1, 2, 3  ], [4, 5, 6] ]
```

flattenDeep() will return

```
[ 1, 2, 3, 4, 5, 6 ]
```

The next thing we have to do is to produce an array of the appropriate length, with elements in the correct order. The reason we have to do this is because of the basic logic here: given an array (call it our "winning" array) with numbers as elements (tile face values) in the correct winning order, ensure that each element of another array (the flattened array of virtualTile objects we just created) matches the corresponding value in the winning array. I'm sure there are other ways this could be accomplished, but this struck me as the most straightforward.

So, we need that winning array.

```
const numberOfTiles =
  this.state.numberOfTilesAcross * this.state.numberOfTilesDown;
const winningArray =
  Array.from({ length : numberOfTiles - 1 }, (v, k) => k + 1);
```

The numberOfTiles gives us the necessary length of the array, and then we can use the Array.from() method to populate the array with ascending numbers. Remember that the blank tile will always be at the end in the winning position, which means the length of the array is actually one *less* than the number of tiles, and the values in this array begin with one, not zero (by virtue of k starting off as 0, so the first element is k + 1).

With both these arrays ready to go, now we must iterate over one and compare each element to the corresponding element in the other.

```
let playerWon = true;
for (let i = 0; i < virtualTiles.length; i++) {
  if (virtualTiles[i].tileNum !== 0 &&
    virtualTiles[i].tileNum !== winningArray[i]
  ) {
    playerWon = false;
    break;
  }
}
```

Well, it's not *quite* that simple, because, of course, in the winningArray, the elements are tile face values, while in the virtualTiles array (the flattened version, remember), each element is an object, and it's the tileNum attribute of each that we must compare to the associated number in winningArray. In addition, we must ignore the blank tile too, because that will be the last one encountered in the loop. These minor quibbles aside, we assume the player wins, unless and until we find a mismatch, at which point, playerWon gets flipped to false.

It's that playerWon variable that ultimately matters here.

```
if (playerWon) {
  this.setState({ wonVisible : true, controlMenuButtonDisabled : true });
}
```

When wonVisible in state is set to true, and controlMenuButtonDisabled is set to true, using a setState() call, the result is that the Control Menu button is disabled and the You Won! screen is shown, using the conditional rendering discussed in the previous chapter.

That's all there is to this function—very simple and very straightforward.

alterMatrixSize()

The final function to look at is a small one, but a vital one. It's the alterMatrixSize() function in the alterMatrixSize.js file, and it's the function called when the player adjusts the grid size sliders on the control menu.

```
module.exports = function(inWhichDimension, inValue) {

  switch (inWhichDimension) {
    case "across":
      if (inValue !== this.state.numberOfTilesAcross) {
        this.setState({ numberOfTilesAcross : inValue },
          global.buildMatrix
        );
      }
    break;
    case "down":
      if (inValue !== this.state.numberOfTilesDown) {
        this.setState({ numberOfTilesDown : inValue },
          global.buildMatrix
        );
      }
    break;
  }
```

Yep, that's it! The `inWhichDimension` argument tells the code whether it was the horizontal (`"across"`) or vertical (`"down"`) slider that changed, and `inValue` provides the new value, which is the number of tiles across or down. As long as the value changed (because this function will be called even if it didn't), all that's required is to set the new `numberOfTilesAcross` or `numberOfTilesDown` attribute in `state`, depending on which switch case is hit, and make a call to `buildMatrix()`. Again, because `buildMatrix()` relies on those two `state` attributes, and because the `setState()` call is asynchronous, we have to use the callback form of `setState()` again, so that `buildMatrix()` only gets called once `state` has actually been updated.

And with that, our exploration of the code of FunTime is complete!

Ruminations on Debugging

In Chapter 4, I touched on the topic of debugging and introduced you to the in-app developer menu and what it offers. I described the errors and warnings that you can sometimes see in a running app (and what options are available when you do see them). I also briefly described the remote debugging capabilities that React Native offers by way of Chrome Developer Tools in your desktop Google Chrome browser. I'd like to go into a little more detail on this last approach, because I suspect it's the way most React Native developers will want to debug their apps (along with good old `console.log()` debugging, but that only gets you so far), and I also want to touch on a few other things under the heading of debugging.

More with Chrome Developer Tools

As discussed in Chapter 4, Expo automatically sets up remote debugging for you, such that you can launch a remote debugging session from the in-app developer menu and have it automatically fire up Chrome. You can then open the Chrome Developer Tools and use many of its capabilities to debug.

While it's true that not all the tools available will work for a React Native app, one essential tool does, and that's the ability to debug. For example, in Figure 8-1, I've set a breakpoint on a line of code in the `tilePress()` function, and you can see that the debugger has paused execution on it.

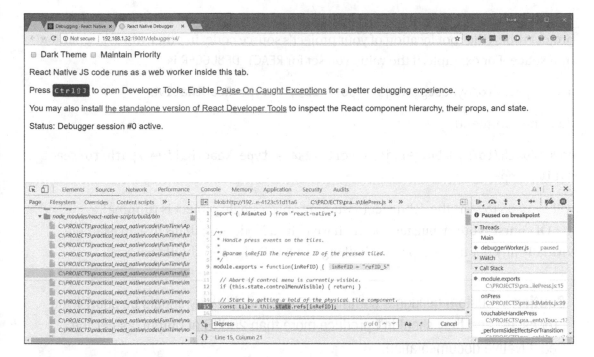

Figure 8-1. *A breakpoint hit in Chrome Developer Tools*

It can be a little tricky to find on the left the source file you need, because of how it all gets bundled together, but once you do, you can then do all the usual debugging things as with a non–React Native app: resume, step over, step out, etc. You can add watch expressions and examine the call stack, etc.

Using a Custom Debugger

If you aren't a fan of the Chrome browser, you don't have to use its developer tools for remote debugging. You can use a custom debugger, if you prefer. To do so, you have only to configure an environment variable on your desktop named REACT_DEBUGGER. The value of this variable should be a command to start your custom debugger. With that set up, you'll be able to select the Debug JS Remotely option from the in-app developer menu, and that custom debugger will launch.

The debugger will, as part of its launch command execution, receive a list of all project roots (the root location of your project's source code, in other words), separated by a space. For example, if the value you set for REACT_DEBUGGER is

```
node /path/to/myDebugger.js --port 1234 --type ReactNative
```

then the command

```
node /path/to/myDebugger.js --port 1234 --type ReactNative /path/to/react_
native/app
```

will be used to start the debugger (assuming only a single project is running).

Of course, your debugger doesn't have to be a Node app; that's just an example. Virtually any debugger capable of talking to a JavaScript app should work.

Caution   Custom debugger commands executed this way should be short-lived processes, and they shouldn't produce more than 200KB of output, as per the React Native documentation.

React Developer Tools

React offers a Chrome extension called, obviously enough, React Developer Tools. This extension adds React-specific tooling to Chrome Developer Tools, something you don't have by default. (Chrome Developer Tools doesn't inherently know you're debugging a React Native app, in other words.) Unfortunately, this extension doesn't work for React Native apps (at the time of writing, at least). However, understanding how useful this extension is, the React development team has also created a stand-alone version of React Developer Tools that *does* work with React Native apps. To use it, you'll first have to install it, and given that it's available as an NPM package, that's as easy as

```
npm install -g react-devtools
```

If you prefer to have it installed as a project dependency rather than globally, that will work just as well, simply drop the -g switch. Once that's done, you can launch the tools by simply executing this command at a command prompt:

```
react-devtools
```

When you do so, you'll be greeted with a new window, such as that shown in Figure 8-2.

Figure 8-2. *The React Developer Tools initial display*

Once it launches, simply start the app you want to debug in the Expo client, as always, and React Developer Tools should automatically connect after a few seconds. I've done so, as in Figure 8-3, and have also expanded the resultant display a bit, to give you something interesting to look at.

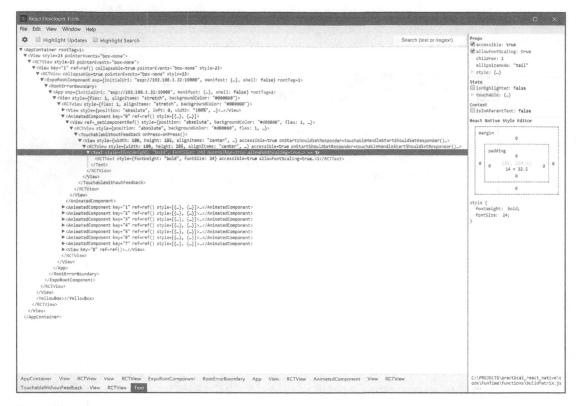

Figure 8-3. *Digging down into the FunTime app via React Developer Tools*

If you look at the branch in the tree I have expanded, it should look familiar. It's the Text component inside the first tile! Moving up the hierarchy, you should be able to identify the various components in the hierarchy, culminating in the View with the backgroundColor of #000000. You'll notice that there are some components above that, however, and these are things that React Native builds automatically to contain your app, but that view, the fourth from the top, is the outermost View in our code in App.js. You can click each component in the hierarchy, to see details about it on the right, as shown here. This includes the props of the component, which is something you can't do easily any other way, even in Chrome Developer Tools (without the React Developer Tools extension, that is).

Unfortunately, what you see here in this tool is all read-only, so there's no on-the-fly editing of props and such and immediately seeing the result in the app, but, hey, we can't have everything. I wouldn't be totally shocked if that capability arrived later, but it's not available at the time of writing. In the meantime, you can do some helpful things, such as right-click a component to copy its name or props, and you can right-click a component to show only components of that type. Just being able to inspect components like this, at a React Native level (meaning where you can see things like props), is extremely helpful and keeps you from having to do a lot of console.log() debugging.

On the View menu here, you'll find an option to show Chrome Developer Tools too, so you can effectively use that tooling right along with the React Developer Tools, all in the same window, and with all the same capabilities.

Performance: It's Not Just for Games

When writing games, performance is of paramount importance. You want the frame rate (how many times per second the screen is refreshed to reflect changes to what the player sees) to be as high as possible. It's generally accepted that 60 frames per second (FPS) is the sweet spot where animations become very smooth. While this is of primary importance for games, it's just as crucial for non-game apps. While React Native provides outstanding performance out of the box, with 60FPS very much being the goal, it's often the case that it can't manage it without your help.

There are some things you should consider when writing your code—common "gotchas" for performance to keep in mind that should keep your app's frame rate humming along nicely.

console.log() Statements

First, given that we just talked debugging, including the console.log() function, keep in mind that such function calls can bottleneck the main JavaScript thread that is running your app's code. That's because they ultimately have to make calls out to native code that writes to the file system, something that may be synchronous and can be expensive even if it's not. Therefore, you'll want to take care to remove or comment out such statements when you're doing your final build for deployment to users.

ListView Performance

If you decide to use the ListView component, be aware that it can have render speed as well as performance issues when scrolling large lists of items. Fortunately, there is a straightforward way to deal with this problem: use the FlatList or SectionList component instead. Their performance is much improved, owing to a near constant memory usage pattern, regardless of the number of items to be displayed, and they also have a simpler API to deal with.

You should, if possible, also implement the getItemLayout prop. This is a function that should return the height of each item in your list. This isn't always possible, of course, especially when the item contents are variable, but if your usage pattern allows it, this will improve performance considerably.

Also, look at implementing the rowHasChanged prop for a ListView as well. This is an optional function that you can provide to the data source for the ListView that, in its most simple form, when you are dealing with immutable data, can just be a reference equality check. The result of executing this function is that the ListView can determine when an item must be re-rendered and only does so when it has to, cutting out a lot of potential work.

Doing Too Much Work on the Main JavaScript Thread

Always remember that JavaScript execution is single-threaded, so you have to avoid doing a lot of lengthy work in that thread. Anytime you fail to follow this rule, the result will usually be dropped frames, which means "janky," or stuttering, animation. This is most frequently seen in navigator transitions, because setting up a new scene tends to require some work, and that work, if you aren't careful, can bog down the thread. But it's definitely not the only place it can happen.

For example, given that FunTime uses the Animation API, it's beneficial to know that the API will calculate keyframes for the animations it's running on-demand on the main JavaScript thread. This means that if you try and run too many animations simultaneously, or perhaps if you decide to do some particularly complex animation, you may start dropping frames. And never forget that this will also depend on the device the code ultimately runs on.

What you can do about dropping frames isn't something you can put any global rules on, because it's always going to come down to looking at what your code is doing and merely trying to ensure that you don't have any long-running code. Tight loops, for example, are a notorious source of dropped frames. Just think about the work you're doing. Try to determine if any of it can be deferred, and do what you can to avoid any code that blocks for more than a few milliseconds. Remember that 60FPS means that each frame requires 1000ms/60=16.6ms per frame. That's the total amount of time you have to finish up any work that has to be done, leaving time for React Native and, eventually, the OS to render the frame to the screen. That can either be a long time or not nearly enough, depending on what your code is trying to do.

Tip   One of the key goals of the React Navigation library is to avoid the performance issues associated with some of the navigators React Native provides natively. It does this by running the animations related to its navigators on the native thread, not the JavaScript thread. So, while you aren't required to do so, this is another good reason to use React Navigation.

Moving a View on the Screen Reduces FPS

Anytime you want to move a View component, or you want to scroll, translate, or rotate it as well, you can start dropping frames, if you aren't careful, especially when that View contains content such as text on top of a transparent background, or text positioned on top of an image.

An excellent way to avoid these problems is to enable the shouldRasterizeIOS prop, and/or the renderToHardwareTextureAndroid prop on the View. These can help a great deal, anytime alpha compositing is required to redraw the view with each frame.

Caution   Be careful with these options, however, because overusing them can result in memory usage ballooning, and then you'll have a whole other set of problems to deal with!

An iOS-Specific Issue: Animating the Size of an Image

Say, for example, that you want to zoom an image to full screen when the user taps it. On iOS only, every time you make an adjustment to the width or height of an Image component, iOS will have to re-crop the image and scale it from the original image. For small images, this won't matter very much, but for larger, higher-resolution images, it can quickly become a performance bottleneck.

One way to deal with this is to use CSS `transform` properties to do the scaling instead. CSS transforms are very efficient and done at a native level, so they tend not to incur the performance hit of merely changing width and height attributes.

In fact, as a more general comment, you may sometimes consider using CSS for animations and visual changes over something that uses JavaScript, especially on iOS, which is highly optimized for CSS transformations. This concern has some validity on Android as well but tends to not be quite as big a problem there, owing to the nature of how things are implemented at the OS level.

Touchable Components Aren't As Reactive As They Should Be

With any of the `Touchable` components, `TouchableWithoutFeedback`, for example, as used in FunTime, it's possible to run into a situation in which your code is trying to update something on the screen—the opacity or highlight of a component, for example—within the same frame during which the touch is being responded to. When this happens, it can sometimes lead to the visual response not occurring until after the `onPress` function has returned. (Refer to the previous point. If the code you put in `onPress` takes too much time, this can happen.) This can be true especially if the code in `onPress` must make a `setState()` call, because these calls can result in a lot of work behind the scenes, so even though *your* application code seems pretty tight, the resultant React Native work can take a long time, which leads to dropped frames and an unsmooth UI.

One way to deal with this is to wrap any code you must put in `onPress` handlers inside a `requestAnimationFrame()` call, like so:

```
myOnPressHandler() {
  this.requestAnimationFrame(() => {
    this.doLengthyOperation();
  });
}
```

These are just a few points to keep in mind with regard to performance. Fortunately, unless you really make some bad decisions, React Native will generally keep your app running pretty smoothly, without you having to do very much work at all!

Summary

In this chapter, we finished the FunTime app, turning it into an actual game, with the final bits of code, rather than just an app for displaying a pretty matrix of tiles. We also talked a bit more about debugging, saw some alternative options available to you, and talked about performance considerations in React Native apps.

I'd like to thank you for reading my book, and I hope you've both enjoyed it and learned a lot from it. Now, go forth and create some great apps with React Native and make this author proud!

Index

A

AboutScreen.js file, 245–246
AccessibilityInfo API, 62–63
ActionSheetIOS, 54–55
ActivityIndicator, 50–51
AdminModal.js file, 243–245
Alert API, 64–65
AlertIOS API, 64–65
Android Developer Bridge (ADB), 172
Android-specific components
    DatePickerAndroid, 57–59
    TimePickerAndroid, 59–61
    ViewPagerAndroid, 61–62
Animated API, 65–66
APIs
    AccessibilityInfo, 62–63
    Alert and AlertIOS, 64–65
    Animated, 65–66
    AppState, 66–67
    BackHandler, 67
    Clipboard, 67–68
    Dimensions, 68
    Geolocation, 68–70
    InteractionManager, 70
    iOS/Android, 62
    Keyboard, 71
    LayoutAnimation, 72
    NetInfo, 72–73
    PixelRatio, 74–75
    Platform, 75–76

    StyleSheet, 77
    ToastAndroid, 78
    Vibration, 79
AppState API, 66–67

B

BackHandler API, 67
Button component, 45–46

C

ChoiceScreen
    animationType, 150
    CustomButton, 151–152
    filteredRestaurants, 155
    firstName and lastName, 156
    FlatList, 156–158
    getRandom(), 159
    map(), 155
    Modal, 147–150, 152–154, 156
    onRequestClose, 150
    participants array, 155
    participantsList, 148, 158
    participantsListRefresh, 148, 156, 158
    presentationStyle, 150
    render() method, 148
    ScrollView, 154
    selectedVisible, 148, 150
    state object, 156–157
    Test, 156

S

T, U

V

W, X, Y, Z

Printed in the United States
By Bookmasters